First World War
and Army of Occupation
War Diary
France, Belgium and Germany

38 DIVISION
113 Infantry Brigade
Royal Welsh Fusiliers
14th Battalion
1 December 1915 - 30 April 1919

WO95/2555/2

The Naval & Military Press Ltd
www.nmarchive.com
Published in association with The National Archives

Published by

The Naval & Military Press Ltd

Unit 10 Ridgewood Industrial Park,

Uckfield, East Sussex,

TN22 5QE England

Tel: +44 (0) 1825 749494

www.naval-military-press.com

www.nmarchive.com

This diary has been reprinted in facsimile from the original. Any imperfections are inevitably reproduced and the quality may fall short of modern type and cartographic standards.

© Crown Copyright
Images reproduced by permission of The National Archives, London, England, 2015.

Contents

Document type	Place/Title	Date From	Date To
Heading	WO95/2555/2 14 Battalion Royal Welsh Fusiliers.		
Heading	38th Division 113th Infy Bde 14th Bn Roy. Welsh Fus. Dec 1915-Apr 1919		
Heading	14th R.W. Fus. Vol.1 Decbr 1915		
War Diary	Winchester.	01/12/1915	01/12/1915
War Diary	Southampton.	01/12/1915	01/12/1915
War Diary	Havre	02/12/1915	02/12/1915
War Diary	Aire.	03/12/1915	03/12/1915
War Diary	Rebecq.	04/12/1915	18/12/1915
War Diary	Laventie.	18/12/1915	26/12/1915
War Diary	Merville.	26/12/1915	26/12/1915
War Diary	Les Puresbecques	27/12/1915	31/12/1915
Heading	14th Battn R. Welsh Fusiliers Vol.2		
War Diary	Les Puresbecques.	01/01/1916	30/06/1916
Heading	113th Inf. Bde. 38th Div. 14th Battn. The Royal Welch Fusiliers. July 1916		
Heading	War Diary For July 1916 14 Batt. R.W.F.		
War Diary		01/07/1916	31/07/1916
Heading	14 Batt. RWF. War Diary For August 1916. Vol.9		
War Diary		01/08/1916	31/08/1916
Heading	War Diary 14th Battalion R.W.F. For September 1916. Vol.10		
War Diary		01/09/1916	30/09/1916
Heading	War Diary Of 14th Battalion. Royal Welsh Fusiliers. October 1916. Vol.11		
War Diary		01/10/1916	31/10/1916
Heading	War Diary For November 1916. 14th Battalion Royal Welsh Fusiliers. Vol.12		
War Diary		01/11/1916	30/11/1916
Heading	14th Battn Royal Welsh Fusiliers War Diary For December 1916. Vol.13		
War Diary		01/12/1916	31/12/1916
Heading	War Diary For January 1917. 14th Batt. Royal Welsh Fusiliers. Vol.14		
War Diary		01/01/1917	31/01/1917
Heading	War Diary 14th Battn. R.W.F. February 1917. Vol.15		
War Diary		01/02/1917	05/02/1917
Diagram etc			
War Diary		06/02/1917	28/02/1917
Miscellaneous	38th Division No. G.S.4123	22/02/1917	22/02/1917
Heading	14th Batt. Royal Welsh Fusiliers War Diary For March 1917. Vol.16		
War Diary		01/03/1917	01/04/1917
Heading	14th Battn. Royal Welsh Fusiliers. War Diary For April 1917. Vol.17		
War Diary		01/04/1917	04/04/1917
Diagram etc			
War Diary		05/04/1917	22/04/1917
Diagram etc			
War Diary		23/04/1917	30/04/1917

Heading	14th Royal Welsh Fusiliers. War Diary For May 1917. Vol.18		
War Diary		30/04/1917	31/05/1917
Heading	14th Batt Royal Welsh Fusiliers War Diary For June 1917. Vol.19		
War Diary		01/06/1917	26/06/1917
Map			
War Diary		27/06/1917	30/06/1917
Heading	14th Bn. Royal Welsh Fusiliers War Diary July 1917. Vol.20		
War Diary		01/07/1917	31/07/1917
Heading	14th Battn. Royal Welsh Fusiliers War Diary August 1917. Vol.21		
War Diary		01/08/1917	31/08/1917
Heading	14th Batt. Royal Welsh Fusiliers War Diary For September 1917. Vol.22		
War Diary		01/09/1917	30/09/1917
Map			
Heading	14th Batt. Royal Welsh Fusiliers War Diary For October 1917. Vol.23		
War Diary		01/10/1917	31/10/1917
Heading	14th Batt Royal Welsh Fusiliers War Diary For November 1917. Vol.24		
War Diary		01/11/1917	30/11/1917
Heading	14th Batt Royal Welsh Fusiliers War Diary For December 1917. Vol.25		
War Diary		01/12/1917	31/12/1917
Heading	14th Batt. Royal Welsh Fusiliers War Diary For January 1918. Vol.26		
War Diary		01/01/1918	31/01/1918
Heading	War Diary 14th Battalion Royal Welch Fusrs February 1918. Vol.27		
War Diary		01/02/1918	28/02/1918
Heading	14th Battn Royal Welsh Fusiliers War Diary For March 1918. Vol.28		
War Diary		01/03/1918	31/03/1918
Heading	113th Inf. Bde. 38th Div. 14th Battn. The Royal Welch Fusiliers. April 1918		
Heading	14th Battalion R.W. Fus War Diary April 1918. Vol.29		
War Diary		01/04/1918	30/04/1918
Map	Map. A.		
Map	Map B.		
Map	Map C Artillery Barrage.		
Heading	War Diary For The Month Of May 1918 14 R.W.F. Vol.30		
War Diary		01/05/1918	31/05/1918
Heading	14th Batt. Royal Welsh Fusiliers. War Diary For June 1918. Vol.31		
War Diary		01/06/1918	30/06/1918
Operation(al) Order(s)	14th Battalion. Royal Welsh Fusiliers. Operation Order No. 30	12/06/1918	12/06/1918
Map	Map Showing Assembly Formation, Positions On Objective, Routes. And Information Regarding The Enemy.		
Map	Reference Enemy Trenches-Wire.		

Heading	14th Batt. Royal Welsh Fusiliers War Diary For July 1918. Vol.32		
War Diary		01/07/1918	31/07/1918
Heading	14th Batt Royal Welsh Fusiliers War Diary For August 1918. Vol.33		
War Diary		01/08/1918	15/08/1918
War Diary	Sheet 57c. S.E.	15/08/1918	31/08/1918
Heading	War Diary For September 1918. 14th Batt. Royal Welsh Fusiliers. Vol.34		
War Diary		01/09/1918	30/09/1918
Heading	14th R.W.F. War Diary For October 1918. Vol.35		
War Diary	In The Field.	01/10/1918	31/10/1918
Heading	14th R.W.F. War Diary For November 1918. Vol.36		
War Diary		01/11/1918	30/11/1918
Heading	14th R.W.F. War Diary For December 1918. Vol.37		
War Diary		01/12/1918	31/12/1918
Heading	14th Battn. Royal Welsh Fus. War Diary For January-1919. Vol.38		
War Diary		01/01/1919	31/03/1919
War Diary	Blangy Tronville.	01/04/1919	30/04/1919

WO/95/2555/2

14 Battalion Royal
Welsh Fusiliers

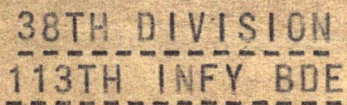

14TH BN ROY. WELSH FUS.
DEC 1915 - APR 1919

I.C.
11 sheets

14 to R.W. Fox:
Vol: I
Decby 1915:
121
7824

38

Dec '15
Ap '19

Army Form C. 2118

WAR DIARY
or
INTELLIGENCE SUMMARY
(Erase heading not required.)

113th Bde. 38th Div.

Diary of 14th Royal Welch Fusiliers

War

From 1st Dec. to 31st Dec. 1915

Instructions regarding War Diaries and Intelligence Summaries are contained in F.S. Regs., Part II. and the Staff Manual respectively. Title Pages will be prepared in manuscript.

Place	Date 1915	Hour	Summary of Events and Information	Remarks and references to Appendices
WINCHESTER	1st Dec	6.30 a.m.	Battalion paraded preparatory to march to SOUTHAMPTON: moved off at 7.0 a.m; on arrival at SOUTHAMPTON proceeded to Docks loaded up baggage; 2 officers and 90 men with Regimental Transport embarked on S.S. Blackwell. the remainder of the Battalion with Headquarters embarked on S.S. Empress Queen, viz 29 officers and 904 men, n.c.o.s and making the total strength, including attached, 31 officers and 994 n.c.o.s and men. Proceeded to HAVRE having an extremely rough passage during the night, of 6 hours duration.	
SOUTHAMPTON				
HAVRE	2nd Dec	6.0 a.m.	Arrival in early morning, disembarked and unloaded baggage and transport, the battalion marched to a rest camp, which was under water, had dinner there; in evening marched to Railway Station and entrained, after toiling ankle deep in mud. Baggage and transport; officers and men were supplied at a stall by English ladies. Train left at 11.0 p.m.	
		11.0 p.m.		
AIRE	3rd Dec	11.40 p.m.	Proceeded via ABBEVILLE, BOULOGNE, and CALAIS to AIRE, where we detrained and after unloading and tea the battalion marched to REBECQ; a guide who was sent by the 19th Division lost his way which caused the battalion to go very much out of its course, and a march of 5 miles was converted into one of about 15 miles each of the result that the destination was not reached until 6.30 a.m. after many halts and delays caused by transport getting stuck in mud, and saddles on mules becoming loose and having to be adjusted. The men were put into their billets, which were not by any means good and required much cleaning	
REBECQ	4th Dec	6.30 a.m.		

WAR DIARY
or
INTELLIGENCE SUMMARY

(Erase heading not required.) 14th Royal Welch Fusiliers

Army Form C. 2118

Place	Date 1915	Hour	Summary of Events and Information	Remarks and references to Appendices
REBECQ	5th Dec	10.0 a.m.	The battalion paraded for Divine Service in a field, the service being conducted by Rev. Hugh Jones, chaplain to the battalion. Battalion Headquarters were in the red brick house facing the church	
"	6th Dec	9.30 a.m.	Battalion paraded for a route march, proceeding via CLARQUES. Artillery formations were practised	
"	7 Dec		Ordinary routine, a battalion parade was cancelled on account of wet weather.	
"	8th Dec	8.45 a.m.	Battalion paraded for time march by platoons, dinners cooked out at WARDRECQUES: march back to billets by companies	
"	9 Dec	8.30 a.m.	Two platoons of "A" Coy did musketry practices on short range at CLARQUES	
		8.45 a.m.	Machine Gunners paraded under Lieut. W.J. Williams. Ordinary Routine	
		12.0 noon	Machine gunners proceeded to the range for firing instruction. Other parades under company arrangements. 2 Platoons of "A" Coy proceeded to short range for firing instruction	

1875 Wt. W593/826 1,000,000 4/15 J.B.C. & A. A.D.S.S./Forms/C. 2118.

WAR DIARY
or
INTELLIGENCE SUMMARY

(Erase heading not required.) 14th Royal Welch Fusiliers

Army Form C. 2118

Place	Date	Hour	Summary of Events and Information	Remarks and references to Appendices
REBECQ	9th Dec 1915		The Divisional orders drawn strict attention to Guard Duties and sentries, and states that any slackness in this respect will be severely punished. The C-in-C directs that any sentry found sleeping on his post will suffer the extreme penalty. It was directed that this order should be read on 7 successive parades.	
REBECQ	10th Dec	8:30 a.m.	2 Platoons of B. coy. Musketry on short range	
		12.30 a.m.	2 Platoons of B. coy. Musketry on short range. Parades under company arrangements	
		6.0 p.m.	A & B Coys. night operations.	
REBECQ	11th Dec	8.45 a.m.	A, B, D. Coys. one hours route marching. Bayonet fighting, Physical Drill, Musketry, Visual Training. Coy drill under coy arrangements.	
		12.30 p.m.	2 Platoons C. Coy firing on range.	
		1.3 p.m.	A & B Coys Wood fighting	
		1.30 p.m.	D. coy. Bombing, Visual Training	

Army Form C. 2118

WAR DIARY
or
INTELLIGENCE SUMMARY
(Erase heading not required.) 14th Royal Welch Fusiliers

Instructions regarding War Diaries and Intelligence Summaries are contained in F.S. Regs, Part II. and the Staff Manual respectively. Title Pages will be prepared in manuscript.

Place	Date 1915	Hour	Summary of Events and Information	Remarks and references to Appendices
REBECQ	11th Dec	4.0 p.m	Lectures to C & D. Coys by Medical Officer	
		6.0 p.m	C & D Coys. night operations.	
REBECQ	12th Dec	9.45 a.m	Church parade for Battalion, C of E.	
		10.30 a.m	Roman Catholics church parade	
		11.30 a.m	Muster Parade. Arms and kit inspection	
			Evening service held in barn.	
REBECQ	13th Dec	8.30 a.m	2 Platoons D. Coy fired on short range	
		9.0 a.m	A. Coy and 2 Platoons D. Coy went to GORSE HILL for Engineering work.	
		11.15 a.m	2 Platoons D. Coy paraded under Coy. arrangements.	
		11.0 a.m	A. Coy Sav helmet parade	
		11.0 a.m	B. Coy. Engineering Field work	
		1.30 p.m	2 Platoons A. Coy fired on range.	
		1.30 p.m	C. Coy. Field Engineering work	
		2.0 p.m	B. Coy. Route March	
		6.0 p.m	night operations by all Coys under Coy arrangements.	
		6.0 p.m	Lecture by M.O. to A. Coy	
		6.30 p.m	" " " B. Coy	

1875 Wt. W593/826. 1,000,000 4/15 J.B.C. & A. A.D.S.S./Forms/C. 2118.

Army Form C. 2118

WAR DIARY
or
INTELLIGENCE SUMMARY

(Erase heading not required.) 14th Royal Welch Fusiliers

Instructions regarding War Diaries and Intelligence Summaries are contained in F.S. Regs., Part II. and the Staff Manual respectively. Title Pages will be prepared in manuscript.

Place	Date 1/15	Hour	Summary of Events and Information	Remarks and references to Appendices
REBECQ	14th Dec	8.30am	Snipers, scouts and stretcher bearers paraded under their own officers	
		8.30am	2 Platoons of D. Coy fired on range.	
		9.30am	2 Platoons of D. Coy fired on range.	
			A. Coy fired on range.	
		1.30pm	B & C Coys timed route march.	
		1.30pm	12 N.C.O's from each Coy went for engineering instruction under R.E officer at GORSE HILL.	
			An estaminet in village was placed out of bounds for selling unauthorised spirits.	
REBECQ	15th Dec	8.30am	B & C Coys had engineering instruction from R.E officer at GORSE HILL	
		9.0am	B & C Coys fired on range, also had bombing instruction	
		1.30pm	A & D Coys timed route march	
		6.0pm	Lecture by M.O. to A Coy	
		6.30pm	" " " B. Coy	
			21224 C.S.M. Weaver H.E was sentenced to be reduced to the ranks by sentence of F.G.C.M.	
			20090 Sgt. Wildon E reverted to the ranks at his own request.	
			Another estaminet was placed out of bounds.	

1875 Wt. W593/826 1,000,000 4/15 J.B.C. & A. A.D.S.S./Forms/C. 2118.

Army Form C. 2118

WAR DIARY
or
INTELLIGENCE SUMMARY

14th Royal Welsh Fusiliers

(Erase heading not required.)

Place	Date 1915	Hour	Summary of Events and Information	Remarks and references to Appendices
REBECQ	16 Dec	8.45am	A & D coys paraded for firing on range & bombing instruction. Other parades under coy arrangements	
		12.30 p.m	B & C coys fired on range & had bombing instruction.	
REBECQ	17 Dec	9.30 am	A & D coys sent 50 N.C.O's and men for engineering instruction by R.E. officer at 60 RSF HILL	1
		8.30 a.m	A coy fired on range	
		10.15 am	C. Coy carried out a scheme on digging ground under the superintendence of the Brigadier-General, the machine gun section also attended.	
		1.30 noon	B & D coy fired on range	
		5.15 p.m	Lecture by Brigadier-General to all officers	
REBECQ	18 Dec	8.45 am	Battalion paraded on Batt. Alarm Post, but did not move off until 9.45 a.m. in motor lorries via LE VENANT & MERVILLE to area of Guards Division left lorries on LA BASSÉE Rd at nearest point to LAVENTIE and marched to latter place for 6 days instruction in trench warfare with Guards Division. The battalion was attached to the 1st Guards Brigade as follows:— A coy to 2nd Grenadier Guards B coy to 2nd Coldstream Guards C coy to 3rd Coldstream Guards D coy to 1st Irish Guards	1

Army Form C. 2118

WAR DIARY
or
INTELLIGENCE SUMMARY

(Erase heading not required.)

14th Royal Welch Fusiliers

Place	Date 1915	Hour	Summary of Events and Information	Remarks and references to Appendices
LAVENTIE	18th Dec		A & B coys were sent up to 1st line trenches with 2nd Grenadiers & 2nd Coldstream Guards. C & D coys going into billets at LAVENTIE with 3rd Coldstream Guards & 1st Irish Guards. The Commanding Officer was attached to 2nd Grenadier Guards. The 2nd in command to the 3rd Coldstream Guards, the Adjutant to the 1st Irish Guards. Casualties in Batt. was sustained no 20357 Pte H. Hughes A coy being slightly wounded, bullet wound.	
LAVENTIE	19th Dec		A few German shells fell in the town, one bursting in the garden of Headquarters mess of 3rd Coldstream Guards caused cancelling of Church Parade. 2050 Pte J. Peake A coy was seriously wounded in back by rifle fire. 2nd Guards Brigade relieved 1st Guards Brigade, & coys were attacked as follows:-	
LAVENTIE	20th Dec		A coy to 4th Grenadier Guards in billets in LAVENTIE B coy. to 1st Welch Guards " C. coy. to 2nd Scots Guards in trenches D coy. to 1st Grenadier Guards " C.O. & Adjutant were attached to 4th Grenadier Guards, 2nd in command to 2nd Scots Guards. Each battn. was 48 hours in trenches & 4 hours in rest billets in LAVENTIE	
LAVENTIE	21st Dec		Each coy was divided up so that 1 platoon was attached to a company of Guards, and 1 section to a platoon. By this means it was ensured that the fullest individual instruction possible was obtained, each Fusilier being looked after by a Guardsman.	

Army Form C. 2118

WAR DIARY
or
INTELLIGENCE SUMMARY
(Erase heading not required.) 14th Royal Welch Fusiliers

Instructions regarding War Diaries and Intelligence Summaries are contained in F. S. Regs., Part II. and the Staff Manual respectively. Title Pages will be prepared in manuscript.

Place	Date	Hour	Summary of Events and Information	Remarks and references to Appendices
LAVENTIE	22nd Dec	4.30 p.m	Relief of trenches; 'C' Coy going into billets in LAVENTIE with 2nd Scots Guards, 'D' Coy with 1st Grenadier Guards, A & B Coys going up to trenches with 4th Grenadier Guards & 1st Welsh Guards respectively.	
LAVENTIE	23rd Dec		Usual routine in trenches, nothing unusual occurring, desultory firing	
LAVENTIE	24th Dec 3.30 p.m		Heavy bombardment by our artillery at night, with satisfactory results. Relief of trenches the reverse detail of 22nd inst. The following casualties occurred on this day to men of the battn. were slightly wounded by shell from one of our own batteries. Has since been unofficially reported dead. 20432 Pte. E.R. Jones B Coy was severely wounded by shell from one of our own batteries. 10583 Pte. H.Y. Jones 'D' Coy was killed in a dug out by collapse of the roof. 21207 Pte. O. Griffiths B Coy was slightly wounded in hand	
LAVENTIE	25th Dec		Attempts at fraternising by Germans & British troops, on our side more especially on the part of Coldstream Guards, severe measures were however taken to stop this state of affairs, disciplinary action taken. Headquarters of 2nd Bn Scots Guards was shelled by enemy to the discomfiture of occupants, who left their hunch hurriedly, took refuge in dug outs etc.	

1875 Wt. W593/826 1,000,000 4/15 J.B.C. & A. A.D.S.S./Forms/C. 2118.

Army Form C. 2118

WAR DIARY
or
INTELLIGENCE SUMMARY

14th Royal (Erase heading not required.) Welch Fusiliers

Instructions regarding War Diaries and Intelligence Summaries are contained in F.S. Regs., Part II. and the Staff Manual respectively. Title Pages will be prepared in manuscript.

Place	Date 1915	Hour	Summary of Events and Information	Remarks and references to Appendices
LAVENTIE	26th Dec	6.30am	The battalion was withdrawn from the Guards Division proceeded by motor lorries to MERVILLE, went into billets at LES PURESBECQUES, 20165 Pte. E.O. Ylenderson was wounded by a dugout falling in.	
MERVILLE				
LES PURESBECQUES	27th Dec	4.0 pm	Parades under coy arrangements 1 Corpl. + 5 Ptes proceeded to Divisional Headquarters for instruction in trench mortars. In the case of Coy Sergt Major H.E.Weaver were quashed.	
LES PURESBECQUES	28th Dec		Proceedings of Court Martial Ordinary Routine; Parades under coy. arrangements	
LES PURESBECQUES	29th Dec		Parades under coy arrangements.	
LES PURESBECQUES	30th Dec		Parades under company arrangements	
LES PURESBECQUES	31st Dec		Parades under company arrangements Officers, n.c.o.'s and 48 i/ranks from each coy proceeded to Brigade Headquarters and received instruction in method of putting on gas helmets quickly, afterwards were subjected to a discharge of gas to test the efficiency of gas helmets	S As

12th Batn R. Welch Fusiliers

Vol. 2.

Ten

Army Form C. 2118

WAR DIARY
or
INTELLIGENCE SUMMARY
(Erase heading not required.)

Instructions regarding War Diaries and Intelligence Summaries are contained in F. S. Regs., Part II. and the Staff Manual respectively. Title Pages will be prepared in manuscript.

Place	Date	Hour	Summary of Events and Information	Remarks and references to Appendices
LES PURES BECQUES	1916 Jan 1st		Holiday. An Estaminet placed out of bounds by Order of C.O.	
	" 2nd		Battalion paraded for Divine Service at 10.45 am 16 Officers attended lecture at Corps Headquarters by Lieut. Gen. Oshiug. Comdg. XI Corps.	
	" 3rd		Parades under Company arrangements.	
	" 4th		Ordinary routine. Parades under Company arrangements - 8 Officers attended Lecture on Sanitation.	
		5.30pm	Lecture to N.C.O's by Major Gwyther on Discipline and Esprit de Corps. From the BASE. came official notification of deaths of following men:—	
			20850 Pte. Clark J. "A" Coy. 19.12.1915.
			20583 " Jones J.H. "D" " Died of Wounds. 24.12.1915.
			20432 " Jones R.E. "B" " Killed in Action. 24.12.1915. Died of Wounds.
			21207 Pte Griffiths O. "B" Coy. Wounded to England. 29.12.15.
			20327 Sergt Hughes J. "A" " Sick to England. 29.12.15.
			Major G.A. Gwyther assumed Command of the Battalion during the absence on Leave of Lt. Col. D. Davies.	
	" 5th		Parades under Company arrangements.	

Army Form C. 2118

WAR DIARY
or
INTELLIGENCE SUMMARY
(Erase heading not required.)

Instructions regarding War Diaries and Intelligence Summaries are contained in F. S. Regs., Part II. and the Staff Manual respectively. Title Pages will be prepared in manuscript.

Place	Date	Hour	Summary of Events and Information	Remarks and references to Appendices
LES PURESBECQUES	Jan/ 6th	9. a.m.	Musketry – 100 men of "C" Coy and 100 men of "D" Coy fired on range.	
"	7th	7.15 am	Battalion paraded and marched to the Reserve billets of the 56th Infantry Brigade at KING'S ROAD, RUE DES CHAVATTES.	
"	8th		Paraded under Company arrangements. Officers & N.C.O's of "A" & "C" Coys visited the front line trenches and island positions on right and left front respectively.	
"	9th		Officers and N.C.O's of "B" & "D" Coys visited their positions in support holes by day. Officers of "A" & "C" Coys visited front line trenches and island positions by night. LA COUTURE heavily shelled today.	
"	10		Battalion relieved 13th R.W.F. in front line and support trenches. Battalion Headquarters RUE DE BOIS, S. 14 Central. Relief commenced 4.30 p.m and was completed at 6.40 p.m. Distribution A. Coy. Right sub sector, occupied 20 islands with the balance in NEW ROPE KEEP. C. Coy. occupied 12 islands with balance between LEPINETTE NORTH B. Coy occupied TUBE STATION with parties in DEAD COW and CHOCOLATE POSTS. D. Coy occupied RUE DES BERGAUX with parties in ORCHARD POST.	

1875 Wt. W593/826 1,000,000 4/15 J.B.C. & A. A.D.S.S./Forms/C. 2118.

WAR DIARY
INTELLIGENCE SUMMARY
(Erase heading not required.)

Army Form C. 2118

Place	Date	Hour	Summary of Events and Information	Remarks and references to Appendices
	1916. Jan 10		The night of Jan 10/11 was quiet, weather mild, no rain. Enemy's machine guns were active during night. Our machine guns retaliated at intervals. Our Artillery commenced at 7.0 a.m. to bombard enemy's line and continued until 7.15 a.m. Enemy's snipers active. The parapet was raised and strengthened in each sector.	
	11.		Heavy bombardment by our Artillery at 3.30 p.m. The night was fairly quiet but very bright owing to the moon. At 3 p.m. Enemy's guns opened fire on ORCHARD POST, but were silenced by our guns. An Officer's patrol went out from 5.15. d. 7. 3. in the left sector; they heard parties going on near the Enemy's line; a Lewis gun was turned in direction from which sound proceeded; patrol reported that our wire was in good condition. No 1. 7 & 8 posts in left sector were joined up and a new post between 3 and 4 posts commenced. Water gauge showed drop of 3 in. in 64 sector. No 1. post Right sector was withdrawn by night to TUBE STATION POST as it was considered untenable in the event of an attack. Wind N. N. W.	
	12		A & C Companies were relieved by B & D Coys respectively. Enemy's Artillery was very active shelling Princes Road. Our Artillery replied and silenced them on right sub-sector. Our snipers were very active and claim two victims in old German sap. S.21. D. 9. 8	

WAR DIARY
or
INTELLIGENCE SUMMARY

(Erase heading not required.)

Army Form C. 2118

Place	Date	Hour	Summary of Events and Information	Remarks and references to Appendices
	1916 Jan 13		A German machine gun was located at S. 22. c. 1. 8. Lewis opened fire on it. Our Artillery bombarded enemy front line during night; Enemy put up white flag during a bombardment at 1.0 p.m.; it was fired on. Wind rose during the night and was from S.W. The Brig-gen visited front line trenches by night. Casualties: B men wounded.	
	13.		Enemy's artillery active during intervals in the day, shelling PRINCES RD. Our machine guns active during day. Enemy machine guns on right sector fairly active during the night. Snipers active on this side. At 1.40 p.m. the company on the left sub-sector report that a small party of Germans approached our wire and threw three bombs at our parapet. We retaliated with bombs rifle and machine gun fire. Enemy's machine gun played at intervals on the orchard behind TUBE ST. They seem to have found the entrance to TUBE ST. Casualties — one man wounded (accidentally) and J.H.S.	
	14		Our artillery active at intervals. Little retaliation by the Enemy. The Battalion was relieved by the 4th K.L.R. and the 9th Welsh Regt. The 4th Kings took over 14 posts from QUINQUE CROSSING to RUE de CAILLOUX	

WAR DIARY
or
INTELLIGENCE SUMMARY
(Erase heading not required.)

Army Form C. 2118

Place	Date	Hour	Summary of Events and Information	Remarks and references to Appendices
	1916 Jan 14		The 9th Welsh took over from RUE de CAILLOUX to FARM CORNER, 16 posts. The 11th Kings occupied Battalion Headquarters at RUE DE BOIS. The 9th Welsh occupied Battalion Headquarters at ALBERT POST and took over posts at RUE DE BERCEUX, TUBE ST., DEAD COW, CHOCOLATE. Relief started 5.10 p.m. Relief completed 7.40 p.m. On relief being completed Battalion marched to Billets at CROIX MARMUSE.	
	15		Bathing parades for baths at VIELLE CHAPELLE. Attention paid to cleaning up of Billets and cleaning of the men who after bathing received a fresh change of underclothing and towel.	
	16		10. a.m. Divine Service in field near "C" Coy. Headquarters. Bathing at Pont du Hem 40 men per Company. Inspection of Billets by Brigadier. Conference at Brigade Headquarters of all C.O.'s in the Brigade after tea with Brigadier. Jollies entertainment at LESTREM.	
	17		Bathing at LOCON. Parades under Company arrangements. C.O. and Coy Commanders went out on reconnaissance scheme with a view to finding suitable number for counter attack in Brigade Reserve area. Jollies entertainment at LESTREM.	

Army Form C. 2118

WAR DIARY
INTELLIGENCE SUMMARY
(Erase heading not required.)

Instructions regarding War Diaries and Intelligence Summaries are contained in F. S. Regs., Part II. and the Staff Manual respectively. Title Pages will be prepared in manuscript.

Place	Date	Hour	Summary of Events and Information	Remarks and references to Appendices
	1916 Jan 18.		Bathing at LOCON. Parades under Company arrangements	
	19.		Bathing at VIEILLE CHAPELLE. A Divisional Entertainment was held at LESTREM and was attended by Officers and men of the Battalion. Ordinary Routine.	
	20		Parades under Coy. arrangements. Inspection of Companies at work by Brigadier General.	
	21		Battalion Route march via LESTREM, NERVILLE, PARADIS.	
	22		Parades under Company arrangements. Inspection of A, B, C & D Companies in marching order.	
	23		Battalion paraded at 10.0 a.m. and marched to Billets in Brigade Reserve area at KINGS ROAD, LACOUTURE, route 2 ELOBES, LOCON, LES FACONS. On arrival Billets were taken over by us from 9th Welch Regt. We furnished garrison at L'ORCHARD and ALBERT POST, and controls at SHRINE and RUE de L'EPINETTE	
	24		Ordinary Routine	
	25.		Ordinary Routine - Improvement of Drainage	
	26		Lt. Col David Davies resumed Command of the Battalion on return from Parliamentary Duties. Improvement of drainage system around billets	

1875 Wt. W593/826 1,000,000 4/15 J.B.C. & A. A.D.S.S./Forms/C. 2118.

Army Form C. 2118

WAR DIARY
INTELLIGENCE SUMMARY
(Erase heading not required.)

Instructions regarding War Diaries and Intelligence Summaries are contained in F.S. Regs., Part II. and the Staff Manual respectively. Title Pages will be prepared in manuscript.

Place	Date	Hour	Summary of Events and Information	Remarks and references to Appendices
	1916 Jan 29		The Battalion relieved the 13th R.W.F. in front line trenches. Distribution:- A. Coy Right Subsector C. Coy Left " B. Coy in right support in TUBE STATION, with posts in DEAD COW and CHOCOLATE. D. Coy. in Left support with two Platoons at dugouts at TEETOTAL CORNER and two at new breastworks behind old British line.	
	29/28		Relief was completed at 7.35 p.m. During the night Enemy's machine Guns were fairly active on both sub-sectors. Enemy's trench mortars fired at breastworks at TEETOTAL CORNER. We retaliated with artillery fire. On the left subsector the Enemy's artillery fired on our front line. We retaliated with artillery. The wire in front of right sub sector was examined and found to be in very good condition. Intelligence A large Enemy's patrol was seen near FARM CORNER. A whistle was blown in the enemy's line opposite N9.14 post of the right sub-sector. Work Parapets have been lengthened and thickened. New fire-steps were put in posts on the right sub-sector, boards laid down where ...	

1875. Wt. W593/826. 1,000,000. 4/15 J.B.C. & A. A.D.S.S./Forms/C. 2118.

WAR DIARY
or
INTELLIGENCE SUMMARY
(Erase heading not required.)

Army Form C. 2118

Instructions regarding War Diaries and Intelligence Summaries are contained in F. S. Regs., Part II. and the Staff Manual respectively. Title Pages will be prepared in manuscript.

Place	Date	Hour	Summary of Events and Information	Remarks and references to Appendices
	Jan 28/24		**Operation.** The enemy were fairly quiet until about 12.0 midnight, when he became active for a short time. A considerable artillery duel took place starting from 11.0 a.m. The enemy got a few direct hits on our parapet but did little damage. **Intelligence.** An Officer's patrol went out from the Left sub-sector. They found no difficulty in proceeding along ditch which runs immediately the other side of our wire. Another patrol went out from Left sub-sector from S.15.d.7½.2. & proceeded E about 300 yards. They found no obstacles. An Officer's Patrol went out from Right sub-sector at S.21.B.5.2. They proceeded along Old German trench; this trench is in good condition from S.22.c.1.8 to S.22.d.9.8 and from there to our line under water. This trench is evidently being used by the enemy as there are new sand-bags and hurdles in it. Enemy sent up a red rocket at 12.15. a.m. Our Artillery sent Darros over the German front line at intervals during the night. One of our listening posts was seen by enemy's machine guns, who played on it for some time, 3 men were wounded.	

1875 Wt. W593/826 1,000,000 4/15 J.B.C. & A. A.D.S.S./Forms/C. 2118.

WAR DIARY
or
INTELLIGENCE SUMMARY

(Erase heading not required.)

Army Form C. 2118

Place	Date	Hour	Summary of Events and Information	Remarks and references to Appendices
	1916. Jan 28/29.		On this occasion a gallant act was performed by 2nd Lieut. Venmore and Corpl. Williams of "C" Coy. who went out to this listening post, which was very isolated, and brought in a wounded man under heavy machine gun fire to a post of security; on arrival it was found that a rifle and 12 bombs had been left behind, and Corpl. Williams at great personal risk undertook to return to the listening post and secure them, which he did successfully; it should be noted that barbed wire had to be negotiated during this double journey. Work. Parados of No. 1. post improved. Also lengthening of parapet and heightening same; firesteps were made in various posts. The path at each end of new breastwork near TEETOTAL CORNER was improved.	
	Jan. "29/30		Operations. – The two Companies in the front line were relieved by the two companies in support. Relief was completed at 8.5 p.m. Intelligence. The enemy were very quiet during the night. Nothing unusual happened. Work. Parapet strengthened on whole front, posts being connected up on right and left subsectors.	
	30/31		Operations. Patrols went out from left Company at 4.15 p.m. – one went from c. d. 7. b. 2. and proceeded along old communication trench for about 100 yards; it is waterlogged all the way; they found 5 dead Germans in	

WAR DIARY
or
INTELLIGENCE SUMMARY
(Erase heading not required.)

Army Form C. 2118

Place	Date	Hour	Summary of Events and Information	Remarks and references to Appendices
	1916 Jan 30/31.		the trench, the patrol remaining out acted as a listening post for about 4 hours but were driven in when the fog lifted by machine gun fire; they reported German working party driving stakes in at S.16.c.w.1. **Intelligence.** A fairly thick fog screened the trenches all day. A patrol went out from the right Company consisting of 1 Officer, 1 N.C.O. and 2 men; they proceeded up old communication trench from S.21.d.6.8. to S.21.d.10.2. They went out to test German wire but found German working party mending it. returned. Machine Gun was turned on the working party. Two prisoners were captured at 8.45 a.m. in the 30t and at S.21.b.L.L.; they were sent to Battalion Headquarters and thence to Brigade H.2. they were Reservists belonging to Guards. Reserve Division, and were armed with revolvers, they had apparently been on patrol and stated they had lost their way in the fog when challenged by one sentry they were 20 yards from our parapet and put their hands up when told to do so. Further work was carried on with the parapet and parados. **N0TB** The wire was examined all along the line and repaired when necessary. New floorboards were put down. Drains were cleared in TUBE STATION and PRINCE'S ROAD cleared of mud.	

Army Form C. 2118

WAR DIARY
or
INTELLIGENCE SUMMARY
(Erase heading not required.)

Place	Date	Hour	Summary of Events and Information	Remarks and references to Appendices
	1916 Jan 31.		The Battalion was relieved by the 13th Battalion R.W.F. in the front line and supports and on relief proceeded to billets in KINGS ROAD, GRUB STREET and KING GEORGE ROAD. G. B. Gwyther Major for O.C 14th Royal Welch Fusiliers	

Army Form C. 2118

WAR DIARY
or
INTELLIGENCE SUMMARY
(Erase heading not required.)

Instructions regarding War Diaries and Intelligence Summaries are contained in F.S. Regs., Part II. and the Staff Manual respectively. Title Pages will be prepared in manuscript.

Place	Date	Hour	Summary of Events and Information	Remarks and references to Appendices
	1916			
	Feb 1st		Ordinary Routine.	
	" 2nd		Ordinary Routine.	
	" 3rd		Baths for men at RICHEBOURG.	
	" 4th		The Battalion relieved the 13th K.R. Inniskns in front line and supports: relief complete at 7 p.m.	
	" 5th		Between 7.0. and 7.30 a.m. enemy shelled the vicinity of Battalion Headquarters; no damage done, retaliation called for obtained. "B" Battery claiming to have hit & exploded a German bomb-store at S.22.c.6.1. Our front was quiet. A German working party was heard near FERME DU BOIS. At 7.30 p.m. a brilliant white incandescent light appeared in the direction of FERME DU BOIS, and flashed like a signalling lamp, a machine gun was turned on it from FARM CORNER. A patrol went out from S.16.c.2.9 at 10.30 p.m. for the purpose of locating a sniper, who has been troubling this part of the line lately. They came across a strong enemy patrol (exact number not known) at fallow tree S.16.a.4.1 and threw three Mills hand grenades at them; they think they struck two Germans, but had to retire later they claim to have killed these two men. Our Machine Gun was also turned on the enemy, and the patrol went out again at 12.45 a.m. to try and find traces of wounded, but did not succeed. A patrol went out at S.21.d.9.7 and proceeded down old communication trench for 150 yards for the purpose of trying to ascertain whether enemy very lights were being fired from	

WAR DIARY
or
INTELLIGENCE SUMMARY

(Erase heading not required.)

Army Form C. 2118

Place	Date	Hour	Summary of Events and Information	Remarks and references to Appendices
	Feb 5/6		NO MAN'S LAND, but after being out for three hours they returned and reported having heard a German working party at S.22.a.5.v. Artillery were called up and a salvo was fired at 2.26 a.m; this went too much to the right, and the battery on being re-directed fired 3 salvos at the spot, but result could not be ascertained. A machine gun was also directed on the spot, but result could not be ascertained. Very lights were found to give better results by pushing up and half an inch down the cartridge. Enemy's artillery was very active during the whole day. Four whizz-bangs dropped on TURF STATION and the Orchard behind it. 8 rounds were also fired at ROPE Communication trench; They shelled TEETOTAL CORNER at 8.20 a.m and again at 2.30 p.m. Our Artillery replied to this bombardment, but it did not have any effect on the enemy for a long time. Patrols were sent out from Right and Left Coys. 2 men and was sent out to locate a sniper's post believed to be in old communication trench S.22.c.37.½. They found a sniper between two trees at S.22.c.2.8. and a strong working party in the trench on the road at S.22.c.3.7½. The patrol returned and the Artillery were turned on the working party. A second patrol went out from the Right Coy. They proceeded to the corner of the ditch S.22.a.23.9 when they came across were entanglements; they then worked SE to point S.22.a.3.7½. They found a break in the wire and when they attempted to get through it, they were challenged by a sentry, who threw a bomb, two other Germans then appeared on the scene and also threw bombs. Own N.C.O. in charge of patrol fired two shots with a revolver and they retired: one man was injured by the bomb. Artillery was turned on the point S.22.a.3.7½.	

1875 Wt. W593/826 1,000,000 4/15 J.B.C. & A. A.D.S.S./Forms/C. 2118.

WAR DIARY
or
INTELLIGENCE SUMMARY

(Erase heading not required.)

Army Form C. 2118

Place	Date	Hour	Summary of Events and Information	Remarks and references to Appendices
	Feb 5/16		A patrol went out from the left Coy along S.16.c.2.6; they found it very dry in parts and quite passable; after proceeding along it for 200 yards they returned. Divine Service held at HAYSTACK POST at 9.15. a.m.	
	Feb 6/7		Morning very quiet along our whole front. Patrols were sent out from Right & Left Coys. German artillery active at 4.15. P.M. Shells seemed to come across from S.23 central. The right Coy. "B" sent out a patrol from S.22.C.1½.5. which proceeded due East for 75 yards, and then turned half left, making for QUINQUE RUE at S.22.C.2½.8. Within 12 yards of the road they heard a working party estimated at 12. They could be heard on the road working on wire or breastwork, the sound of hammering being clear. There was a sentry on duty near this party. A sniper was mounting about from one position to another in the willows at S.22.C.4.8. Another patrol was sent out by "B" Coy from S.21.b.9.7½, towards FME COUR D'AVOUÉ alongside what is reported to be an old French running E.N.E. from S.21.b.9.7½. The patrol met enemies with obstacles, but advanced about 250 yards, when a flare suddenly exposed two enemy working parties, working on each side of the gateway leading to the farm, each party consisting of 8 men. The patrol thought there was a sentry posted in the old French along which they had come: the enemy working parties were very silent, probably wiring. Machine Guns were turned on parties found by both patrols. The left Coy. "D" sent out a patrol from S.16.c.1.3. consisting of 1 N.C.O. & 5 men towards point S.16.c.5.0. patrol reported that snipers did not fire while patrol were out: very lights were observed sent up from S.22 a S.9. in three directions.	

WAR DIARY
or
INTELLIGENCE SUMMARY

(Erase heading not required.)

Army Form C. 2118

Place	Date	Hour	Summary of Events and Information	Remarks and references to Appendices
	Feb/6/7		Another patrol of 1 NCO and 5 men went out at 2.15. a.m from S.16.c. 27 towards S. 16.c. 5. 7 returning at 4.15. a.m. This patrol was unable to locate exact position of the sniper who has been troubling this part of the line lately but they think he is in communication trench at S.16.c.6.7. The first patrol of the left Coy. "D" went out at 12 midnight and returned at 2.5. a.m.	
	7/8		The morning of 7th instant was quiet. In the afternoon an operation by order of the 113th Brigade, was carried out. At 2.40. P.M the French Mortar Battery opened fire on the point S.22.O.4½.8½ in the German line, the mortars fired from the point S.21. d.9½.9½ in our line. Two guns were used and each fired 10 rounds 16 of which were very effective and fell right into the German trench. The remainder were nearly all very short. At 2.45.p.m. the Artillery started to bombard the same place. They fired about 150 rounds most of which found the mark, but quite a number were in direction and fell to the South at point S.22.c.5.5. and S.22.e.4.5. Considerable damage and lots of loose earth were thrown up. Our machine gun fired during the stay at points in the German line and at point S.22.a.5.8½. at 4.45. from the enemy retaliated by a short bombardment of our front line from S.21.d.9½.5½ to S.21.d.9.7. Their 18 pounders fired about 30 rounds of these only 3 did any damage to our parapet, the damage was slight one dugout roof being blown in, and a few snollops knocked off the top of parapet. At 10.5am the enemy shelled Batn.Head Qrs with about 20 shrapnel, no damage done. Retaliation was given from "C" Battery R.F.A. the line "B" Battery being broken. Patrols went out from both "B"& "D" Coys.	

WAR DIARY or INTELLIGENCE SUMMARY

Army Form C. 2118

(Erase heading not required.)

Place	Date	Hour	Summary of Events and Information	Remarks and references to Appendices
Febry 7/8			7. At midnight 7 February 7/8, 10 rounds rapid fired along the whole line, the object being to make the Germans man their parapets. To soon as the rifle fire ceased, the artillery & motor machine guns opened fire on their night lines. An officer patrol under Capt. J.G. Jones went out from the point S.22.c.4.3.6.5. along the communication trench to find out if the Germans were working on the point S.22.c.4.3.8.2. but found S.16.c.3.7 and 8.30 p.m. a listening patrol went out from the left bay at its point to find him. The patrol returned at 11.0 p.m. Enemy's snipers were active on both sides & englobate a portion of our trench between Nos. 6 & 7 from trenches were seen to be in the ruins of the Ferme au Bois. He fires down a portion of our trench by Nos. 7 bays, and fires 8 rifles were placed in parapet. In the night our front 1 at No. 15, 1 at No. 13, 1 at No. 12, 1 at No. 11, 1 at No. 7, 1 at No. 5, 1 at No. 4, and 1 at No. 3 three trench mortars & artificial awning the could object was to catch any working parties which was trying to repair trench at S.22.c.4.3.8.2. They were fired at regular intervals during the night. A hole looking like a special form of traverse at S.22.c.6.7 was knocked down during the day by machine gun fire.	
Febry 8			2. Relief of Battalion in front line and supports by 10th Welsh Regt. after relief companies & Head Qrs moved to LA CROIX MARMUSE	
Febry 9			3 and 8 Coy recalayer killed otherwise camps in own billets as before. Battn. Chaplain in charge of underclothing and cleaning generally.	
	10		Ordinary routine	
	11		—do—	
	12		—do—	
	13		Battalion paraded for Divine Service at 11.30 a.m. the Rev. Lewis officiating.	
	14		Ordinary Routine. Great attention being paid to instruction in Bomb throwing.	

WAR DIARY or INTELLIGENCE SUMMARY

Army Form C. 2118

Place	Date	Hour	Summary of Events and Information	Remarks and references to Appendices
	2 May 15		Ordinary Routine	
	" 16		" "	
	" 17		Battalion paraded at 8 a.m. and marched to GORRE via VIEILLE CHAPELLE and LA COUTURE. Headquarters and C & D Coys billeted in GORRE CHATEAU, A & B Coys in farms outside.	
	" 18		Ordinary Routine	
	" 19		" "	
	" 20		Battalion paraded for Divine Service in GORRE CHATEAU C. of E. Wesleyans' paraded with Irish troops in attendance. A brandon battalion of Lancashire Fusiliers arrived at GORRE CHATEAU for attachment to Battalion in 113 Brigade, one Coy remained, 1 Coy going to 1st Battalion, after all had their dinner in Courtyard de la Courtyard. Shortly from the other Battalion for attachment, band played in the Courtyard. About 6 p.m. a false alarm for gas was given and the Coys and Battalion paraded outside their billets with gas helmets on, the alarm not in command until 7.30 p.m. 9.30 p.m. and 11.30 p.m.	
	" 21		relieved 13th Battn in right front subsector of Scottries Farm at ST VENANT. 1st Battn. Suspecting a relief at 50 yards distance between Givenchy companies marching by Coy in columns. Relief was completed at 9.15 pm. A.13 & in front line & support, D Coy in reserve, at GUNNER'S SIDING.	
	2/22		Operations. The enemy was very quiet with occasional shortbursts of machine gun fire. During the relief our artillery was very active, enemy replied to our fire by Sap G. at 6.30 pm. 21.2.16 we had one man killed and one slightly wounded. We received the order and the men made no attempt to occupy it. A Battery fired 115 rounds. B. Battery 63 rounds of shrapnel during the day.	
			Intelligence. It was reported by 13 Batt. that probably a German working party would be found between	

1875 Wt. W593/826 1,000,000 4/15 J.B.C. & A. A.D.S.S./Forms/C. 2118.

WAR DIARY or INTELLIGENCE SUMMARY

Army Form C. 2118

Place	Date	Hour	Summary of Events and Information	Remarks and references to Appendices
	27/23		enemy line and that of "C" sap; bombing officer and two men found a string of unstrung enemy strands to have a few special rifles which fire unusually "C" sap but used tea no underparty; the sentry at the sap also heard no sound of working. Enemy appear to have a few special rifles which fire unusually at intervals on gray stedach. A working party was observed at 1.0 am at F.9.D.6.7 at 1 am the night. A German working party was observed in that was not known. Work on firing loophole in B. Sap commenced, also strengthening parapet and building up traverses; drainage of communication trenches taken in hand. Operations: Enemy machine gun traversed our parapet at "Sand 6" m 12 pm about F.9.D.5.10 two machine gun retaliated effectively; the enemy also fired rifle grenades at intervals all day; we retaliated by sending over two or three to their own. A German sniper was very active opposite F sap, but could not be located. As soon as it was observed that the snow was likely to remain some while single quits for patrols were made and sent up to front line but an account of bright moon patrols were unable to go out. (Loopholes) 250 rifle grenades were fired by us. Two snipers made their way out to the edge of the crater of the mine exploded on 24/2/16 by the enemy; no enemy movement was observed about F.9.D.22.93 not F.9.D.1.1 as reported previously. Indeed no forms a new crater but to enlarge the old one of the N. side; it has made no difference to our front at 11.15 pm a 2/L. and snipers were heard as the B.F. officer had a immediate party would rap the other had a German working party dimming in stature. Whistling laughing it was decided not to take offensive action; the working party's fault was masked on their right by luftmines who fired regularly on our sap; they were too far away to be [illegible] At 9.0 pm A/L C of [illegible] sniper working parties in F.9 of craters; the boy bombers were organized for rifle grenades were fired enemy, enemy were discreetly hard in direction of talk and work fire which was not effective WORK A J.A.A 13 mdr also was started panel of Chickened revetted dugouts built off KINGS ROAD.

WAR DIARY
or
INTELLIGENCE SUMMARY

Army Form C. 2118.

Place	Date	Hour	Summary of Events and Information	Remarks and references to Appendices
	Feb 23/24		Operations. Our machine gun fired at working party Sq.d.7.4 and at another party at A9.D.6.6.1 and at. They also frequently searched the enemy's parapet. The enemy's snipers were active during the night and fired frequently. Fq.d.2/2.1 at 8.0 a.m. 23.2.16 the artillery bombarded enemy trenches in SUNKEN RD rather in advance with perfect results which it was gathered that casualties were inflicted. In all 250 rifle Grenades were fired from enemy shelled Coy HQrs Fq.a.b./2.2/2 at 8.10 p.m. They obtained no direct hits but no damage was done. Intelligence. A patrol of two men went out under Lieut. Ward at 8.30 p.m. 23.2.16 from F rap. patrol followed an old trench running due EAST, until the enemy's wire. Patrol reports enemy wire to be strong and deep, for about 80 yds in length, being the area they were able to examine; no sentry was seen at the vicinity of the F rap. Sap E F (there was no indication of work. There were sounds of sawing and chopping also much talking to the south). This was probably a working party of 80 to 100 at ruff patrol returned 9.50 p.m., & machine gunfire and rifle grenades turned on the party. One sniper claim one victim in the crater opposite point Fq.d.1/2.4. He was seen to fall back. Officer's patrol went out at 9.0 p.m. from Sap F under Lt. Newman to reconnoitre the ground to the right of craters & find a way round the crater, to the right of Sap F. To the rear of the craters adjoining also to ascertain enemy working party on the far side of the crater. The patrol went SE along our wire to about 100 yds and then struck N.E. to the south side of the crater for about 100 yds distance Very lights were thrown up from the far side of the crater and a machine gun opened fire from the enemy's parapet on the right of the patrol at 9.40 p.m. our artillery opened heavy fire not the Several enemy patrol came in. The patrol were unsuccessful in reaching the feet, but have been [?] and retired, by a our ground, to the wire, the feet and the knees' for straining and climbing whilst marcets within range could be felt. No wire was seen near the crater except in am. A sniper's post was located opposite Sap C at Fq.d.7.2.12. A German working was seen from sap @ in vicinity of Fq.d.7½.1.½ and it was noted that they wore white caps, the party was fired on with rifle. Grenades from three different points simultaneously and dispersed.	

#353 Wt. W3544/1454 700,000 5/15 D.D.&L. A.D.S.S./Forms/C. 2118.

Army Form C. 2118.

WAR DIARY
or
INTELLIGENCE SUMMARY.
(Erase heading not required.)

Instructions regarding War Diaries and Intelligence Summaries are contained in F. S. Regs., Part II. and the Staff Manual respectively. Title pages will be prepared in manuscript.

Place	Date	Hour	Summary of Events and Information	Remarks and references to Appendices
	23/24		WORK. Thickening parapets and making new traverses in sector of No. 3. platoon, A. Coy. Further proposed parapet S. of REGENT ST. cleaning trench boards and wiring then continued. Wiring done S. of Regent St. R.E. fatigues and carrying parties. An unfortunate accident occurred to Pte Williams of "C Coy" who was accidently shot by a man of Border Regt. Lieut Bracken died from his wounds.	
	24/25		OPERATIONS. Enemy shelled GIVENCHY from 2.0 pm to 2.30 pm obtaining one direct hit on the tunnel of sheet. Heavy active with machine gun between 6.0 pm and 6.30 pm. 24.2.16. Firing on GUNNERS SIDING and MARIE KEEP on machine guns retaliated and fired 1180 rounds at enemy wire and parapet. Our auxillary Trench mortar battery fired at A9.d.6½.6. From about 2.30 pm to 3.30 pm 24.2.16 it took the artillery considerable time to get the range, but when they did they seemed to be doing good work. The Stokes howitzer well and accurately established with 7.7m incredibly searching for trench mortar batteries but caused no casualties at 9.55pm we fired 10 rounds rapid fire, also machine gun and rifle grenade fire at the gap in enemy's wire at A9.d.6½.6. The enemy retaliated with machine gun, shrapnel and rifle grenades, their rifle fire noticeably weak. In every rifle grenade he sent over we replied with two. In all 500 rifle grenades were fired and very few were blind. Intelligence. The enemy grenade shooting is not too accurate, most of them falling between front line and support trench. The night was very foggy & Fogg's siren & F. Sap 9 in front of it heard a German working party in the area of the mine exploded on 21.2.16. The party is apparently employed in pumping water and repairing the gallery. It is proposed to organise an attack on this party. The wiring in support trench was completed & Bond St. several government repair of parapet, laying trench boards, making traverses, and ammunition store. Old dug-outs running along Queen's Rd. facing the railroad in A9C were cleared. Many fatigue and carrying parties and rifle grenade.	
	July 25		Our artillery in conjunction with Trench mortar batteries and rifle grenades bombarded enemy's salient at parish.	

#353 Wt. W2541/1454 700,000 5/15 D. D. & L. A.D.S.S./Forms/C. 2118.

WAR DIARY or INTELLIGENCE SUMMARY

Army Form C. 2118.

Place	Date	Hour	Summary of Events and Information	Remarks and references to Appendices

Points

July 25

A10C 1½. To cut wire and at A9.d.6½.6½ widen the gap. Bombardment began at 1.0 a.m. with good results as wire still appeared to be dropping nightly on to the wire, gaps being made and several small gaps are now to be seen. Two Bangalore Torpedoes set of which exploded with good effect and must have thrown up enemy wire beyond with 3 minenwerfer which was effectively replied to by our bombs and 4.2 m GIVENCHY Church, which attracted two direct hits. Very few rifle grenades and no trench mortars were fired during the night and at "stand to" this morning enemy machine guns instead of being quiet, kept up a hot being fired. Our bombers fired about 200 rifle grenades during the day giving the enemy chance to say me they sent our trenching parties was observed from about A9.d.3.8. Fire was opened which dispersed them and was trenching party was observed from about A9.d.3.8. Fire was half an hour taking enemy undoubted the gap.

Intelligence. An officer patrol went out at 6.0 p.m. from A9.d.3.8 and found a German working party in the crater to the left. Probably big a mortar. They came as heard distinctly working and pumping. This night flared was chased by snipers and a party of 4.0 placed on the far side of the crater. The party was too far away to be forced the officer then took a patrol in a S.E direction towards the German lines and came to widen 25 yards of German working party at about A9.d.6½.6 the patrol returned in. A German line was tuned in to the working party, a German in which was punched the news of the taking of ERZERUM was taken out by an officer's patrol at 6.0 p.m. and tied to a permanent stake facing the German line. At 8.0 p.m. an officer's patrol went out from about A9.d.6½.2 (approximately) "C" safe crawled forward up to their front, sloping down from which was a crater which dropped away slightly for about 50 to 60 feet; from this point a sniper could be heard humping and alternately firing to his rifle and firing it, a machine was also located which fired until over the backs of its patrol in a S.W direction this. This but cannot be approached to a bomb throwing distance from this direction and must be tackled from further west, a sniper's loophole was spotted at about A9.d.3 9½. The loophole is in top of the parapet and a flash of the rifle was distinctly seen, the German's were

A/B.S.S./Forms/C. 2118.

WAR DIARY
or
INTELLIGENCE SUMMARY.
(Erase heading not required.)

Army Form C. 2118.

Place	Date	Hour	Summary of Events and Information	Remarks and references to Appendices
West Ham	24/7/15		Ringing went down English snipers opposite part of our lines; a patrol went out from A9.a.6.8 to ascertain exact position of working party in front of MACKENSEN's TRENCH who were preventing our working party at work and the snow who was beyond SUNKEN RD (H.q) said prior to advance Enfilade Austrian material untaken was being rung in the German front line trenches; an officer's patrol from about A9.a.9.2½ went out at A9.a.4.45 a.m. proceeding N. of the station to the rear of the enemy's outpost at A9.a.6.1.4 running along the N. side of their trench was able about 15 feet deep and within the ridge ends of by the wire breaking; the wire was about 18 yards strong, enemy was heard talking in the trench, but no one was seen; the sentry at the whole way along their front made movement away talking was heard away to the front left, which seemed to be in advance of MACKENSEN's TRENCH, a sentry was heard to challenge in front of the patrol, he said "halt" & somebody unintelligible. A machine gun was located firing from the crest of the crater about opposite A9.d.2.9.3.	
			YORK Dugouts constructed general improvements to his accommodation trenches. At 6.15 p.m. the 14th Batt. was relieved at GUNNER'S SIDING by 13 BATT. By 4 hr relief 14 Bn took up support position in VILLAGE LINE, A Coy. holding HILDER, GIVENCHY, MOAT HOUSE & HERTS. redoubts. "C" Coy in lubis at LE PLANTIN N ⅔, B Coy in billets at HB ?? WINDY CORNER and adjacent lines. D Coy in harn stores and dugouts near Batt. H.G.	
			Attention devoted to cleanliness generally; many fatigues for R.E. carried out.	
	July 26		Same as above	
		do	do	
		do	do	
		07		
		8	On relief by 16th Bn. in VILLAGE LINE and keeps in left Bn. relieved 13 BATTN in right front line to GUNNER'S SIDING. A Coy on to GUNNER'S SIDING A/D Coy on ?? clearing ? Dugout positions A Coy sent to GUNNER'S SIDING. 'D'Coy to mightily front line Central was not completed until 12.25 a.m. on 1/3/16 as the 9th 9th Bn could not move until they had been relieved by the 16th Bn who in their turn had to wait until they were relieved by the 15th Bn from YORK.	

S. H. Singleton
MAJOR, 1st R. ? ??

WAR DIARY
or
INTELLIGENCE SUMMARY.

(Erase heading not required.)

Army Form C. 2118.

Place	Date	Hour	Summary of Events and Information	Remarks and references to Appendices
	1/3/16		ST DAVID'S DAY. Messages of good wishes passed between the different battalions in the Regiment and the Brigadier. Leeks were worn by Headquarters.	
			Operations - Our Machine Guns were active during the night, firing 880 rounds at working parties which were reported to be at A.15 & 8.7 - A10.c.1.1 and A.16 a.2.8.; 350 rounds at A9.d.6½.6 and along the German parapet. During the bombardment of the enemy's billets in the night a few rifle grenades were fired by the enemy, but we retaliated with the usual 3 to 1, firing 50 in all.	
			Intelligence - The enemy was very quiet during the night.	
			Work. - Cleaning trenches & rebuilding after thaw; cleaning Lewis & rifles.	
	2/3 March		Operations - Our artillery on the morning of the 1st March fired at the enemy's line about A9.d.6½.6. and the supporting line in rear of that. A proportion of our shells were duds, but one burst prematurely about 30 yards in rear of our front line; 30 ft. high; the enemy during the day was remarkably quiet; at 2.0 a.m. a patrol of one man under Corpl Savage went out at point A9d.7.5. The object of the patrol was to carry out a scheme to induce the enemy to desert 2 sandbags containing 30 rifle & 17 rounds of rations and letters in German purporting to be written by a french soldier were taken out. The patrol had orders to dump these near some isolated old German knife rests about A9.d.10.1. and return by same route; at 2.45 p.m. they reported that they had found a deep ditch and had 16 bear to the right but that they had dumped the bags near they enemy wire, on examination it was found to be running from A.15.c.7.5. and dumped them too close to our own parapet; struck the short ditch running from A.15.c.7.5 and dumped them too close to our own parapet; a second attempt was then made; this time 20/70 Corpl. J.R. James took a man patrol of two men of from Days A about A9.d.7½ at 2.45 p.m. they took an entirely direction skirting the Southern boundary of rations and making for the above mentioned knife rests a then running line up laid from a fishing rod resting in Days A about A9.d.7½ and suspended on short stakes; at the end a small blue flag was fixed. The patrol reported having completed its work about 4.30 a.m. The patrol took samples of rations along this wire and dumped them a few yards away from the blue flag. The lettering of the German language made it clear to the enemy	

WAR DIARY
or
INTELLIGENCE SUMMARY
(Erase heading not required.)

Army Form C.

Instructions regarding War Diaries and Intelligence Summaries are contained in F. S. Regs., Part II. and the Staff Manual respectively. Title pages will be prepared in manuscript.

Place	Date	Hour	Summary of Events and Information	Remarks and references to Appendices
			that if they wish individually to surrender to us they must come in to the flag and follow the line unarmed with the hands up, and that they must not come in chargers harder than [?]th at a time. The whole operation was completed by 5.20 am, the garrison of o/p's warned, and extra sentries posted. Another patrol went out with the same object and similar samples of rations and letters from "B" boy in the Centre. They went out from F Sap about A.9.d 9.4; patrol went out at 2.0 am and returned shortly after 4.0 am. Patrol followed along the line of stakes to a point where these stakes run to the South; at this point they left the old fibres and bore to the North for about 60 yards from the point reached, the patrol worked back, firing Verey lights at intervals, to a point in front of our parapet where there is a short unused sap at junction of BOND STREET and front line. Our rifle grenades evidently annoyed the Germans who turned their machine gun activities our Lewis guns replied. — A patrol also went out from A.9.d 2.5 at 7.30 pm from A.9.d.2.8 under Serjt J? Venmore, the Germans threw a heavy trench mortar bomb into the trenches about 15 were killed and 1 wounded — two of the former being Bantams of 15th Cheshire Regiment attached. Traverse was wrecked also the entrance to COVENTRY STREET to also blown up & caused considerable damage, D'troop Headquarters A.9.d 3.2 at 6.20 am 2.3.16 and caused considerable damage. Intelligence — The patrol which was sent out by "B" boy found that there was only one sentry on the front of the enemy trenches apparently. A considerable amount of work was going on inside the German trenches but none outside. The patrol which went out from the left boy at A.9.d.2.8 under Lieut. J.J. Venmore proceeded along S. side of Crater and reported a covering party 60 yards away; the patrol then went due South and found that there was a working party at about A.9.d.6?.6. mending the wire; machine guns were turned on this point as soon as patrol returned. Rifle grenades were fired at a German working party in the Crater near A.9.d 2.8 and also a machine gun, the bombers organised a rifle grenade attack on the crater and the machine gun was knocked out. Work — Repairing trenches and parapets, clearing trench boards, one traverse in front-line rebuilt, Sap E cleared and revetted, work on parapet South of REGENT STREET continued, garrison at MARIE greatly improved, Lewis communication trench by pumping out water, new parapets were repaired and cleaning trench boards, this was also done in the MARIE Redoubt; at GUNNERS SIDING was also built. KINGS ROAD Communication trench scraped and cleaned; work on bomb proof shelter carried on in left Coy, walls built and steel girders put over them, roof timbered and parapet repaired, wiring done before front line N & S of	

E. Sap.

WAR DIARY or INTELLIGENCE SUMMARY

Army Form C. 2118.

Place	Date	Hour	Summary of Events and Information	Remarks and references to Appendices
	2/3 Mar		**Operations.** - At evening "Stand-to" a heavy artillery bombardment started on our right; artillery fire being continuous; retaliation on part of Enemy Artillery was weak; our own "obds to" until 7.20 p.m., and opened rifle & machine gun fire; rifle grenades were also fired, enemy sent up red rockets, which were supposed to be signals for reinforcements. Our Stokes guns fired during the night at enemy working and wiring parties at A.9.d.6.3.6., and A.10.c.1.1; own Mobile guns fired from A.15. B.8.9. at enemy snipers situated about A.9.d.9.2. during "Stand to" on 2.3.1916 rifle grenades were fired from all along our line, most of these exploded; not more than 5% being blind. Mobs were fired at a flat periscope observed at A.9.d.8.6½; it disappeared after the third grenade had exploded; about 250 grenades were fired in all. Our patrol under Sgt Egerton mentioned in yesterday's report went out again from A.9.d.3.4. to complete the work of taking the samples of ration and german letter so close as possible to the german line. Patrol left ration & bread at end of line, which they had fixed on the previous night. The patrol went near the German line. **Intelligence.** - The above mentioned patrol reported much noise and talking & movement in the German trench to their front, which seemed much more full of troops than last night. The patrol thought a relief was taking place or reinforcements coming up; patrol returned at 2.30 a.m. An officer's patrol went out under Lt. A. Foy's Jones from A.9.d.2.3. to reconnoitre the front before our men started sewing; they found front clear, but enemy could be heard driving stakes, singing & whistling in the crater. During the day a telephoned observation was obtained from Sap F. with a telescopic periscope; there were many signs of activity to work Sap F. has lately been subject to very deadly sniping & from these movement was observed about 70 or 100 yards off; that of a man's face was observed above the parapet; it was withdrawn & shown again at intervals; it was decided that it was a mask put out as a bait; from the listening post position in the sap a man's face was seen along parapet(?) he was wearing a round grey cap without a peak and was at another part of the crater about 20 or 30 yards from the mask; turning to the northern side of the crater an object grey in colour was seen a little further off, about 100 yards off, with a black object like a small post in front; the black post was withdrawn and the grey object was turned slowly round and was disclosed to be a box periscope; an attempt was made to snipe the man seen from front	

WAR DIARY
or
INTELLIGENCE SUMMARY.
(Erase heading not required.)

Army Form C. 2118.

Place	Date	Hour	Summary of Events and Information	Remarks and references to Appendices
	Nov 3/4		The listening post, but heavy fire from machine guns and rifles made it impossible. The amount of fire from enemy side of his crater is strongly held, rifle grenades were turned on and the enemy retaliated with rifle grenades. Proceeding with bomb proof shelters, dug-outs, repair of parapets etc, renewing sap with parados in wire cap also renewing traverses which had buckled in parapet will up in SHAFTSBURY Street wiring done in front of left bay, thickening of parapet in right bay beginning with the height of each platoon water pumped out of MARIE KEEP, trench boards raised and cleaned, cellars cleaned out and water pumped out, one dug out completed, excavation for another proceeded with, parapet and trench step strengthened. Observation of enemy bombardment by the Artillery and trench Mortar Batteries of the enemy line on our front A9.a.4.2. took place between 12.0.0 & 12.30 p.m. and the firing was effective much material being thrown about. There was also considerable Artillery activity on lighter batteries 2.0 p.m. + 5.0 p.m. Enemy bombarded GUNNERS SIDING at 3.30 p.m. one shell falling in the trench, but no damage was done. Enemy rifle will Minenwerfers fire falling on our support line & rgt front line. The Boy. Dept. Major watched & to trenches about A9.a.3.5. this was very successful and was followed by but shelling and rear a salvo from about A9.a.3.5. this was very successful and was followed by but shelling and remaining of frames and vigorous retaliation by enemy machine guns. At enemy stand 6 enemy snipers were fined and 4 be fired 200 rifle grenades were fired at our support a' A9.a.4. & one [...] about [...] quiet about 12.15 a.m. one rifle At enemy stand loop holes were made from which to fire at enemy snipers who had been troubling our snipers; of late rifle grenades fired by the enemy seem to be greatly reduced numbers at A9.b.2.5. at A9.b.2.7.5 which has been line from a sniper at about A9.b.5.9.7; careful observation & no parapet arrangements for turning the movements were noticed on. Wale in ruining in the trenches in the support line 16 front line. At 9.0 p.m. a patrol under Sec. 2nd Lt. of right company were made damage was done during the morning bombardment. Sg. 2 and g was from A9.b.3.4 to observe what working party 80 yards N of A9.b.10.8 grenade was heard at 10 p.m. and reported from the enemy kept up bursts of machine gun fire for some time, the patrol wire could not be damaged; no fire except the ground patrol German was in boats of loopholes during the morning by of several loopholes it was impossible to reply	

Army Form C. 2118.

WAR DIARY
or
INTELLIGENCE SUMMARY.
(Erase heading not required.)

Instructions regarding War Diaries and Intelligence Summaries are contained in F. S. Regs. Part II. and the Staff Manual respectively. Title pages will be prepared in manuscript.

Place	Date	Hour	Summary of Events and Information	Remarks and references to Appendices
YORK			Hospital much pumping going on at a trench opposite Sap E.	
	4/3/16		Parapets and dugouts knocked about; walls bombed out of MARIE KEEP; new dug out erected at GUNNERS SIDING also knocked. Work done on parapets between CHAFTESBURY & REGENT ST. Sentries repaired at BOND ST. & PICADILLY. Wiring was done in extra cry. several get-rebuying made. The right Coy. to work consisted of rebuilding & putting knocks about parapets, strengthening dugouts in front line. & left Coy repairing trench, cleaning and wiring. Boards broke floor during Sap E and putting down boards and proof shelter and dugouts started.	
	5/3/16		One operator claimed a machine. The enemy sniping officer reporting that a German who casually showed himself above had been answered by a shot. The blend through a snipers loophole. About 20 downfall of snow made conditions in the trenches very trying to all ranks. His lying a great amount of water and mud. The bath was returned by the 13 Battn. the rally filling temptation at 10.0 pm. One bell of our Coy marched back to GORRE. H.Q. Coy & two his holding to the CHATEAU OF CAPOY. In front. Dinner & Coy... service took place at 5.30 pm. and was taken by Rev. Jung & Jones.	
	6/3/16		All Coy bathed, and generally in prepared. The Paid. played in courtyard Coy. during the day; a voluntary 7/3/16	
	8/3/16			
	9/3/16		GORRE Chateau at 11.30 am. Clearing up and back at ESSARS.	
	10.3.16		General cleaning up and back at ESSARS.	
	11.3.16		A Fatigue party of 500 N.C.Os. and 6 officers went to GORRE to undertake a big wiring scheme in front	
	12.3.16		of defences in vicinity of LOISNE. Disposition of arms by Common Sgt. a.k.a inspection under Coy. arrangements.	
	13.3.16			
	14.3.16		Ordinary routine, fatigue parties on wiring at LOISNE 5.0 NCOs and men needed for trenching raids in enemy's	
	15.3.16		front parade until shrubbing. Being much to wire Range under by companies.	
	16.3.16		Fatigue parades at 3.10 pm. Reported to reserve at FESTUBERT arrived in FESTUBERT 6.10 pm. & took over from 102. S.S.B.	
			The Battn. returned to 11 Battn. in the front line left Battalion from RITHESAY BAY to QUINQUE RUE Consisting of 1 Coy left	
			BREWERY CORNER at 7.0 p.m. C Coy took over left front A Coy took over right front 3 platoons of B in supports	
			at RICHMOND TERRACE A Coy and 1 platoon of B. in reserve at OLD BRITISH LINE. Standed cupboard 20 minutes.	
			When the arrival of another platoon. Our Artillery shelled enemy line at S 28 a 2.2 at 11.30 am and our shell appeared to be effective	
	17.3.6		and burst well. Very high considerable amount of hostile rifle fire about 2/3 am behind. Lewis guns fired occasional	
			bursts in front of RICHMOND TERRACE was battered and examined at S28a2.2 and completed at 9.25 pm. to enemy	
			trench at gap in wire at S29a.2.2 and at working party at S.22.C.6.3.	
			Intelligence. The relief of the 19 Battn. Suffks was carried out without incident and completed at 12.15 pm. Artillery fire was	
			not very active. During day considerable amount of hostile rifle fire received at 11.30 and others activity. No news of Sn.che	
			25. Digging party was at work for a time till recommenced at 3 am. M.M. Our wife Lewis guns were opened from 12 and	
			a red & coloured and 6 x H.V. landed near the parapet. The enemy party was again party not altogether night is also so as a result. and 6x H.V. landed near the parapet. Artillery fire was	
			was heard. The enemy party were very noisy and called out "Hullo" several times and there was practically no rifle fire on M14 Drive.	
			until Rumour Storm time. On the right Coy. front there was practically no rifle fire on M14 Drive.	

2353 Wt. W2344/1154 700,000 5/15 D. D. & L. A.D.S.S./Forms/C. 2118.

Instructions regarding War Diaries and Intelligence Summaries are contained in F. S. Regs., Part II. and the Staff Manual respectively. Title pages will be prepared in manuscript.

WAR DIARY

or

~~INTELLIGENCE SUMMARY.~~

(Erase heading not required.)

Army Form C. 2118.

Place	Date	Hour	Summary of Events and Information	Remarks and references to Appendices

The wire in front of RICHMOND TERRACE was found to be weak. An officers patrol under Lieut. T Rees consisting of 1 officer, 1 NCO & 1 man went out from S28 a 3.5. they entered CANADIAN ORCHARD and proceeded along an old trench running in a N.E direction. After proceeding along this sap for some distance they climbed out on the left side and after proceeding about 30 yards they saw two men about 30 yards in front of them. The patrol watched the enemy for some time and Cpl Williams observed more of the enemy approaching from the right flank with the intention of cutting off the patrols retreat along the sap. The patrol then retired to the Sap - fired at the enemy approaching from the right and returned along the old trench through the ORCHARD to the point they started from. The same patrol went out again from S28 a 5½. 9½ and proceeded in an Easterly direction working their way towards a ditch or trench fringed with trees running obliquely towards the Germans line and after crawling for an hour the patrol encountered an enemy sentry throwing up flares and on being discovered had to retire. They heard sounds of hammering and the enemy working party was whistling and singing. The going was good and the Sap was fairly dry.

WORK — New loopholes were erected in the following islands 14, 15, 21, 24 and at S27. a 8.3. and at S27 b 3.1. Parapets were strengthened and new traverses erected, trench boards relaid on the islands. Pumping and repairing of parapet at Cover TRENCH on right Sub Sector. Construction of Parapets and dug-out proceeded with at RICHMOND TERRACE and bomb and Grenade stores examined and checked. Bombs, ammunition and RE material carried up to front line. Parapets also strengthened in O.B.L.

Mch 19 — **Operations** Rifle grenades were used during the day by the left Coy in retaliation for Grenades sent over by the enemy. Our artillery active at 10. AM and in the afternoon. Many heavy shells falling about S21 c central were blind. L.H.V. Shells falling at S28 a 2.2 were observed to burst wire on the German parapet. Two M. G. fired bursts at working parties observed at S28 a 1.1 and S22 c 6.6 respectively.

Intelligence Enemy's snipers inactive during the day but were more active at "Stand to" last night. Enemy sniper suspected at about S27 d 5.6. A patrol of 1 NCO & 7 men went out to examine the gap in the German wire at S28 a. 2.2. The night was very thick and the wire is reported to be strong. The patrol was seen and fired on when approaching the wire. The ground is swampy. Noises as though men working with trowels were heard about S28 a 3.2 all day. Evidently some breastwork being erected. At "Stand to" last night the enemy was noisy and kept calling across to our men to fetch cigarettes and bully beef.

WORK — Snipers Posts started at S28 a 2¾. 6½ and S27 b 10. 4½. Gooseberries were made in the day time and put out after dark, strengthening parapet, clearing trenches and draining has been done also Salvaging and bringing refuse.

Mch 19. — **Operations** The enemy were quiet. There was some desultory rifle fire. Aeroplanes & Artillery were fairly active on both sides. About 33% of our heavy shells falling in direction of S22 C. Central were blind. At 8 pm. enemy's transport was heard on RUE DE MARAIS & our artillery opened fire with two salvos of shrapnel. Our M. G. fired bursts at gap in Hun's wire at S28 a 2.2. and at enemy's working party about point S22. c 6.5. Our snipers claim two victims.

Intelligence. A reconnaissance of the ground in front of the left Coy shows that posts 34 - 31 are connected by the OLD CANADIAN TRENCH, which continues to the listening posts at S28 a 4.7 approx. There is a signboard marked ORCHARD SAP between the listening post and 31 Island. Near the L.P. the road is crossed by old front and support trenches connecting up to Island 30 and the Islands in front of the right Coy. Old trenches in CANADIAN ORCHARD...

WAR DIARY
or
INTELLIGENCE SUMMARY
(Erase heading not required.)

Army Form C. 2118

Instructions regarding War Diaries and Intelligence Summaries are contained in F. S. Regs, Part II. and the Staff Manual respectively. Title Pages will be prepared in manuscript.

Place	Date	Hour	Summary of Events and Information	Remarks and references to Appendices
	Mch 20		one day and forwards gives great cover but that are two exposures lines nearest ARGYLE ROAD and PICCADILLY met in No 30. Sound report seeing enemy a man behind the him keep to their front. A good deal of hammering was heard along enemy line and particularly near QUIN QUE RUE and a effort and much organ dust was heard opposite S.28.a.3.7. The enemy appeared to be endeavouring to induce our men to do likewise. The enemy sniping was more vigorous during the day. An observer in island 14 saw enemy throwing over the parapet at about S.27.d.6.5. WORKS. Construction of snipers loos at islands 35,36,37 proceeded with. Notice Boards engaged as at construction of Nos 3 and 9 the enemy shelled. During mornight of post 11 and in Nos 3 of islands 14, 15 + 16. 60 loopholes were put up to dimensions and put into the tunnel parapets traverses in islands strengthened and repaired and new ones constructed and new loopholes made. Ramping and cleaning trench proceeded with. New trench boards put in + wired in PIONEER ROAD. S.A.A. + R.E. Stores carried to front line	
		9.0pm	Operations. The Snipers Officer reported about RUE DE MARAIS. About 9.0pm. No word was heard at RUE DE MARAIS and the Artillery fired two salvos shrapnel about 10.30 p.m. a small working party about S.22.0.6.0 opposite post 31. Two men of the patrol moved into the old french wire left and fence 2 bombs each machine-gunners were seen of the working party. Artillery was now carried out. An officer and two men left POST 16 at 8.0pm to find a enemy wire reported to be in front of post 34 (Arista) own front was heard but he was not there. Patrol returned 10 p.m. a patrol of 1 NCO + 6 men left POSTS 25 at 10.30 p.m. no hostile patrol was met. The enemy was heard working and talking in his trenches. Patrol returned at midnight. Owing to very light and moonlight the General Work. Training and cleaning bottom of trenches and up to the Scots. Building traverses in islands also loopholes. Wiring done. Battalion relieved by 13th Win J and cond to support line of FESTUBERT Relief completed at 9.0 pm. C.pl met. Pauleau news received that Luit J. Vanmere had been granted demobilisation leave and Naval Routine Fatigue party to R.E. work.	
	" 22		Usual Routine.	
	" 23		Bath relieved the 13th Win J. in the front line. The 16th Win J. relieving us in support line - Relief.	
	25		completed at 9.45 pm. Operations. Relief of 13th Win J. very quiet night. An Officers patrol went out and returned in half an hour as they were plainly visible in the snow at a distance of men 50 yds	

1875 Wt. W593/826 1,000,000 4/15 J.B.C. & A. A.D.S.S./Forms/C. 2118.

WAR DIARY or INTELLIGENCE SUMMARY

Army Form C. 2118

Place	Date	Hour	Summary of Events and Information	Remarks and references to Appendices

Mch. 26.

Patrol went out 9.30 pm.

Intelligence. The enemy heard walking along RUE DE MARAIS at 1.45 am.

Work. Carrying up R.E. stores. Jumping up of 27, 28 dugouts + 36 + 37. Also ORCHARD TRENCH and M.G. islands. Trench boards laid down on right of front line. Lengthening parapets of dugouts.

Operations. Three patrols went out. An officers patrol left at 9.0 pm from S.27.b.3.0 to reconnoitre suspected M.G. emplacement at S.27.a.9.9 p.m. The M.G. opening fire abruptly to S.W. when every light 70 yds away. The officer crawled up to once the whole area was lighted up by very lights. The patrol returned at 10.30 pm and from S.27.b.6.3 an 9.0 pm to examine enemy wire. A patrol of 1 NCO + 6 men went to investigate trickle work in Cg opposite line. It was met left S.28.a.4.4.3 proper. Reconnaissance made for gridded rifles. No wire was found.

Intelligence. The enemy's wire was seen to be high and strong. An patrol from S.27.b.6.3 reported no trip wire in front of enemys wire. It met two battle patrols apparently working in trenches and retired. Its patrol entered an wine it was hundred once and reconnoitred. The going was good and the ground clear. The enemy during the night fired rockets which burned with flame on reaching the ground & burnt for about 30 minutes. The light is yellowish and burns out about 3 feet if ground very fairly.

The enemy fired 27 m.m. at RICHMOND TERRACE during the day. An excellent burst message was sent by the 2nd Cay at 10.35 am. Opening at 10.29 pm first shells in at 10.35 am. O.P. had to obtain observation before firing. B.19 does not cover the point where enemy's line crosses RUE DE MARAIS S.28 a Central. These Cokes are rifle grenades and cannot be carried well. The enemy sent in burst in return which did not reach our entrance trench. Enemy's snipers quiet.

Work. Repairing parapet and making firing steps of ORCHARD TRENCH. Manning, hunting trenches. Pumping and cleaning. Connecting up islands 27 + 29, and 36 + 37. Monthly tub dug-outs Crossties made and taken up.

Mch. 27.

Operations. Rules lay relief completed at 9.0 pm. Three patrols went out. A patrol of two officers went out, Lieut T. Rees + J. Venman went out at 9.0 pm from Island 23 about S.27.b.7.3. to investigate and cut wire. Patrol

WAR DIARY or INTELLIGENCE SUMMARY

Army Form C. 2118

Place	Date	Hour	Summary of Events and Information	Remarks and references to Appendices

operation of ditch which runs Eastwards from S.27.d.7.5½ for about 150 yards and then bears slightly to the North and advanced till they came to a ditch running parallel to enemy trench at about S.27.d.7½.2. The ditch was about 5 feet wide and deep. The water level being about 6" below the bank. The enemy wire was immediately in front of the ditch and there were Germans working on their wire. Patrol of men moving through high wire was clear. L/Cpl Willis crossed the ditch and found a gap in the wire through which he and funnel onwards the patrol to do so. Since very light was observed Germans took a special small very light which dropped in the German wire late. Germans opened fire with about 5 of at me and fell with its rifles. One of the first shots hit the mission and remained covering it. The bodies of the men was shot through his cap and one through his bomb pocket - both without injury. It was deemed inadvisable to continue to try and get the wire under these conditions and whilst the last of the party returned L/Cpl Willis had to return and get the wounded under rifle fire of two wounded of 1 N.C.O. and 5 men. Wounded men from 30 sland (S.28.a.3.6) at 8.0 pm which matured to reexamine the ruin on the right of Rue de Marais at S.29.a.4.6. They lay for hours in a ditch undergrowth that they had arranged up to within fifty they could not pass through. They believe that they had moved mine of two more nettling which they put of the original ditch. There were no bombs or anything noticeable in the ruins. Small patrol under L/Cpl Jones inspected my wire from about S.29.a.4.4 to S.29.b.6.1 and reported that high and strong all the way except in spot near the ruin on Rue de Marais. There was no one in the ruin.

Intelligence. Enemy's army strengths opposite believed to be about S.29.c.6.2. Where appeared to be a fly dugout with two wire veins. At Stand 6" last night a man's head appeared near the parapet, and some new timber being carried could be seen. A light railway runs near the German line. There is also a narrow plank with a small self over a small sniper bombhole in a most M.G. loophole. A vantage on the N. side of Rue M G opposite S stand 31. An enemy sniper was spotted at S.29.a & 2. 7. Snipers were spotted at S.28. c & 7. Sniper fires at him and he fell Enemy parapets at S.29 c.6.2. Sniper seems to be covered and along enemy front.

WAR DIARY
or
INTELLIGENCE SUMMARY
(Erase heading not required.)

Army Form C. 2118

Place	Date	Hour	Summary of Events and Information	Remarks and references to Appendices
	Mch 28.		WORK. Operations made. Pumping and draining. Relaying wire carried up. R.E. material and their own rations. Trench Boards on RICHMOND TERRACE completed. Dugouts strengthened. Wiring done at 1"N3.H 70.0.t. and at QUINQUE RUE R.E. parties working on the new 30A. Post. Drew a fellow recce for Vermorel sprayers. Searching flare troops and dug-out given a visit at new crater O.P. Operations. A patrol of 1NCO and 7 men went out at 10.0 pm from S.27.b.9.3. To search for and attack enemy patrols. The enemy was quiet and none was found and the patrol returned at 11.0 pm. Intelligence. About 15 L.H.V. Shells sent into RICHMOND TERRACE about 3.45 pm and again at 9.30 pm. A sentry from the extreme left of ORCHARD TRENCH noticed several Germans working near the FME DU BOIS & called the attention of the sniping officer to this. The sentry fired 3 shots and after the 3rd shot one of the men was seen to fall. WORK. Trench Boards to knitt up planks brought up and laid down. 3 Bumps joined by Trench 96 and brought in. Deepening and thickening was in front of No.14 Island – 40 yds of high Apron wire with gooseberries and loose wire in outer edge was constructed from QUINQUE RUE in front of the portion in the centre of ORCHARD Trench to enemy FME DU BOIS Trench. Snipers loopholes constructed and deepened drain near RUE DE CAILLOUX. Battalion photograph taken. Relief of Battalion by 13th R.W.F. Relief completed at 9.50 pm. Baths.	
	Mch 29		Usual Routine. Baths arranged.	
	" 30		Usual Routine.	
	" 31		Relief by 14 Welsh Regiment the Bath. marched to Drummed Barracks districk at LES HARISOIRS, moving off at 1.30 pm via BETHUNE arriving at DROUINEN at 5.36 pm.	

S.W. Smyth MAJOR
for O/C. 11 (S) BATTALION
ROYAL WELSH FUSILIERS

WAR DIARY or INTELLIGENCE SUMMARY

(Erase heading not required.)

Army Form C.2118

14 Welsh
Vol 5

5.C
14 Welsh

Place	Date	Hour	Summary of Events and Information	Remarks and references to Appendices
	1.4.16		General cleaning up of billets and equipment. Concerts in evening, football in afternoon	
	2nd/4/16		Church Parade at 9.30 a.m. C of E and Nonconformist.	
	3rd/4/16		Ordinary routine. 330 men on fatigue wiring at LE TOURET.	
	4th/4/16		The Battalion marched to LE PANNERIE for inspection by the Corps Commander, Lt Gen Sir R.C.B. Haking K.C.B. & were drawn up in Battalion mass. After the inspection the Corps Commander expressed himself as being very pleased with the general bearing & turn out of the men, and Companies marched back to billets independently.	
	5th/4/16		Ordinary routine, a fatigue party of 100 men proceeded to LE TOURET for wiring.	
	6/4/16		The Second in Command, Adjutant, four Company Commanders and four Coy. Sergt. Majors proceeded to new sector of front line at GIVENCHY, which will be occupied by the Battalion on the 9th instant. - Parties from each Company went to bathe at LOCON; 320 men went to LE TOURET in evening for wiring fatigue.	
	7/4/16		Parades under Company arrangements.	
	8/4/16		Battalion marched to GORRE at 8.30 a.m. via BETHUNE and took up quarters in the ancient Chateau. C & D Coys however found rest in billets in farmhouses outside, we relieved the 10th S.W.B.	
	9/4/16		The Battalion relieved the 16th Welsh Regt. in the Right Sub-sector, GIVENCHY, the leading Company moving off by sections at 8.50 a.m. A.B.C. Coys occupied the front line in that order from the right, D Coy being in support at PONT FIXE, the left Company	

1875 Wt. W593/826 1,000,000 4/15 J.B.C. & A. A.D.S.S./Forms/C.2118.

WAR DIARY
or
INTELLIGENCE SUMMARY

(Erase heading not required.)

Army Form C. 2118

Place	Date	Hour	Summary of Events and Information	Remarks and references to Appendices
	9-10/4/16		found a garrison of 1 platoon for MAPLE KEEP, the centre company ½ platoon for ORCHARD FARM and the right company ½ platoon for SPOIL BANK. Relief completed at 12.45 p.m. Enemy active with rifle grenades, to which we replied vigorously; sniper claimed one victim at 6.30 p.m. at A.9.a.9.2; at 2.0 p.m. the Artillery attempted to detonate Bangalore torpedo, which had been left in Hun wire at A.15.c.15.6, but met with no success. Machine guns very active all night on both sides. Intelligence – A patrol of 3 Officers and 2 men of the 16th Batt" Welsh Regiment went out from Sap A.16.c.1.7 to find and bring in a wounded Officer of their Regiment, who was supposed to be lying out in front of our parapet, the patrol, however failed to find any trace of him, a second Officers patrol under Capt. G.P. Williams went out at 2.0 a.m. with the same object, they followed the route which the raiding party had taken up to the third telegraph pole about 150 yards from the Hun line, the patrol then wheeled to the left and came back in splinter order; they picked up two separate bombs and an apron containing 11 bombs, which were brought in, but they found no traces of the missing Officer and returned to our line at 3.15 a.m. An Officers patrol under 2nd Lt. Blue Jack went out from A.15 to A.9.0 at 8.0 p.m with the object of discovering hostile patrols or working parties in the event of finding any to send back for a fighting patrol and attack. The enemy's patrol; they returned at 10.0 p.m. & reported that they had seen no hostile patrol or working party and that the enemy was quiet. Works – Snipers loophole reconstructed at Sap C.A.; cleaning up trenches, wiring in front of left of A.Coy, drawing CHEYNE WALK, work on left flank of A.Coy. to link up with B.Coy.; drainage and new trench boards at ORCHARD KEEP. Wiring continued to right of A.Sap, parapet strengthened and rebuilt.	

1875 Wt. W593/826 1,000,000 4/15 J.B.C. & A. A.D.S.S./Forms/C. 2118.

WAR DIARY
or
INTELLIGENCE SUMMARY

(Erase heading not required.)

Army Form C. 2118

Place	Date	Hour	Summary of Events and Information	Remarks and references to Appendices
	10-11/4/16		**Operations** – A patrol went out at 8.0 pm from A 15 d 9.1 & went across the Centre Boyshront at about 200 yards distance without finding any hostile patrol or working party, patrol returned at 9.45 p.m.) There was great activity during the day at Duckshill with rifle grenades; we retaliated & silenced the enemy; rifle grenades were fired at frequent intervals on the gap in the show were made by the 16th Welsh Regiment. **Intelligence** – Sniping loophole discovered at A 9 d 8½.2, enemy's working party at A 16. C 6.8, wearing round dark grey caps; enemy very quiet until 9.30 pm when machine gun and rifle fire was opened and kept up for some time ; our working parties were stopped there for a short period having to cease work ; ours wire was broken but repaired ; enemy machine gun traversed our parapet during the night. Artillery took carried out successfully by Centre & left Companies at 8.30 a.m. on 11th instant. "D" Coy relieved "C" Coy in left front trenches and saps A, B, C & C. & "D" relief completed at 10.0 am when "C" Coy proceeded to quarters in village but at PONT FIXE, vacated by "D" Coy. **Work** – 3 recesses for S.A.A., rifle grenades made, many goosekries made & at night the parapet 18 night Company was extended and a new fire trench completed, wiring for 50 yards from A 15 B. 9 4 commenced, & single apron made. Jumping, cleaning trenches & laying curved tracks boards, removing full gas cylinders from many fire step in night-loop; extended parapet in gap in our line towards Centre Coy; steamed pills for 2 dug outs, drained entrance to "D" Sap. 3 sinitied parts & front-line trenches resown S.A.A. Area constructed. Fixed rifles mounted at BAYSWATER HILL and GUNNER'S SIDING.	

WAR DIARY or INTELLIGENCE SUMMARY

Army Form C. 2118

Place	Date	Hour	Summary of Events and Information	Remarks and references to Appendices
	11·12/1/16		**Operations.** A patrol went out under 2/Lt Upman from A.15.d.9.9. composed of 1 officer and 6 men to capture a sniper reported to be about A.16.c.5.9½. The patrol went out at 7.20 and returned at 8.30 p.m., a thorough search was made but no signs of a sniper having occupied this spot were discovered, no tracks patrol was seen. A patrol under Lt. A.E. Jones went out at 7.45 p.m. returned at 9.30 p.m. went out to ascertain if there is any threat running into the German lines from the old trench parallel to the trench and about 50 yards out at this point. Also to search for hostile listening posts and patrols. A dinner truck entering parallel with our old trench right top front did not lead anywhere to the enemy. The patrol then went out to a distance of 250 yds and carefully examined the tracks without seeing any traces of enemy patrols. Rifle grenades fired at A.16.c.6.7 and A.16.c.5.5. **Intelligence.** Enemy accidentally burnt in our front for the last 24 hours. The extra garrison appeared to be on the firestep as early flares "A" in the German trench opposite the entire bay. The snipers were not active; one flare was seen at point A.16.c.6.7 and A.16.c.5.5. as the latter point two men exposed themselves as snipers in O.P. BAYSWATER HILL saw the flashes of 4 enemy guns at A.16.d.0.8. at 4.50 p.m. **Work** wiring, relaying trench boards, heightening parapet on back sides of gap between right and centre Coys frontage, and draining improved and lives making good damage of straightening apron wire in front of entire englace; distance 6 gaps in c-D-bays, other dugout improved; improvements made for rifle grenade rifle 2 new latrines made ampex/proto renewals and sanitation cleaned and 2 dugouts commenced; nos 1+2 with no ablution from rifles; respond to firing wells have grenades. The 16/K.R.R.C. are on our right. The 15/K.R.R.C. are on our left. Up to date there have been casualties as follows: Killed, died of wounds + disease 27 Wounded + sick to England 73.	

Place	Date	Hour	Summary of Events and Information	Remarks and references to Appendices
	12-13/16		Operations At 12.10pm we fired 10 rounds rapid at enemy's parapet and threw bombs and rifle grenades; the latter appeared to take effect, as cries were heard opposite the gap. The artillery opened fire at the same time. Cheers were raised after firing 10 rounds rapid at about 12.15 am. 5 rounds rapid were fired immediately after the buglars sounded the charge and the men cheered with a view to induce the Huns to man their parapet in anticipation of an attack and rifle grenades were then directed at their loop hole trench. The enemy retaliated with L.H.V. shells towards the canal without effect. A patrol went out from A15.B.g.o at 8.0pm. They went out about 150 yards and crossed 16 yards of the centre Coy; there were notable patrols or signs of activity seen and on the return of this patrol they located a small working party opposite parapet. Rifle grenades and machine guns were directed on the working party. Intelligence. The enemy was active with rifle grenades on the left about 8.30pm (6 which we effectively replied, judging from the volume of rifle fire from the enemy front line trench it would seem to be lightly held; the snipers claim a victim at AQ.D 7.3 at 6.20pm. WORK Completed a fire bay in the gap on the right & a subtantial part of new traverse made. Wiring in the centre of old line from WIKLOW R.D completed with double apron for 50 yards C + D gaps widened and truck niches made in gaps, revetting with hurdles on the left ground.	

WAR DIARY
or
INTELLIGENCE SUMMARY.
(Erase heading not required.)

Army Form C. 2118.

Place	Date	Hour	Summary of Events and Information	Remarks and references to Appendices
	13.14/16		laying trench boards; one dug out erected in the right and two dugouts commenced in the centre of the line. Sniping, cleaning ditches, cleaning up of trench hills at PONT FIXE, burying rubbish what had accumulated there. No 1 snipers post completed. Nos 2 & 3 continued. Operations relieved by the 13 Kn? in the night front line and support posts, the relief started at 6.30 am and was completed at 10.30 am. The 1st Batt. R.W.F. then proceeded to the portion of support baths in the VILLAGE LINE. A Coy. occupying Brewery at PONT FIXE & B Coy the farm ruins by Batt. Hd Qts. C Coy GIVENCHY HILDER, MOAT FARM & HERT redoubts & D Coy houses by NINDY CORNER & LE PLANTIN SOUTH. Intelligence by snipers. Five (5) men reported to have been seen working about A16 c.9.7 from O.P. at BAYSWATER HILL. A Hun was seen to walk quickly past the repaired trench where the victim was claimed yesterday at A9 d 7.3. No 5.6.7 & 9 snipers post constructed at A9 a 7.1?, two Hun H.E. shells dropped near S.E. corner of GIVENCHY KEEP at 5.0 am. WORK Cleaning up Keeps, collecting salvage, revising cleaning under trench boards, making knife rest obstacles for roads. Burying and draining water out of Keeps, R.E. fatigue. A party of officers of 12 Royal Sussex Rgt. including C.O.	

Army Form C. 2118.

WAR DIARY
or
INTELLIGENCE SUMMARY.
(Erase heading not required.)

April 1916

11th Welsh Fus.

Place	Date	Hour	Summary of Events and Information	Remarks and references to Appendices
	14/4/16		and 4 coy officers paid a visit to the support line. Ordinary Routine	
	15/4/16		The battalion was relieved by the 12th Batt. Royal Sussex Regt & in relief marched to billets formerly occupied at RIEZ DU VINAGE, taking over from 12th Royal Sussex Regt.	6150
	16/4/16		The Battn. marched to ESTAIRES taking over billets from 10th Durham Light Infantry. Landed over late billets to 16th Sherwood Foresters	
	17/4/16		The Batt'n marched to PONT DU HEM taking over billets from 16th Royal Warwicks. T became Battn in support of the left sub-sector of MOATED GRANGE section	
	18/4/16		Ordinary routine, companies latched 50 men pe hour at Baths in "B" Coy area.	
	19/4/16		Parades under coy arrangements, route marches by platoons & bathing and bombing. Brig. Gen. Price Davies V.C. D.S.O. inspected the coy billets. C. O. and Coy offrs. visited front line trenches.	
	20/4/16		In the morning parades under Coy arrangements. at 8.6 pm the battalion relieved the 13th R.W.F. in front line sub-sector the relief was completed at 9.30 pm A B & C Coy occupied the front line in order named; D Coy occupied posts at WINCHESTER, TILLELOY NORTH, DREADNOUGHT, GRANT and ERITH pro. the line extended	

WAR DIARY or INTELLIGENCE SUMMARY

Army Form C. 2118.

49069

Place	Date	Hour	Summary of Events and Information	Remarks and references to Appendices
From M29d.9¼.7½ to M.24 d.1.5. Bathn. HQrs at MANCHESTER HOUSE. 15th Rd.W. on right, 16 Welch Regt. on left.	April 20/21		Intelligence:- Wire examined in the centre and found to be poor, except for 40 yards single apron made recently at 57. It stands to one of our Snipers that about 30 Huns working at right railway head about N.19.c.6.10, this was reported to Artillery but no rounds were fired at this target. The night was bright on account of moon and men could be seen at a distance of 50 yards. Machine gun traversed the tape during the night; rifle & machine gun fire took place by friend & foe during the night. Works:- Adjusting parapet & fire step to correct height; thickening parapet in places; wiring was done in front of centre & left companies, but work had to be suspended by latter owing to chances of night & machine gun fire on our party; repairing banquettes; removing obstructions in fire trenches; some berm steps fixed in parapet; pumping. Similar work carried out in Keeps.	

WAR DIARY
or
INTELLIGENCE SUMMARY.
(Erase heading not required.)

Army Form C. 2118.

Place	Date	Hour	Summary of Events and Information	Remarks and references to Appendices
	22-23/7/16		Snipers Report. Snipers in M.5.a.6 shot claim victim at 6.30 a.m. at M.30.a.6.5. Snipers in post no.19 claims a victim to-day at 11.10 a.m. at M.30.a.4.3. the latter victim was seen by a trench mortar officer who was observing at our loophole. Enemy uniforms, round grey caps. FIRES numerous fires in enemy's front line throughout the day. Progress of work. No. 39 post; new loophole plate fixed to command good field of fire, half right; general improvements. Bombardment 7.0 a.m. on 22nd inst enemy exploded mine at M.30.a.2.4½ about 80 yds. from our parapet in midst of craters already existing, and at same time commenced an intense bombardment at points M.29.b.9.2. and M.30.a.1.3. with shells of all calibre and 3 in. bombs, which fell slightly in rear of our line and did no serious damage. After examination of crater there seemed to be no advantage in their occupation to ourselves or enemy's headquarters. Lasted about half an hour; our casualties were not at all serious, one man being slightly wounded and one suffering from shell shock. Some damage was done to parados and WINCHESTER TRENCH was also damaged; several rifle grenades were fired at enemy's front line and	6.9.p

WAR DIARY or INTELLIGENCE SUMMARY

Army Form C. 2118.

1849

out 2 M.G's registered with one round only. Trench Hyphens were dropped in enemy front line trenches.

Intelligence: At 1.30 a.m. an Officer's patrol, Capt: J.P. Williams and I, were went out from M.30 a 1½ 4 for the purpose of examining new craters made by the mines yesterday of yesterday morning, and investigating old craters. The new crater was found at M.30 a 3.4, and measured about 15 feet wide by 12 ft deep; it was perfectly dry, and all other craters had water in them, numerically E of next crater no lip, crater full of water. The patrol went completely round the new crater, but found no traces of enemy occupation. There is no trench leading to it from Germans front line trench. Our any were between them. The ground round the crater is full of Shell holes giving good cover. Patrol watched among the craters for 3/4 hour, but saw no signs of enemy and returned at 2.45 a.m.

At 1.15 a.m. a patrol under 2nd Lt J. Pack went out to inspect the new crater. They went into the old crater at about M.30 a 4.5 and found their passage obstructed by barbed wire in their endeavors. The water prevented the wire being followed, but it appeared to be continuous. The patrol found the new crater. It was

6696

dug and not bigger than an 8 inch shell hole; these were no signs of enemy or of any work having been done by them. The patrol came in at 2.30 am; another patrol under Lt. B. Blackie went out to reconnoitre ground in front of M 24 C.10.3 at 12.30 am; our wire is poor and the front contains live ditches and an old trench roughly parallel to our parapet; the going was good and the patrol carefully examined the ground and any obstacles; there were no signs of the enemy's the patrol returned at 2.30 am.

Sniping. 1 victim was claimed by one of our snipers at 6.30 p.m. at M.30.a.6.5. Another victim was claimed at 11.10 a.m. at M.30.a.4.3. Both victims were grey uniforms and round caps. The latter victim was observed by a T.M. Officer who was observing at the time.

Work. Wiring + pumping ~~front~~ — and drainage repairs to parapet + parados in front line and bays making good wire, clearing MINCHESTER trench where hit by shell, new bomb shelters dug into parapets, trench boards laid on piles new pump placed in GRANT'S POST.

WAR DIARY
or
INTELLIGENCE SUMMARY.
(Erase heading not required.)

Army Form C. 2118.

Place	Date	Hour	Summary of Events and Information	Remarks and references to Appendices
	23-7-17		**Operations** We fired about 25 Newton Bippers into enemy's front line from BIRDCAGE during the day. A patrol went out from M36.a.4.9 to search for hostile patrols at 9.30pm. and returned at 11.30pm with no result. A patrol under Lieut. B.B. Cattime left M24d.2.4 at 8.30 p.m. after going some distance the noise of uncoiling wire and driving in piles could be distinctly heard at M24.d.4.1. The patrol returned at one and the artillery, who had registered the points on the previous day fired four rounds, the effect of same is not known, no hostile patrols were met. **Intelligence** A quiet day generally, machine gun flashes observed at M30A4.0. A little working party about M30 B.23.9b. reported by our evening party, at 12.15 A.m. they were dispersed by machine gunfire, the enemy was busy on his wire last night. **Snipers** Snipers claim victim as follows, 1 at 1.0 p.m at M30A4.3 from post No. 19, 1 at 3.30pm at M30A4.3 from No.19 post, 1 at 8.0 am at M30A52.5 from post No.9.0, 1 at 3.45 p.m at M30A3.4 from post No.46. The enemy has worked hard fully to day and in some cases has been seen firing over the parapet.	6709

Army Form C. 2118.

WAR DIARY
or
INTELLIGENCE SUMMARY.
(Erase heading not required.)

Instructions regarding War Diaries and Intelligence Summaries are contained in F. S. Regs., Part II. and the Staff Manual respectively. Title pages will be prepared in manuscript.

Place	Date	Hour	Summary of Events and Information	Remarks and references to Appendices
			WORK Wiring continued to left of circle at M24 d.14, wiring 40 yards single apron by entire company and wiring by right company continued; goatskins made and put out. Repairs to parapet & parados effected and dugouts made in front line and sups; draining and clearing drains effected and cleaning water level appreciably lowered, bombstore taken down and re-erected, new dugout completed and another commenced, firesteps remade; clearing up WINCHESTER trench, french boards laid and cleaned in several places; pumping also continued. A good many rifle grenades fired by enemy causing three casualties, one man severely and two slightly wounded; our trench mortars and left evening battery retaliated, the enemy artillery fired almost but were quickly silenced by our guns. We fired MARTIN pistols at their front line trench.	
	24/16		The Bath. were relieved by 15th Welsh Regt. on relief at 11.10 p.m. marched to billets at LA GORGUE arriving at 2.30 am on 25 Apl. Several cleaning up of billets & equipment. Backing of whole Battalion.	

Army Form C. 2118.

WAR DIARY
or
INTELLIGENCE SUMMARY.
(Erase heading not required.)

Place	Date	Hour	Summary of Events and Information	Remarks and references to Appendices
	26/16		Inoculation and parades under company arrangements.	
	27/16		Parades under Coy arrangements. Pantomime at Div. Recreation Room.	
	28/16		Parade under Coy arrangements. Pantomime in Divisional Recreation Room.	
	29/16		Parade under Coy arrangements. Football & athletic exercises in afternoon. In evening "Welsh" and all Coy messes dined together in B.Coy's mess. A very pleasant evening was spent.	
	30/16		150 NCO's men of the Battn. attended church parade at Divisional Recreation Room at 11.0 A.M. and after service medal ribbons were presented to an officer and some NCO's and men of 1st Division, who had gained them by acts of gallantry, by General Monro, commanding the 1st Army.	

S.B. Gwyther MAJOR. Commanding
14(S) Battalion.
Royal Welsh Fusiliers

6726

14TH BATTN. ROYAL WELSH FUSILIERS.
WAR DIARY
or
INTELLIGENCE SUMMARY.
(Erase heading not required.)

Army Form C. 2118.

/14 Welsh Fus
XXXVIII   Vol

6.C.
6238/
813
29 Melos

Place	Date	Hour	Summary of Events and Information	Remarks and references to Appendices
	May 1st 1916		Battalion marched to LAVENTIE. Relieving 13th Roy. A.C. (less 1 platoon) D'Coy going into billets in the town, while B. Coy furnished garrisons to MASSELOT, WANGERIE & ROAD BEND POST, while one platoon of C. Coy formed a garrison for ESQUIN POST.	
	2nd		Ordinary Routine parades under Coy arrangements.	
	3rd		Ordinary Routine. The enemy dropped three incendiary shells into FORT ESQUIN which at the house on fire immediately totally destroyed it. Many men losing all their possessions. Two enemy "sibs" also burnt into billets occupied by "A" Coy. There was only one casualty as the result of the bombardment.	
	4th		Ordinary Routine. Parades under Coy arrangements.	
	5		The Battalion relieved the 13th R.W.F. in the right front sub-sector, relief started at 8.0 p.m. & was completed at 9.35 p.m. Order of Coys in line from right A.B.C.D REDOUBTS. "A"Coy 1 platoon in ELGIN, C Coy 1 platoon in FAUQUISSART, D'Coys 2 sections in FELON. Enemy machine guns active throughout the night. Our Machine Guns kept up a brisk fire all along the line. At 2.50 am enemy commenced severe	

of the front line trenches of our two left coys. especially round Drury Lane Gun emplacements and in Drury Lane. N13c5b.8. we called for instant retaliation & the operation reported on acknowledgment, though the left coy alone was subjected to about 300 L.H.V. Trench Mortars & nearly 100 rifle grenades. It was not until after about 30 minutes that B199 Battery fired 28 rounds & C132 Howitzer Battery 24 rounds, on being asked to continue the retaliation C132 Battery reported that they could fire no more rounds without the permission of the Officer I/c Group, who ordered them not to continue firing if the enemy had stopped shelling. Our retaliation was insufficient, our casualties 3 killed & 7 wounded & 2 men suffered from shell shock. One of our own shells struck our parapet, some of the enemy shells fell within his parapet.

Intelligence. Parties were sent out to examine the wire, the right coy, A Coy report the wire to be very poor, the left Centre coy. reports that there are many weak places, and the wire is on the whole a fair obstacle. An officer patrol under 2/Lt Aponious went out at 12.45 am to inspect all communication trench leading to an old French running parallel to our line, but it returned

WAR DIARY or INTELLIGENCE SUMMARY

Army Form C. 2118.

625/3

Place	Date	Hour	Summary of Events and Information	Remarks
	6-7 5/16		two feet of water, and could not be utilised. WORK Cleared four parts of STRAND trench below RUE TILLELOY, which had fallen in during the shelling of the 5th inst. Firestep in right Coy raised. Repaired damaged parapet at M26 B75 reported parapet shattered by steel fire in the Rups. Operations About 1.20 pm our howitzer fired 8 rounds at night of enemy salient opposite N13.4 four were duds, two got [struck out] home on its mark. At 4.0 pm our artillery shelled communication trench near N14 c 5.2 & obtained several good hits. There was a further shelling of salient opposite N13.3 with better results. A trench was made in the enemy parapet. Our Lewis gun were directed on it's at N13 d.0.3 at 4.45 pm the artillery registered with 7 rounds on N13 d.2.8 four of these were duds, as a result of this activity the enemy fired about 50 L.H.V. which fell about M12 c 7½ · 8½ at 5.15 pm. An sniper claim one victim. At 1.30 pm the enemy put 20 & 25 grenades no 2 slightly wounded no man. Intelligence Two Germans were seen looking over parapet, one wearing a light grey tunic and round cap, the other a civilian cap. Parties of the enemy were seen approaching at LE PIETRE making their way to	

WAR DIARY or INTELLIGENCE SUMMARY

Army Form C. 2118.

Place	Date	Hour	Summary of Events and Information	Remarks and references to Appendices
			the communication trench to the German line they seemed too lightly equipped to be a relief, but may have been returning to the trenches for the night. Our artillery fired on these parties, their being directed on N 30 B 3.3. A patrol under Cpl Wrekenin went out from N 12 c central to reconnoitre ruin at about N 11 a 2½.9 & found no sign of the enemy there. A fighting patrol from 13th RWF of 3 officers & 28 men under Lt Wynne Edwards went out at 11.0 pm from M 24 d.2.5 with a view to capturing any Germans who might be occupying the suspected listening post at M 24 d 5.6. no trace of the enemy was seen in no mans land; the patrol was out until about 1.45 am. WORK Previous R.E. fatigue: general trench repair, left centre Coy (C) pushed out and placed in position & packed with wire obstacle in front of No 10 Bay, commencing at 11.0 pm finishing at 2.20 am. Left Coy were employed in clearing the trenches DRURY LANE & FELON POST of debris caused by heavy bombardment.	
	7.8 15/16		Operations Usual rifle & machine gun artillery exchanges. About 15 H.E. shells were fired by the enemy at FAUQUISSART POST about 6 of	69/69

6276

which fell right into it doing considerable damage to parapets and dugouts, our artillery retaliation was slow, nine minutes elapsing between call for same firing of first round, very few rounds were fired, artillery Obs. were carried out afterwards in every case a round was fired within two minutes of the call for same.

Intelligence. A German wearing a dark brown sheepskin was seen from No. 3. Sniper Post at M.24.d.25.7. Germans were seen returning from line near LE PIETRE wearing while Evans & they appeared to be carrying spades. An enemy machine gun at about N.13.C.10.4 fired bursts N.N.E & S of our Cuinchy machine gun was observed at N.19.a.4.2.8, the enemy is putting a lot of work into his trench at about this point, he was heard driving in stakes. M.24 d.2.6 appears to be a new tender spot in the dam line as when our Machine Gun opened fire on it the Bosch immediately retaliated with machine gun rifle fire. A covering party went out in advance of our wiring party at M.24.b.6.0, followed the line of weeers and climbed about 150 yards in direction of German trench. The party remained there 2 hours, but no noise of any description was heard in the enemy's trench and was observed in no man's land. At 9.0 p.m an officers patrol of 12 men under 2/Lt Jack went out from M.21 b 8.9 for the purpose of taking prisoners. The patrol returned at 11.0 p.m. No signs of enemy were seen about 9.50 a.m and 10.25 a.m enemy machine gun fired near N.13 a 8½.7½. This was repeated during the afternoon and the gun was watched the bearing (true) is 172° from head of No.14 drain at M.13 b 1.11½ which was given to the artillery. There is probably an emplacement at this point in the front of the left battalion 15 Divn.

Reports of hand grenades were heard at 1.55 a.m. Enemy sentries in our front became very active but were lost sight of by our machine guns. WORK Right Coy (A) Sandbagging ERITH TRENCH. General trench improvements. Wiring at M.21 b 6.0 Right centre coy (B) R.E. fatigue, repairs to parapet at M.34 b 7.5 clearing trench boards and wiring, left centre coy 'C' wiring from 10.30 p.m to 2.15 a.m, covered by scouts they employed 50 x of gotch wiring on left of ditch N30.3½.½ started on night of date. General French improvements. Left Coy (D) Revetting DRURY LANE clearing out drains. Repair of breach in parapet, new M. G. emplacement for No.5 gun. Day T

WAR DIARY
or
INTELLIGENCE SUMMARY.
(Erase heading not required.)

Army Form C. 2118.

Place	Date	Hour	Summary of Events and Information	Remarks and references to Appendices
	3.5.16		Work, extension of sufficient good dirt to thicken the whole of apron put down last night, two new rifle grenade stores made, washing stand for No. 10 platoon made, hurdle revetting of parapet damaged by shell fire. Repair of parapet firestep at night. Operations Reckonedly quiet day, at 8.15 p.m. red & green rockets were seen well away to our left at 9.0 p.m. the right coy. was subjected to several rifle machine gun fires, four rifle grenades being fired at us, three of which fell about some 6 yards behind our parados, the coy. stood to and returned with rapid fire our machine guns and rifle grenades, this silenced the enemy but he frequently opened bursts of rifle machine gun fire during the night. At 7.0 am enemy parties were observed on bicycles & a foot passing cross roads at N.15.b.4.3. Some trucks were also seen coming down that road towards the trenches, a salvo of 15 rounds was quickly put [out?] and men had fire 100' to the right of the mark. The artillery fired two more salvos at this point during the night. INTELLIGENCE. An officer patrol from 13 R.W.B. under 2 Lt. Hughes went out at	6092

WAR DIARY
or
INTELLIGENCE SUMMARY.
(Erase heading not required.)

Army Form C. 2118.

Instructions regarding War Diaries and Intelligence Summaries are contained in F. S. Regs., Part II. and the Staff Manual respectively. Title pages will be prepared in manuscript.

Place	Date	Hour	Summary of Events and Information	Remarks and references to Appendices
			M 24 & 4.7 became enemy wire, patrol went out at midnight returned and returned at 2.10 am and reported enemy wire thick at about M 24 d 8.6 a sentry was heard working up and down the trench the front frequently. No sign of the enemy in No man's land. Patrol of 3 men under Lt. A. H. Williams went out from M 24 b 5. 3 patrol reports an old fire trench immediately in front of our line and an old dugout in front of Bay 45. There is a sandbagged machine gun emplacement, its parapet is not however bullet proof, it has two loopholes one facing half right and the other half left, the patrol examined the distance the one to the left of Bay 45 being 18 feet wide & 2 feet deep & the one to the right 3 ft deep & 5 ft wide. at 11.0 p.m. a small patrol under L/Cpl Toy left our trenches at N 13 c.5.5. to patrol found before reaching our wiring party, found was reported clear & a strong wiring party went out. At 2.0 am a big explosion similar to a trench mortar bomb took place in No man's LAND giving out a large cloud of whitish smoke, the enemy at once threw up many lights towards towards it, suspected rally post" with wire gap in wire in front of it was located 114° true bearing from junction of of Drain 15 and trench line N 13 c 7.6½., a fixed rifle was put up in the extreme right of left coy, &	620

WAR DIARY or INTELLIGENCE SUMMARY

fired during the night, a Lewis gun also registered on it. At 9.30 pm 2nd J/Lt Lewis and two men left our sally-port near ditch N13c73.7 which opens to breast along ditch & find whereabouts of enemy working party, a Lewis gun was trained on end of ditch where enemy was supposed to be working & the presence of a patrol of enemy having been reported the Lewis gun & artillery opened fire. At 6.45 pm the enemy artillery shelled the batt'n on our left, some of the shells dropping in ~~Rotten~~ ROTTEN ROW, our guns retaliated quickly and effectively at WICK SALIENT.

WORK. Right Coy. R.E. fatigue, traverse and cleared French boards & holdied on pickets constructed gooseneck revmnt, partly strengthened work put up on 9th inst. Right Centre Coy. R.E. fatigue, improved French boards & made gooseneck repaired parapet and bay to completed work to parados at Bay 33, wired 50 paces on left of Coy. front.
Left Centre Coy. R.E. fatigue wired N°6 right of ditch N13 c 23.3 cleared trench boards, made gooseneck, cleared & repaired damage done by trench mortar. Left Coy. Demolished old French shelter now embrasure.

639b

Date	Hour	Summary of Events and Information
		hostile rifle fire kept up repaired trench after damage by stokes. telephone trench towards DRURY LANE, new working towards hill. R.E. fatigue finished loopholes in FELON.
9/6	5	OPERATIONS. The Bothas in night of CC officer & made good practice. bursts of Huns again seen on RUE D'ENFER N25 b 4.3. Artillery were informed and fired a salvo which fell well on the target. R119 ranged on X roads N26 c.8.3½, which can be ranged on X roads N26 c 8.3½ (which can be observed from No.5 cupola loophole) so as to get fire brought quickly up parties passing there. It transpired with O.C. R/119 to call it TRAMWAY CORNER. Intelligence. It transpires a bomb went out at 8.30 p.m. last night L5 became aware of last night's explosion and found a 3" pole similar to small telegraph pole past erected with Cossery with detonators and connecting wires. Enemy observed moving from N5 loophole a new place put up in No.3 loophole. The Bn. Hrs. was relieved by 13th H.L.I. in front line tranches in relief. 6 billets in LAVENTIE, with the exception of troops which occupied posts as follows :– 1 Platoon at WANGERIE POST, 2 platoons at MASSEKOT POST

WAR DIARY
or
INTELLIGENCE SUMMARY

Army Form C. 2118.

Place	Date	Hour	Summary of Events and Information	Remarks and references to Appendices
	10/5/16		1 platoon at ROAD BEND POST, 7 Coy which occupied FORT ESQUIN POST with one platoon. Relief was completed at 9.25 p.m.	
	11/5/16		Bathing parades for companies.	
	12/5/16		Ordinary routine, parades were by accoutrements.	
	13/5/16		Ordinary Routine. Companies employed on working parties. The Battalion relieved the 13th KRRC in the right front sub-sector, the Coy taking up positions in following order from the Right. A, B, C & D. Roy furnished garrison of 1 platoon at ELGIN POST, 2 Coy, 1 platoon at FAUQUISSART and 2 Coy 2 section at FELON POST, relief commenced at 8.0 p.m., relief complete at 9.50 p.m.	
	13/14/5/16		Operation. At 12.30 a.m. a patrol of 16 men under Lt. A.R. Jones left our trench at N13 c 8½ 6½ with orders to examine the enemy's wire for gaps and if possible capture enemy patrols, ground was wet and going bad, the patrol got within 30 yards of enemy wire and found no enemy patrols, it was then getting light and patrol had to return. At 3.15 a.m. enemy fired about a dozen rifle grenades,	

WAR DIARY
or
INTELLIGENCE SUMMARY.
(Erase heading not required.)

Army Form C. 2118.

Place	Date	Hour	Summary of Events and Information	Remarks and references to Appendices
			a few of which dropped over own parapet, trench mortar batteries light and medium retaliated quickly & effectively, our artillery also fired 10 rounds, we let off rifle grenades, this silenced the enemy, our machine guns were active during the night and fired 2000 rounds. Intelligence Listening post at M.24.d.2.7 reported no signs of the enemy in No Man's Land. WORK. Right Coy continued wiring at M.24.B.6.0 lowering front of parapet, in place. Right centre coy. strengthening parapet in Bay 38, clearing trench boards, lowering parapet in Bay 43. filling sandbags. Left Centre Coy Continued work on a sandbag parados which has been started as the for Left Centre. General trench improvements. Operations. At 3.30 pm enemy shelled the immediate rear of RUE TILLELOY with about 50 H.E. shells, he seemed to be searching for notes machine guns, which have been very active during last two nights, our artillery retaliated Enemy fired 6 rifle grenades at about M.24.D.4.5 at 3.30 pm. & Shell	
	14/5/16			

6357

rifle grenades at 4.30 p.m. no casualties resulted, we retaliated at once and 20 riflegrenades fell in the enemy trenches. The line of melinite at M.24.d.4.6 adjoining the old communication trench was traversed during the night by machine guns. A fixed rifle was placed at sniper loophole No. 5, in the RUE D'ENFER, cross roads N25.b.4½.½. (N25.b.4.25) and fire frequently during during the night.
Intelligence listening post at M.24.d.3.7 was sent out from 8.45 a.m. until 2.0 a.m. they heard nothing of the enemy, a movement was observed in NO MANS LAND, enemy party in front of our wire at M.24.b.6.0 made the same report. Landrop of different colour observed at N.19.a.5.5. there is evidently much work going on there. At 9.45 p.m. a fighting patrol 16 strong went out under Lt. REES from N13.c.93.83 with the object of reconnaisance in the direction of WICK SALIENT and capturing any hostile patrols, about 30 to 40 yards from our own wire the patrol advancing in a wedge formation saw a small group of Germans about 20 to 30 yards ahead, whilst waiting to draw up our flanks

and envelop it. the enemy threw 2 bombs and ran away. whilst we were then seen following the men back towards enemy line, which suggests that they had been advancing in similar formation to our own. our patrol handed them vigourously of pushed forward, but no casualties were found. patrol returned at 10.55 p.m. and our 2nd Lieut Sims reached "No Mans Land". A patrol of 1 NCO and 3 men went out at midnight from M24 b.7.5. to the purpose of searching for enemy patrols. Patrol proceeded along ridge leading towards enemy line and encountered no opposition. They heard a working party working about 50 yds to their left. After they had proceeded 150 yds. patrol returned. and machine gun fire was directed on working party. The enemy sent us a few light bombs of which the following is a rough sketch.

Propeller
wing heavy here (about 1½ lbs)

WORK. Rifle Coy.

Work continued at M34 b 6.0 two loops were kept down knife rest taken out

and placed in position, trench reconstructed, cleared and repaired on forepart, pickets pulling away frieze & revetting with hurdles, clearing and dugouts in support trench, R.E. fatigues, wiring parties, no enemy grenadiers during the day.
Right Centre Coy. Raining and clearing trench trench improving Trenches except weak defence round dangerous part in the trench and cleared space for new dugouts, fifty yards of apron wire laid, raising enclosed overhead traverse.
Left Centre Company, trench troops cleared and repaired drains reconnoitred providing air space in roof, parados built. MASSELOT STREET cleared. General trench improvement at FAUQUISSART POST. S.A.A. boxes lot in C bay.
Artillery —
R.E. fatigues - DRURY LANE + trench mortar emplacement, relaying and wiring trench boards, revetting on left continued, wire apron continued to one compressor before and camel attack

6376

Army Form C. 2118.

WAR DIARY
or
INTELLIGENCE SUMMARY.
(Erase heading not required.)

Instructions regarding War Diaries and Intelligence Summaries are contained in F. S. Regs., Part II. and the Staff Manual respectively. Title pages will be prepared in manuscript.

Place	Date	Hour	Summary of Events and Information	Remarks and references to Appendices
	15.16/5/16		20* men duck running from Centre of N.13.3. OPERATIONS from 2.45 pm to 6.0 pm our light and heavy artillery medium and light trench mortar batteries bombarded the WICK SALIENT at N.13.d.2.7½. at 5.30 pm our trench from DRURY LANE to the left of our line at POTTER ROW was cleared except for a bombing party of 1 NCO & 8 men left at a point opposite trench entrance to PARKLANE, our men holding these of FELON POST went to Reserve line until 6.0 pm when they re-occupied the trenches. At 3.0 pm the Trench Mortar Batteries opened fire under cover of artillery on the salient N.13.d.2.7½ to N.13.d.12.5½, a good rate of fire was kept up, at first directed on the Southern Side, two gaps were seen made and after trench fire, sandbags, trench boards and dugouts were flying about in profusion, direct hits were obtained by trench Mortars and artillery. Rifle grenades and Light trench mortar bombs were fired on the flanks of the salient of our line at the same time. great numbers which good result. At 4.0 pm the heavy howitzers joined in. Enemy retaliation did not begin until 3.25 pm. when	6381

T/134. Wt. W708—776. 500000. 4/15. Sir J. C. & E.

WAR DIARY
or
INTELLIGENCE SUMMARY.
(Erase heading not required.)

Army Form C. 2118.

Place	Date	Hour	Summary of Events and Information	Remarks and references to Appendices

Eny commenced searching for our Batteries, this was followed by several attempts at the O.P's on RUE TILLELOY N130.52.3 with H.E.S. Several of them blind, but 2 direct hits were obtained an enemy air "burst" mortar continued vigorously until about 4.45 p.m. these went on intermittently heavy batteries became prominent now. at 4.10 p.m. the enemy fired on ROTTEN ROW & FLEET ST. getting several hits in trenches causing some damage in all about 20 H.E's fell on FLEET STREET. At 4.45 p.m. an air "burst" searched for enemy guns and fired at grenade in WICK SALIENT. 40 minutes, the brick building also fired on until 5.30 p.m. when enemy parapet was widely breached enine and parapet damaged. Towards "Sena Co" the enemy became very active with machine guns and rifle fire, at 10.0 p.m. a lg being patrol of German milled their 3rd A Major Jones went out from N13 C 9.8.6 found a fair extent of damage from afternoon bombardment and if possible they were ordered to return as the moon was so bright, however they entered a working party opposite N13 C 9.8½ came in at 11.0 p.m.

6 792

WAR DIARY or INTELLIGENCE SUMMARY

640b

enemy Company "close to" and fired 15 rounds rapid, while machine guns kept up a high rate of fire, rifle grenades revelling forming in. The enemy appeared nervous and hopped up repeated signals, he also threw up many Very lights from WIEK SALIENT, we had the "last word" in the duel finishing up with rifle grenades and artillery fire.

Intelligence parties of men were seen walking along road at LE PIETRE N20 b to b at 4.30 p.m. also men were seen entering houses at N20 b 2 3½ at 11.0 am. Snipers report enemy has returned his wire a distance of 25 yards at N19A 3.4. Artillery machine gun emplacements observed by snipers at N19A 3.4. during the night were informed of and machine guns fired at it after during the night.

3 men unfortunately injured accidentally by rifle grenade.

WORK Right Company cleaning dugouts between ELGIN POST & GLOUCESTER HOUSE trench, improvements and making of gooseberries.

RIGHT centre Coy. Repairing and revetting parapets and parados, wiring & relaying trench boards, cleaning filling reserve water tank.

WAR DIARY
or
INTELLIGENCE SUMMARY

Army Form C. 2118.

641b

Place	Date	Hour	Summary of Events and Information	Remarks and references to Appendices
			LEFT centre Coy. Three parados built, facing trench boards in support line, commenced, deepening of communication trench to FAUQUISSART KEEP, finished.	
			LEFT Coy. R.E. fatigues on DRURY LANE and French mortar emplacements, commencement of work on support trench.	
	16-17 5/16		Operating. At 12.0 p.m. enemy commenced bombarding our line with 5.9 with an artillery O.P. in RUE TILLELOY, this was at once followed by shrapnel with a variety of 4.2 and 5.9 shells on FLEET ST. Shelling was more intense on the support line on the front line, and consequently the HUN is under the impression that the support line is held by us. The enemy obtained two hits on the parapet of our left Coy. which did little damage, as the men had been cleared to the flanks, enemy also obtained a direct hit on a suppos loophole in right centre company. Our artillery retaliated with good effect and caused considerable damage to the enemy line. French Mortar Batteries also joined in the retaliation and rifle grenades were	

WAR DIARY
or
INTELLIGENCE SUMMARY.
(Erase heading not required.)

Army Form C. 2118.

Place	Date	Hour	Summary of Events and Information	Remarks and references to Appendices

fired at enemy, our batteries continued firing until 2.0 p.m. we obtained a distinct mastery over the enemy's batteries. At 4.0 p.m the enemy started a most violent bombardment of our front line and old support trenches, shells of all descriptions came in quick succession invading the area with smoke and debris. Capt. GLYNN JONES O.C. left Coy. with great coolness cleared his way to a flank, detailed a bombing party to be at head of PARK LANE communication trench & guarded weak points by machine guns. The enemy did not confine his attention to the left Coy but bombarded the whole line, though its bombardment was most more intensive on our left. The retaliation of our guns was quick and effective, our 18 pounders seemed specially live. A continuous bombardment on back rills was kept up until 5.30 p.m, and it was found that most of the enemy's shells had fallen on FLEET ST. & on the old divisional support trench, the parapet of the left coy. was damaged in nine places, the headed dug out was knocked down, but the breaches were mended & our

64¾

WAR DIARY
or
INTELLIGENCE SUMMARY

Army Form C. 2118.

64¾

Place	Date	Hour	Summary of Events and Information	Remarks and references to Appendices

Casualties NIL. A Trench Mortar Battery had several killed and another wounded while in their dugouts. The explosions did damage in remaining in dugouts under heavy trench mortar shell fire. Our artillery yesterday fired on the new machine gun emplacement at N19 a 3.0, two direct hits were obtained and a great quantity of new bricks thrown up.

Yesterday Green & white lights were sent up by the enemy to the left rear of WICK SALIENT. Flashes of two guns seen in front of house with two clouds of smoke at N26 d 2.8.

WORK Right Coy. continuation of work clearing old dugouts near ELGIN. Repairing front line after bombardment.

RIGHT CENTRE Coy. Repairing snipers post near breastworks, also repairing dugout.

LEFT Cent Coy. Repairing trenches after shelling, putting fire steps on dugouts. General trench improvements.

LEFT COY. Repairing trenches after bombardment.

T2134. Wt. W708-776. 500000. 4/15. Sir J. C. & S.

WAR DIARY
or
INTELLIGENCE SUMMARY.
(Erase heading not required.)

Army Form C. 2118.

14th Welsh Fus   May 1916

644

Place	Date	Hour	Summary of Events and Information	Remarks and references to Appendices
	1.7/16		Nothing unusual occurred in the trenches in the day a party was seen in German Lines with "An Artillere" on it, but the rest of the notice was obliterated. The battalion was relieved in the front line by 14th WELSH REGIMENT and luckily got out without casualties as the Huns shelled the heads leading up to front line with shrapnel in response to fire opened on their reliefs by our own Artillery. Companies marched back to billets at 1A 6 OR 6 VE, relief effected at 7.15 pm completed at 9.15 pm	
	15/5/16		All Companies Pacloon	
	19/5/16		Parades under Company arrangements	
	20/5/16		Parades under Company arrangements	
	21/5/16		Church Parades	
	22/5/16		New method of wearing Gas Helmet with Steel Helmet exemplified. Lecture in afternoon on theatre on subject of aeroplane work and methods of photography of same. In evening lecture by Brigadier to COs and Company Officers.	

WAR DIARY
or
INTELLIGENCE SUMMARY.
(Erase heading not required.)

Army Form C. 2118.

645b

Place	Date	Hour	Summary of Events and Information	Remarks and references to Appendices
Gas Demonstration	23/5/16		Parades under Coy. arrangements.	
	24/5/16		Parades under Coy. arrangements. Large fatigue parties provided for work on trenches, resembling those of the Hun.	
	25-26/5/16	5pm	OPERATIONS. Batt. moved up to left sub-sector of front line support trenches, MOATED GRANGE SECTION relieving 11th Batt. Durbordieux in the front line and fork. D Coy. moved off at 5.0 pm. and took over WINCHESTER, GRANTS, ERITH, N.TILLELOY and DREADNOUGHT Pts., the remainder of the Batter. paraded at 6.30pm and marched via LAVENTIE & LAFLINQUE cross road to front line trenches, relief was complete at 10.10 pm. Very quiet night. Intelligence A patrol of 5 men under Capt. W.K. Jones which went out from M 30 c.w.1.4.4 to reconnoitre the ground and the condition of the enemy's wire reported finding trip wires to the depth of about 15 feet and apron wire on the German side at M 30 a 6.2.2½. The aprons were not many strong. Considerable movement was heard in enemy trench, double sentries were posted at 20 or 25 yards interval, who fired frequently. The Hun front line at this point appeared very irregular, it was found difficult to approach	

the German wire unobserved as the long grass in NOMANS LAND gave away much movement. At 11.0 pm the O.C. Coy. unarmed sent out an officer's patrol to reconnoitre German wire in front of M24 d 1.5 and it came across a German patrol, the patrol were withdrawn and our machine guns were turned on to the enemy patrol. The entire Coy. R. Coy. put loop-holing posts in front of every platoon and a N.C.O. patrolled the front, no sign of the enemy was observed.
WORK. Wiring in front of our parapet, general trench improvements, pumping.
A. B. & C. Coys. held the front line in that order from the right.
15 O.R's. were on our right.
1st Bn "The Welsh Rgt." on our left.

26-27/5 OPERATIONS. We registered on enemy's line at M30a H.2 with Stokes mortars and on M30a H.2.2 with Rifle Grenades, our Artillery fired H.V. Shells on enemy's line at M30a H.1 with good effect, enemy retaliated with H.V. & L.H.V. shells which cleared our front line and fell in rear near WINCHESTER Trench. At 4.0 pm enemy opened fire on our left company with 7.7 m.m. H.S. shrapnel and some rifle grenades doing little damage, our Artillery and Grenadiers retaliated. At 12.30 am a wiring party to our working party of the left company had a bombing encounter with a German patrol which retired. About 8.30 am the enemy evidently searching for No Co1 Meeking's and Gallery on our left and right respectively of ERITH POST sent over about 30 L.H. V. bombs, no damage was done.

Intelligence. Listening post at M.30.a.2½ reports work either in or near the craters. A day observer states that a carrying party was also seen in the early morning in the vicinity of craters. This confirms previous statement that work is being actively carried out there. A patrol of 6 men under 2/Lt A. B. Thompson went out from M.24.c.5.1. They proceeded along the right of the ditch bearing to the right after proceeding for about 100 yds. and entering in the direction which with in about 40 yds. of the enemy's trench, they then detected to their front a small working party of about 7 men to their right front. There seemed from sound and movement to be a large working party at work in the craters. About midnight our patrol noticed on their left a party of about 7 men retiring whilst retiring they threw bombs, this was followed by much machine gun and Rifle fire on part of the enemy who also threw up many very lights, our patrol returned safely and machine guns were turned on to the working party, a

WAR DIARY
or
INTELLIGENCE SUMMARY.
(Erase heading not required.)

Army Form C. 2118.

648/9

Place	Date	Hour	Summary of Events and Information	Remarks and references to Appendices
			Hostile Machine Gun was observed at M.24.d.3.0, the enemy is reported to be working on his parapet at about M.24.d.4.1½. The enemy snipers are quiet and their fire is very inaccurate & spasmodic.	
			WORK. Communication and goose-ries made during day put out at night. Space trench repairs including drawing revetting, making new ammunition store. S.A.A. and bomb stores started by left company and empty S.A.A. boxes put in parapet in each section. Trench daily use S.A.A.	
	27.2.16		OPERATIONS. Our artillery with 18 pounders at zero to a turn at about M.30.a.6.1. where a party of the enemy was working, this party was unticendy dispersed, during the night culminage 18 pounders, machine guns, rifle grenades, and rifle fire were directed on a German working party about M.24.d.4.1. who were then ceased. The enemy sent over about 60 H.E. shells at about 3.30 p.m. they fell near ERITH POST causing no damage. Our snipers claim 3 victims. Intelligence An officers patrol under Capt. H.E. JONES went out from M.30.a.1.½ to reconnoitre the ground to observe any movements on the part of the enemy, patrol reported presence of an enemy working party at M.30.a.4.4. Rifle grenades and	

649

machine guns were brought to bear on the spot. Listening patrols were put out in front of every platoon of the entire company and the posts sent out patrols, no signs of the enemy were seen or heard.

WORK. Wiring emcombres and gooseberries and wiring 19 emcombres & 335 gooseberries being taken out and laced firmly in front of 114, 15 & 16 bays, and 114 of each in front of the entire coy. Sap no. 2 bayonetted and fire steps put in. Bay in BIRD CAGE pulled down and partly revetted. Support line & coy. French construction between tramway & WINCHESTER Rd. continued, fire steps rebuilt, new officers latrine made, pumping and draining carried on. Work done on ERITH & support trenches, construction of banketone in left Coy. area continued.

28.29/16 OPERATIONS. Our night Coy. registered with rifle grenades at apparent gap in enemy wire at M30 a 4.1. Our listening post reports that a working party at that point was dispersed by the rifle grenades, we kept dropping rifle grenades those at half hour intervals and no more work was heard done during the night, there was some artillery activity during afternoon evening & following

all quiet along the front. Our Lewis Guns fired about 2200 rounds at enemy parapet revine. *Intelligence* A heavy mist prevailed from dawn until 5.30 a.m. on the 27th enemy working parties could be heard on their wire. Our snipers claim 3 victims at M34 d.4.2 who were shot as soon as the mist began to lift, sniper in J.04.H.5 claims a victim at 11.0 p.m at M30 a 5.5 and another in same place at 7.0 a.m., all were wearing blue uniform with long forearm & dark blue caps. Enemy sniping very quick. One man was seen in enemy trench wearing trench cap with peak, had hands outside hadf. Listening p.ots were put in front of each platoon of the entire Coy. rode Coy. front was patrolled, there were no signs of enemy in NO MANS LAND. An unsuccessful patrol went out on the right Coy. front as far as trench M30 a 1½.2. The trench was dry and the going good, the patrol reports a machine gun at salient M30 a H.1
Work. Concertinas & gooseberries made toward, side cleared in all companies for regulars dugouts, repair to ERITH and WINCHESTER trench, work on support line continued, sally ports almost completed at Bays 111 & 1115, work on making bomb store for No.12 platoon continued

WAR DIARY
or
INTELLIGENCE SUMMARY.
(Erase heading not required.)

Army Form C. 2118.

Place	Date	Hour	Summary of Events and Information	Remarks and references to Appendices
	29/5/16		The Battn was relieved by 13th R.W.F. in front line & on march to billets at PONT DU HEM, with the exception of "B" Coy which took over GRANTS, WINCHESTER, NTILLELOY, MIA LONELY Pts. no incidents of note to record	61/D
	30/5/16		All Coys. took advantage of the back areas alloted to them. All Coys told off as training companies. At about 9.30pm troops of the Battn received orders to "Stand to" on the Battn. alarm Post, in consequence of heavy bombardment of front line & rewards on our right and anticipated German attack. Orders received to lay front ineluding the areas to	
	31/5		Stand down was received at 10.45 pm Parades under Company arrangements	

S.P.B. Guyton MAJOR
14 (S) Battalion
Royal Welsh Fusiliers

WAR DIARY
INTELLIGENCE SUMMARY

Place	Date	Hour	Summary of Events and Information	Remarks and references to Appendices
June 1/16	1st		Parades under Coy arrangements. A + B Coys had a special form of training in attack of trenches and surrounding wire obstacles. Also physical training.	
"	2nd		The Battalion relieved the 13th R.W.F. in front line as follows. A Coy B Coy 2 platoons & C Coy in front line in that order from the right. A Coy finding a garrison of 1 platoon in WINCHESTER POST, 2 Platoons in GRANTS POST & 1 platoon in N.T. HEDGE POST. B Coy 2 platoons in ReDoubt line, one platoon in DREADNOUGHT POST and one in ERITH. Relief was completed at 9.55 p.m. Intelligence. Wiring Pots put in front of the platoon of the centre coy. & vintage patrolled. A patrol of 10 men under Capt. W.E. Jones Lieuts. A. Lloyd Jones & 2/Lt Thompson went out from M.30.a.12.14 with the object of reconnoitring point M.30.a.3.t.4 and also bretly trenches shown on map as running from that fence to M.30.c.5.5. When at about M.30.c.3.8 2 2/Lt A. Thompson was killed by a stray bullet. Capt. Jones then decided to bring his party in and also the body of 2/Lt Thompson. When the party was at about M.30.a.1/2.1 the enemy started our front line at 11.15 p.m. Capt W.E. Jones fell wounded by shrapnel, the party then left the body of 2/Lt Thompson and our four stretcher bearers to	

WAR DIARY or INTELLIGENCE SUMMARY

Army Form C. 2118.
10th BATTN. ROYAL WELSH FUSILIERS

6538

Place	Date	Hour	Summary of Events and Information	Remarks and references to Appendices
		(6)	met there Capt. W.E. Jones was brought in at M30 c. 0.7. Another patrol was quickly organised & taken out by Capt. N. Phosevens to bring in the body of 2 Lt. Thompson, who was successfully accomplished. In the meantime Cpl. Hulse of the first patrol, who had gone for the stretcher bearers who were supposed to have gone into the Padget Posan, on our right was found to be missing, but came in wounded in broad daylight at about 9.0 am.	
	3/4/16		WORK. Wiring & fatigue. General trench improvements. At 5.0 pm. the medium trench mortars under cover of some heavy H.E. shells and 18 pr. shrapnel bombarded the enemy trenches at M30 d 5.3 and M30 b 2.9 whilst rifle grenades were fired at about M30 a 7.5. Chief aims of the stokes bombs were their clay members and many effective work, on freeing over the parapet and appearing to cause great destruction. The medium trench mortar bombing worked tremendous havoc in the enemy line, 5 their only, wire and many frames were thrown into the air, the parapet was breached to the length of about 4 yds. a the wire was broken to stand came under at M34 d 5.3. The enemy retaliated with 7.7 mm. 5.9 M.G.'s behind our Front line in CHAPIGNY & ERITH POST	

WAR DIARY
or
INTELLIGENCE SUMMARY

Army Form C. 2118.

Place	Date	Hour	Summary of Events and Information	Remarks and references to Appendices
			with heavy rifle grenades, but did no material damage. They knocked our parapet at one place but we repaired the damage before dawn. An officers patrol under 2nd Lt. Roberts which went out at night to examine the damage done was unable to advance to the enemy wire as there was a large working party, working on the gap, patrol returned and the artillery, rifle grenades, machine gun rifle fire was turned on the spot and effectually stopped all work. No indication of any work in the crater but there was working going on in front behind the crater.	658
			WORK. Making connecting work on WINCHESTER and support trenches.	
	4/5/16		OPERATIONS at 4.0 pm our medium trench mortars opened heavy fire in conjunction with artillery on enemy trench & mine at M30a H2.1 firing of trench mortars were good and effective, a distinct gap being made in enemy wire, mole of the artillery fire was effective, at 4.5 pm light T.M. fired on trench from M30a5.5 to M30a8.5 also between M30a5½ and M30c5.8, this appeared to be effective. firing was bursts in return. At 4.15 pm rifle grenades fired on M30a9.5 the vicinity of trench mortars in our trench had been shown	

WAR DIARY or INTELLIGENCE SUMMARY

Army Form C. 2118.
14th BATTN. ROYAL WELSH FUSILIERS.

6550

The operation lasted 4.50 p.m. rifle fire commenced soon after our started, the enemy went on artillery & any rifle grenades mostly on the BIRDCAGE being little damage. Firing ceased at 4.50 p.m. at and 5. 45 p.m. the enemy started retaliating again along our whole front, most of this shell fell behind our front line, it appears to be under the impression that we been the support line, my little damage was done, a few small bombs only being made in our parapet. At 9.15 p.m. a listening patrol went out in front of M30a 4.2.1 released by arrangement at 10.30 p.m. reporting everything quiet. At 10.45 p.m. a strong raiding party of 60 men under Capt. N.P. WILLIAMS, Lt. A.L.LLOYD JONES & 2/Lt. BROCK went out from M.30.a.1.5 with the object of:-

1. Killing Germans.
2. Obtaining prisoners & identity marks.
3. Portraying & capturing enemy material. At 11.0 p.m. our artillery commenced an intense bombardment of Hun front line lifting 5 yds at 11.2 & the firing was perfect. From the few very lights that went up & the questions of the enemy he must have been terrorized. At 11.10 p.m. much grenade firing was heard, but no machine gun fire until a few minutes later, the impression made was that a successful entry had been made, the party cannot a gap in the enemy's wire

but not a large one, they entered the enemy first line trenches and found them practically deserted, but there were GERMANS massed together in a support trench only a few yards away rather heavy mortars to [our?] line, our party was outnumbered to a very heavy fire from this trench which was only about 15 yards away, our party hurled on each neighbouring party came upon a deep dugout full of Germans, when they bombed heavily and five exits with revolvers, our party also failed the enemy in this support trench and undoubtedly inflicted heavy loss on them. the left flank supporting party encountered very little opposition, much squealing and yelling was heard, often a well directed shrapnel 10 minutes [?] signal for retirement was given & they were outnumbered to a very hostile fire whilst going through the enemy wire, where most of our casualties occurred. at 11.30pm group of men appeared over our parapet, the raiding party returned in small parties, our casualties were Lieut Rees 5 men missing (totally killed, 24 men wounded (12 slightly) Capt. H.P Williams missing Lt. Allaya Jones wounded. 2nd Lt H.L Brock wounded (slightly) the Second Patrol was sent out to look for the missing officer & men some wounded

WAR DIARY
or
INTELLIGENCE SUMMARY.
(Erase heading not required.)

Army Form C. 2118.

BATTN. ROYAL WELSH FUSILIERS.

Place	Date	Hour	Summary of Events and Information	Remarks and references to Appendices
	5-6	6½	They succeeded in keeping in the labs, but could find no trace of the enemy. WORK. Wiring and work on support trenches. OPERATIONS. Both day & night were exceptionally quiet except for very active hostile machine gun fire in NO MANS LAND at night. Our riflemen fired about 2500 rounds at gaps in the enemy's wire. We also fired intermittently at gaps in front of the left of our line and about 60 R.G. of craters with rifle fire and rifle grenades effectively stopping any hostile work, our rifle battery fired a good deal during the night. INTELLIGENCE. Some flashing of a white object, which might have been a signal from someone in division in NO MANS LAND was observed during the day at about M.30. 3.8. behind a mound of earth just short of the crater. Capt. W.P. WHELDON took a patrol of 4 men to this spot to see if it possibly contained a wounded man who had crawled there, the object was discovered to be an old parachute and although a careful search was made none was found. A patrol of 8 men under Lieut. VENMORE went out on a searching party for a missing man from M.30.a.15. they made two successive sweeps in NO MANS LAND in extended order from old French leading to trench M.30.a.3½.4½ on the	65 YP

Army Form C. 2118.

16th BATTN. ROYAL WELSH FUSILIERS.

WAR DIARY
or
INTELLIGENCE SUMMARY.
(Erase heading not required.)

658

Place	Date	Hour	Summary of Events and Information	Remarks and references to Appendices
			Left to avoid leading into our line at M29dg92.5 but no result was achieved. De holte machine gunfire was heard in No Mans Land. Enemy sniper seen at M30c12.7. Three machine gun emplacements seen on edge of wood at M30b12.2, our men sniped four tempts and fired 5 times at a loophole which was subsequently closed.	
			WORK. Support trench, preparing foundations of new emplacements, to R.E. 16 continue, housing machine gun emplacements to Vickers gun wing, rectifying ERITH trench cleared after clumps done on previous night. Creatinus Redout in front of DREADNOUGHT.	
	6.7.16		OPERATIONS Enemy Quiet both day and night, use played during the night on gaps in enemy's parapet at M24d6.4 and M30b2.8 with rifle and machinegun fire and rifle grenades. A patrol of two men under Sergt Horne left our line at 10.30 p.m and returned at 1.0 p.m. having searched the ground to the right and left of the old communication trench up to M30c32.1 for any wounded or dead from the recent raid, they were under machine gun fire frequently and often had to take cover, our rifle battery fired on gaps at M30c2.8.	

Intelligence. At 12.15 am listening post No. 2 reported that there were 5 Germans in the Orchard about M30a 3.3. 1 an officer went out to the listening post but found the report was incorrect, enemy machine gun fire was exceptionally heavy near M29b.9½.3 and one of our men was slightly wounded. Our Machine Gunners reported that an enemy machine gun was in position in NO MANS LAND in old cap running into enemy line at M30a33.1. On a very light going up our Lewis guns emptied a magazine each at the spot and immediately a second very light went up, 12 rifle grenades were fired with good effect, the hostile Machine Gun did not fire again. Our patrol reported that there was new wiring from the old communication trench about M30a8.1. The report of Machine Gunners confirming this new wiring was new loophole by the sniper's post to cover this spot in Bay 91. Our sniper claim one hit as certain.

WORK Communication loopholes made and put out; work on support and WINCHESTER trenches, drawing, bumping, work on foundation of new Lewis Dugout.

Army Form C. 2118.

14TH BATTN. ROYAL WELSH FUSILIERS

WAR DIARY
or
INTELLIGENCE SUMMARY.
(Erase heading not required.)

Instructions regarding War Diaries and Intelligence Summaries are contained in F. S. Regs., Part II. and the Staff Manual respectively. Title pages will be prepared in manuscript.

Place	Date	Hour	Summary of Events and Information	Remarks and references to Appendices
	4/9/16		OPERATIONS. Enemy very quiet day and night. A strong working party from 13th & 16th Battns in support commenced digging a new trench last night from M80c0.7 to M80a2.3½ with a covering party of 2 officers and 40 other ranks in front, from M__ to 15th Battn. The left working party was subject to severe machine gun fire at times & suffered casualties, viz. 2 killed and 5 wounded; At 2.0 AM covering and working parties retired behind our lines, the trench was only dug to a depth of two feet. Intermittent rifle, machine gun fire and rifle grenades was kept up on gaps in the enemy's parapet at M2 and 6.2 and M38 b.2.8 in hopes claim a certain victim. Intelligence. About 8.0 p.m. there were seen to rise from the enemy lines at about M80 b.12.7, three series of 30 & 40 bubbles, each series being a string of bubbles at regular intervals, which rose about 40 & 50 feet, then went out, at about 50 feet and then disappeared. bubbles seemed to be white with a yellowish tinge. Listening posts were put out in front of entire company and the front patrolled, no sign of enemy seen.	66 of

Army Form C. 2118.

1st BATTN. ROYAL WELSH FUSILIERS

WAR DIARY
~~INTELLIGENCE~~ SUMMARY.
(Erase heading not required.)

661P

Place	Date	Hour	Summary of Events and Information	Remarks and references to Appendices
	8th June		WORK. Making inventories and wiring work on support trenches and machine gun emplacements. Supplied R.E. working parties. Trench improvements generally. Reserve water tanks placed in position erased and filled with water.	
			The Battn. was relieved by the 13th R.W.F. in front line and back, relief started at 8.30 p.m. and was completed at 10.20 p.m. The Battn. on relief marched back & billeted at PONT DU HEM "C" Coy. finding Garrisons in posts as follows:- ETON 1 NCO 4 men, PONT DU HEM MUD POST 1 Section. LONELY POST ½ platoon, CHARTERHOUSE 1 NCO & 4 men, LA FLINQUE 1 NCO & 4 men, HARROW 1 NCO & 4 men.	
	9th "		Bathing parades	
	10th "		do	
	11th "		Battn. paraded at 1.0 pm. for marching to ROBERMETZ, MERVILLE marching in Brigade to rest of next period.	
	12th "		Battn. paraded at 11.15 am. and marched to GONNEHEM district. Weather boisterous and inclement.	

WAR DIARY
or
INTELLIGENCE SUMMARY.
(Erase heading not required.)

Army Form C. 2118.

14th BATTN. ROYAL WELSH FUSILIERS.

Place	Date	Hour	Summary of Events and Information	Remarks and references to Appendices
	13 June		Rested at GONNEHEM started.	
	14 "		Bath, marched to RAIMBERT.	
	15 "		Battalion marched to ORLENCOURT where the billets were dirty and indifferent.	
	16 "		Ordinary Routine. Cleaning of Billets.	
	17 "		Commencement of Company training in manoeuvre area near MONCHY-BRETON from 7.0 am to 1.0 pm. Dinner on ground.	
	18 "		Church parade in event denomination. Instruction for officers in map reading by Capt W.P. Wheldon.	
	19 "		Company Training from 1.0 pm to 6.0 pm. Tea on ground.	
	20 "		Company Training from 9.0 am to 1.0 pm. Dinner afterwards on ground. Rifle calls commence, reveille, retreat, first and last post.	
	21 "		Company Training from 1.0 pm to 6.0 pm. Night march and instruction of working parties with Gas Helmets on.	
	22 "		Battalion baths were allotted to the Battalion and men at TINQUES from 9.0 am to 12 noon. The Battalion commenced Battn. training	

66W9B

Army Form C. 2118.

WAR DIARY
or
INTELLIGENCE SUMMARY.
(Erase heading not required.)

14th BATTN. ROYAL WELSH FUSILIERS

Place	Date	Hour	Summary of Events and Information	Remarks and references to Appendices
	23 June		Training attack and were exercised in information as to junior to neit received instructions and outposts	
			Baths were allotted to remainder of Battn. at TINQUES. Remainder on training during battalion training which consisted of practice of advanced guards, sending of messages, moving forward in extended formation & outposts.	
	24 "		Battalion paraded at 9.15 am and marched to manoeuvre area for Brigade Training. The Battn. took part in attack on an imaginary German Trench System, which was taken by assault and then consolidated. The 13th & 16th R.W.F. first attacked the German 2nd line System and when this had been captured the 14th & 15th R.W.F. on right and left respectively went through the German 2nd line System and attacked and captured 3rd line System which was consolidated, a conference took place when clear operations had ceased and the companies marched back independently to their billets.	
	25 "		Battalion paraded at 7.25am and marched to manoeuvre area	

T2134. Wt. W708—776. 500000. 4/15. Sir J. C. & S.

WAR DIARY

Army Form C. 2118.

14th BATTN. ROYAL WELSH FUSILIERS.

Place	Date	Hour	Summary of Events and Information	Remarks and references to Appendices
			1915	
			For Previous Training. The 113th Brigade was in Reserve in German 1st line system which had previously been captured. The 114 +115 Bdes. made an attack on the information 2nd + 3rd German Trench system. the 14th + 15th R.W.F. then advanced from position of Reserve to 2nd line German system, which was consolidated, information having been received that the enemy were preparing a counter attack against 3rd system of trench. The Battalion was ordered to move forward to meet the attack which was done with great spirit, its progress being then terminated and dinners were served on the ground of what. A message from the G.O.C. in Chief turned attack to the following decorations had been awarded.	
			MILITARY CROSS Capt. T. Glynn Jones.	
			Lieut. A. Lloyd Jones.	
			D.C.M. 20603 Sergeant H. McHale.	
			MILITARY MEDAL 27936 Private H. Noble	
			21206 Corporal D.H. Hughes.	

… 14TH BATTN. ROYAL WELSH FUSILIERS

Army Form C. 2118.

WAR DIARY
or
INTELLIGENCE SUMMARY.
(Erase heading not required.)

Place	Date	Hour	Summary of Events and Information	Remarks and references to Appendices
			20324 Sergeant F GARNER	
			35383 Private W HALL	
			21236 " T.C. JONES	
			The above recipients of merit also Lance Cpl. S. SOAR previously awarded the MILITARY MEDAL attended Brigade Headquarters this day to and had tea with the Brigadier-General.	
	26 June		Packing up and preparation for departure by route to BUIRE au Bois. Medical inspection by M.O.	
	27 "		Marched at 5.30 p.m. from named place, the 14th + 16th Battns. named as right column from OSTREVILLE with R.E. and A.S.C. through ST POL, HERLINCOURT, FLERS and MONCHEL to BUIRE au Bois, the arrival was very late the weather being tripply wet which made the roads very heavy, the rear guard did not reach its destination until 2.50 a.m. lateral communication was maintained with left column to westernion of Bde. H.Q.	
	28 "		The Battalion marched again as above in right column but with no A.S.C. to BEAUMETZ via AUXI-LE-CHATEAU, MAIZICOURT, PROUVILLE	

WAR DIARY
or
INTELLIGENCE SUMMARY.
(Erase heading not required.)

Army Form C. 2118.

Place	Date	Hour	Summary of Events and Information	Remarks and references to Appendices
	29/6		starting at 9.0 p.m. The destination was reached at 1.10 a.m. on 29/6. The 38th Sub Area having supplying the whole BATTALION with tea on arrival. Rest at BEAUMETZ. CO's of Bde met and to Bde HQ where they were introduced to Gen. Jacob. Corps Commander. Forces under Corps arrangements.	
	30/6		Usual tactical scheme for junior officers & NCO's. Battalion paraded at 3.30 p.m. marched to starting point road Junction N. of PtE in BERNAVILLE in rear of 113 Bde Rte. from which point the 113th Bde marched to PUCHEVILLERS arriving at 1.0 midnight, a long halt was made en route at 9.0 p.m. until 10.30 p.m. for refreshment. The column was accompanied by and communicated with air service on this road	

G.W. Gwyther MAJOR
Comdy. 14(S) Battalion
Royal Welsh Fusiliers

113th Inf.Bde.
38th Div.

WAR DIARY

14th BATTN. THE ROYAL WELCH FUSILIERS.

J U L Y

1 9 1 6

WAR DIARY
FOR JULY 1916

14 BATT⁼ RWF

Vol 8

Army Form C. 2118.

WAR DIARY
or
INTELLIGENCE SUMMARY.

14th Battn. Royal Welsh Fusiliers

(Erase heading not required.)

Place	Date	Hour	Summary of Events and Information	Remarks and references to Appendices
July	1/6		PUCHEVILLERS to ARRUEVES. Battalion paraded at 11.0 p.m. At ARRUEVES one hour Company training.	
"	2/6			
"	3/6		ARRUEVES to RIBEMONT by night	
"	4/6		At RIBEMONT	
"	5/6		Coy. officers left to view lines. Battalion moved to MAMETZ and attack under Capt Whelan. Relieved 91st Brigade in front line.	
"	6/6		QUADRANGLE TRENCH and supports in SHELTER WOOD. A+B Coy came to DANTZIE ALLEY. Ve orders to bivouac near CARNOY.	
"	7/6		B+D Coy came to DANTZIE ALLEY, Battalion HdQts came up to old German dugout in POMMIER'S TRENCH	
"	8/6		We moved down to bivouac MINDEN POST	
"	9/6		Battalion moved off at 1.0 am to MAMETZ to take part in an attack but received orders later to return to bivouac	
"	10/6		Attack on MAMETZ WOOD. The 16th R.W.F. moved off to the attack at 4.12 a.m. and at that time our A+C Companies had formed up in four lines behind the 16th R.W.F. and followed up near them in the	

Army Form C. 2118.

14th Batn Royal Welsh Fusiliers

WAR DIARY
or
INTELLIGENCE SUMMARY.
(Erase heading not required.)

Instructions regarding War Diaries and Intelligence Summaries are contained in F.S. Regs., Part II. and the Staff Manual respectively. Title pages will be prepared in manuscript.

Place	Date	Hour	Summary of Events and Information	Remarks and references to Appendices
	10/7/16		c/o rear. At that time the 114th Bde. on our right could not be seen but as the Bangalore was moving into the Hollow by the Railway our Battalion of the 114th Brigade crossed our line from the left. This caused some confusion but did not stop the advance. As soon as our line got within 200yds of the front of the wood they were subjected to heavy rifle and machine gun fire and suffered heavy casualties particularly in Officers and Senior N.C.O's. When within 150 yds of the wood which the main rifle running N. & S. opposite our right a number of men from the preceding lines retired back on shouting "Retire". At this stage Major GWYTHER commanding 14th R.W.F was wounded and Major R.H. MILLS was killed. The process backwards was great and Capt. T. GLYNN JONES gave the orders to reform in a hollow 150 yards from the front edge of the wood and dig in. This was done and a report sent to Bde. About an hour later some of our men were seen advancing on the left along the various strips of wood in which runs STRIP TRENCH. These were our B.D. Companies and the 15 R.W.F. At this time prisoners in some numbers were coming from the	

WAR DIARY
or
INTELLIGENCE SUMMARY.
(Erase heading not required.)

Army Form C. 2118.

1st (S) Batt. Royal Welsh Fusiliers

Place	Date	Hour	Summary of Events and Information	Remarks and references to Appendices
			left and a white flag was shown up near the entrance to the main ride. This was investigated and it was found that the front of the wood was fairly clear and it was decided to move in. This was done and the final objective was reached. 2Lt. STORIK, C.S.M. P. THOMPSON and CPL PUDNER were sent out as a patrol to search the wood. They reported it clear for 200yds except in the direction of WOOD SUPPORT. This was reported to the C.O. 15½ R.W.F. and we received orders to dig in where we were. The line was very slack at this time and Battalions much mixed up. Further enemy were threatened a much counter attack from WOOD TRENCH mid of our M.G. and rifle fire was marked with a great deal of effective fire was lost. The counter attack was however easily repulsed. The Battn. was shaken reorganised but owing to casualties among officers and N.C.O's this work was difficult. Some men were therefore moved back into the line which we had dug in at about 5.0 am. We remained in the	
11 July 16			position during the night of the 10/11 July during which time stragglers were found and attempts to relieve by men of other	

Army Form C. 2118.

1st/6(S)/Batt. Royal Welsh Fusiliers

WAR DIARY
or
INTELLIGENCE SUMMARY.
(Erase heading not required.)

Instructions regarding War Diaries and Intelligence Summaries are contained in F. S. Regs., Part II. and the Staff Manual respectively. Title pages will be prepared in manuscript.

Place	Date	Hour	Summary of Events and Information	Remarks and references to Appendices
		Oct 10	Until we penetrated about now the G.O.C. 113th Bde stood us up a nucleus of 1/6 was used in an attack that was being organized that afternoon. About 4 p.m. we had orders to reinforce the 11th S.W.B. 200 yds to the North East of the same wood running E and W across the wood. At this time we were subjected to our own shrapnel fire. The 11th S.W.B's had pushed on to a point mentioned and we were moved in file in parallel columns to reinforce. The portion on the right met the 11th S.W.B's retiring but they moved up to a line 50 yds from the front edge of the wood. There they dug themselves in and a line was held extending from main ridge to the E & W 300 yds. the flanks being protected by Lewis Guns. About half an hour later the details in 11th under Capt. WHELDON who had been awaiting the order to reinforce just much of the wood came up and extended the line on the right and a few minutes later Capt. HARDWICK and men of the 13th R.W.F. arrived and held the line on the left & still further extended it on the left. A good supply of ammunition and bombs was brought up. About	

T2134. Wt. W708—776. 500000. 4/15. Sir J. C. & S.

Army Form C. 2118.

WAR DIARY
or
INTELLIGENCE SUMMARY.
(Erase heading not required.)

1st (S) Battn. Royal Welsh Fusiliers

Place	Date	Hour	Summary of Events and Information	Remarks and references to Appendices
			About 10.0 p.m. CAPT. T. GLYNN JONES reported the situation to G.O.C. 115th Bde. and he ordered the line to retire to the S. & W. of the traverse in the wood. This was done and we stayed there until relieved by the WARWICKS at daybreak. During the whole time there was a heavy barrage on the S. of the wood by the enemy and on the N. of the wood by our artillery.	
12/7/16			After relief marched through MAMETZ to CITADEL where we BIVOUACED for the day. Later stragglers and at 6.30 p.m. received orders to march to EDGEHILL station (near TREUX) to entrain. Reached there at 9.0 p.m. No train. Bivouaced by the trackside.	
13/7/16			Paraded Battalion 3.0 a.m. and marched to meet motor buses. Entrained in these at 4.30 p.m. and proceeded via AMIENS to LONGPRÉ. On arrival Capt. WHELDON as O.C. reported to Divisional H.Q. and was ordered to proceed to BUSSES. This was done. Battn. in Billets.	
14/7/16			Received order to proceed to EGNIERS. Battn. paraded 11.0 a.m. and marched via entrucation Billets.	
15/7/16			Battalion paraded & proceeded in buses to AUTHIE ST LEGER. Billets.	

Army Form C. 2118.

14(S) Batn Royal Welsh Fusiliers

WAR DIARY
or
INTELLIGENCE SUMMARY.
(Erase heading not required.)

Place	Date	Hour	Summary of Events and Information	Remarks and references to Appendices
	16/7/16		Men bathed. — Kit inspection. Inspected by G.O.C. 113th Bde.	
	17/7/16		Battalion inspected and addressed by Major General Hunter Weston. G.O.C. VIII Corps. Remainder of men bathed at COVIN and Battn. marched thence into huts. 4 officers & 300 men detailed to report to Major RICHARDS 16th R.W.F. at MAILLY MAILET as tunnellers	
	18/7/16		Battn. paraded at 2.30 p.m. and marched to bivouac at SAILLY DELL by COIGNEAUX. Major HODSON 15th R.W.F. took command of the Battn.	
	19/7/16		Bivouacs inspected. Coy. officers re-committed kits had hire. Coy Training	
	20/7/16		Coy Training. G.O.C. 38th Division inspected two platoons respectively equipped with different styles of fighting equipment by way of experiment at 2.0 p.m. O.C. Coys went to view line now held by 115th BRIGADE	
	21/7/16		Instruction of Subaltern officers. All men of Battalion in fatigue training bivouacs improvised.	
	22/7/16		Officers reconnoitre reserve line from HEBUTERNE to GROVENOR FORT. Men of Battalion on fatigue.	

Army Form C. 2118.

1st (S) Batln Royal Welsh Fusiliers

WAR DIARY
or
INTELLIGENCE SUMMARY.
(Erase heading not required.)

Place	Date	Hour	Summary of Events and Information	Remarks and references to Appendices
	23/7/16		Instruction of Lewis officers. Fatigues for men continued	
	24/7/16	12.30 p.m.	B & D Coys go into the Reserve line & relieve 36th Brigade about VIEW TRENCH and TAUPIN TRENCH. H.Q. "A" & C Coys bivouac about R.1.a at 3.0 p.m. Trenches were heavily shelled & three fire wounded.	
	25/7/16		W.R.K. Boupain relieved by "C" Coys and B. D Coys went on R.E. fatigue. A large party was sent on R.E. fatigue. Operations and intelligence N.I.L. His reduced the garrison of ELLES SQUARE to a dangerous degree. Work was carried out on Trench Boarding.	
	26/7/16		B & D Coys holding reserve line. Battalion on fatigue.	
	27/7/16		Relief by 61st Brigade. Battalion marched to BUS encamped in chutes in BUS WOOD arrived 3.0 p.m.	
	28/7/16	11.45 a.m.	Move off from Bus at 11.45 am arrived at SARTON at 3.0 p.m.	
	29/7/16		Roads at SARTON. Instruction parades under Coy. Officers.	
	30/7/16		Leave SARTON by route march and proceed to DOULLENS for entraining. Train leaves DOULLENS at 9.17 pm for HOPOUTRE detrain there at 4.0 am	

T2134. Wt. W708—776. 500000. 4/15. Sir J.C. & S.

Army Form C. 2118.

WAR DIARY
or
INTELLIGENCE SUMMARY.

4th (S) Battn. Royal Welsh Fusiliers

(Erase heading not required.)

Place	Date	Hour	Summary of Events and Information	Remarks and references to Appendices
	3/7/16		Moved to billets in HOUTKERQUE at 5.30 a.m. via WATON arrive 10.30 A.m. Capt. J. C. Ellis (other ranks command) of letter "D" Coy Capt A Lloyd Jones (other ranks command) of letter "C" Coy.	
	3/7/16			P.H.Basham Captain 4th Bn. Royal Welsh Fusiliers

Vol 9

14 Batt.. RWF

War Diary for August 1916

9.C.
7 sheets

WAR DIARY
or
INTELLIGENCE SUMMARY.
(Erase heading not required.)

Army Form C. 2118.

1st/(5th) Bn. Royal West Surreys

Place	Date	Hour	Summary of Events and Information	Remarks and references to Appendices
August	1st	1916	Training of Battalion and Specialists carried out. Visit from Brigadier General commanding.	
"	2nd	1916	Move out from Sheets at 12.30 p.m., halt for ½ hour at HOUTKERQUE. Arrive in camp at M camp POPERINGHE at 4.30 p.m. Officers sent out to reconnoitre roads.	
"	3rd	1916	Training of Battalion in elementary works. Special care being devoted to Lewis Gunners. Lieut H.S. Ormsay from 13th Batt R.W.S & Lt D.C. Morris rejoined Battalion	
"	4th	1916	Training Musketry, two companies on range, 150 mm and 3 officers sent on working party to YPRES. A draft of 9 N.C.O's and 63 men joined Batth	
"	5th	1916	Ten men sent tunnelling. Training of Battalion in close order drill. All specialists under their respective officers.	
"	6th	1916	Draft of 52 men joined the Battalion. Training of Battalion.	
"	7th	1916	Draft of 57 men joined the Battalion. Training, Route March. Officers reconnoitering, Divisional Commander does a tour of inspection.	
"	8th	1916	Training. Wood fighting practised.	

WAR DIARY
or
~~INTELLIGENCE~~ SUMMARY. 14th (S) Bow. Royal Welsh Fusiliers

Army Form C. 2118.

Place	Date	Hour	Summary of Events and Information	Remarks and references to Appendices
August	9th. 16		Training. Route march	
"	10th 16		Training. The Regimental tour for instruction for all officers in wood fighting. Battalion inspected by the Corps Commander.	
"	11th 16		Training	
"	12th 16		Training. Wood fighting.	
"	13th 16		Sunday observed as a day of rest.	
"	14th 16		Training of Battalion in Physical Drill and Bayonet Fighting taken over by Brigade. Senior officers in reconnaissance	
"	15th 16		150 men return from Fatigue at YPRES. Training by Brigade arrangement in Physical Training and Bayonet Fighting Continued.	
"	16th 16		Physical Training and Bayonet Fighting under Bde arrangements. Ordinary Coy. Training. Wood Fighting.	
"	17th 16		Physical Training. Bayonet fighting under Bde arrangements. Coy training.	
"	18th 16		Physical Training. Bayonet Fighting under Bde arrangements. Coy trng. Capt. Badham returns to HQ. Coy. Major Whelan takes over adj. 2nd in Command.	
"	19th 16		Senior officers & C.S. Majors go over right subsector line to be taken over	

Army Form C. 2118.

14th (S) Battalion
Royal Irish Fusiliers

WAR DIARY or INTELLIGENCE SUMMARY.

(Erase heading not required.)

Place	Date	Hour	Summary of Events and Information	Remarks and references to Appendices
	August 20th 1916		one by Brigade. now held by 2nd DUBLIN FUSILIERS and arrange details of relief. Physical training and Bay. Training interrupted by wet weather. Church parade in morning. At 4.15 pm the Battn. paraded to go and relieve 2nd Dublin Fusrs. at POPERINGHE to YPRES at 9.0 pm and proceeded to the line, arrived at POPERINGHE. Relief completed at 2.45 am. Line held "A" Coy on right from D23. B Coy in centre to E25. D Coy on left to E27. "C" Coy 2 PLATOONS at LANCASHIRE FARM 2 platoons on CANAL BANK.	
	21st		C Coy took over on the left the Frontage held by 2 Coy 16th R.W.F. C E28 inclusive and were relieved — at CANAL BANK and LANCASHIRE FARM by B Coy. 13th R.W.F. Enemy quiet - work done on parapet and wiring also cleaning and draining. Patrols sent out from each company. Gas alarm at 10.0 pm.	
	22nd		Line inspected by G.O.C. 36th Division and orders given that front parapet to be thickened by firing in front trench and constructing new firer trench behind parados. Patrols sent out, wiring and parapet work. Enemy quiet.	

WAR DIARY
or
INTELLIGENCE SUMMARY.
(Erase heading not required.)

Army Form C. 2118.

14th (S) Battalion,
Royal Welsh Fusiliers

Place	Date	Hour	Summary of Events and Information	Remarks and references to Appendices
August	23rd 1916		Trenches inspection by G.O.C. 38th Div. Enemy shelled support line, doing little damage. Otherwise enemy quiet. Wiring and parapet work.	
"	24th 1916		Relieved in front line by 13th R.W.F. relief complete 12.35 am 24/25. Enemy quiet during day except for a few Minnie Werfer Bombs fired into trench just before relief. "A" Coy & "C" Coy (less one platoon) marched off to their huts after relief at CHATEAU TROIS TOURS. "B" Coy plus 1 Platoon "C" Coy relieved "Heavy 13th R.W.F. on Canal Bank and "D" Coy relieved "B" Coy 13th R.W.F. on Canal Bank and LANCASHIRE FARM. Orders were given that after relief and in future nights 2 platoons of "B" Coy at LANCASHIRE FARM should hold support line at DAWSON CITY and close over the gap in front line and the 2 platoons on Canal Bank should stay at LANCASHIRE FARM during the nights.	
"	25th 1916		"A" & "C" Coys cleaning up and fatigues. B.Coy in support in the line.	
"	26 1916		A & C Coys training and fatigues, B.Coy in support in the line.	

Army Form C. 2118.

14th (S) Battalion,
Royal Welsh Fusiliers

WAR DIARY
or
INTELLIGENCE SUMMARY.
(Erase heading not required.)

Place	Date	Hour	Summary of Events and Information	Remarks and references to Appendices
August	27 & 28 /1916		A.C Coy. and Training and fatigues. B & D Coy in Support in the line on CANAL BANK. C.W. and some officers attend T.M demonstration at NIEUPORT. Relieved 13th Rwt in front line. The Battalion Frontage being divided by ABD & C Coys. as in the last time in the trenches. Relief complete 1.5 a.m. 28/29. Right new officers reported for duty with the Battalion	
29 /1916			Batt. in the line. Heavy thunderstorms in the afternoon subsequent rain interrupted work and flooded some parts of the trenches. The dugouts of B Coy. a bit new werent. a patrol from right centre, found going very heavy, and could find no gap in German wire. Enemy quiet.	
30 /1916			Battn. in the line. Excessively wet weather and trenches flooded. All work except drainage interrupted. In evening two patrols went on patrol from left Coy. with intention of finding a gap in the enemy's wire & subsequently raiding its trench. The gap discovered and going bad. Enemy quiet. N.W. breeze atmosphere went on patrol from right Coy. found enemy wire strong and forte, no gap and going bad.	
31 /1916			Battn in line. Fine weather, quiet weather, enemy quiet except for saw	

Army Form C. 2118.

14/(S) Bosealon
Royal Welsh Fusiliers.

WAR DIARY
or
INTELLIGENCE SUMMARY.
(Erase heading not required.)

Place	Date	Hour	Summary of Events and Information	Remarks and references to Appendices
Aypul	30-16	out	Settling in outpost line. Work carried on with thickening of parapet, wiring & drainage	
		2i/c	J. Rhodes Major
L/(S) Battalion,
14th (S) Battalion,
Royal Welsh Fusiliers	

Vol 10

10.C
7 sheets

WAR DIARY
4th BATTALION R.W.F.
FOR
SEPTEMBER 1916

WAR DIARY
or
INTELLIGENCE SUMMARY

(Erase heading not required.)

Army Form C. 2118

14th (S) Battalion
Royal Welsh Fusiliers

Place	Date	Hour	Summary of Events and Information	Remarks and references to Appendices
September	1st 1916		Considerable Artillery Activity on both sides and Enemy sent several T.M.S. Relieved at 11.45 p.m. by the 13th Bn. R.W. Fus. "B" Company and "D" Company less one platoon returning to the CHATEAU TROISTOURS and "C" and "A" Company remaining at LANCASHIRE FARM and CANAL BANK, two platoons of "B" Company garrisoning DAWSON CITY by night. Fatigue for front line.	
September	2nd 1916		Company training for "B" and "D" Companies also fatigues and working parties for front line. Battalion in support.	
September	3rd 1916		Church parades and fatigues. Battalion in Support.	
September	4th 1916		Company training and fatigues. Battalion in Support.	
September	5th 1916		Battalion in support at CANAL BANK and CHATEAU relieved by the 17th Bn. Royal Welsh Fusiliers at 11.0 p.m. and marched to "E" Camp A30d.	
September	6th 1916		Batt. at "E" Camp. See men bathed and paid. Battalion fatigue and Battalion marched to "P" Camp A15d.	
September	7th 1916		Company training and 320 men on fatigue at night.	
September	8th 1916		Rest in morning for men on fatigue, coup [?] construction fatigue in afternoon. Formation of raiding party under Capt Glynn Jones and 2nd Lt. Seymour.	
September	9th 1916		Company training, Physical training, made & made arrangements. 320 men on fatigues at CANAL BANK at night. R.O.C. 113 [?] approved with I please with the work.	

WAR DIARY
or
INTELLIGENCE SUMMARY

(Erase heading not required.)

Army Form C. 2118

Instructions regarding War Diaries and Intelligence Summaries are contained in F. S. Regs., Part II. and the Staff Manual respectively. Title Pages will be prepared in manuscript.

Place	Date	Hour	Summary of Events and Information	Remarks and references to Appendices
September	10th 1916		Rest for men in the morning – no parade for divine service but camp construction fatigues occupied the men during the afternoon.	
September	11th 1916		4 days rest and no training under Brigade orders. Footbrace march with Lydia Boots in which the Battalion won by 4-1. Battalion on fatigue at night at CANAL BANK.	
September	12th 1916		Rest during morning. Work in camp during afternoon until 6.0 p.m.	
September	13th 1916		Company training – Physical training in morning, working parties at CANAL BANK at night.	
September	14th 1916		Rest in morning and work in camp in afternoon.	
September	15th 1916		Physical training in morning. Coy. training mainly practice with the new Box Respirators and taking same in Gas chamber. Visit from Sir A. HUNTER WESTON. Capt. Commanders were expressed himself as pleased with the cleanliness and training of the camp. Working parties at CANAL BANK at night carried out for the Base.	
September	16th 1916		Baths in morning and afternoon. Company training. Cleaning up preparatory to leaving camp. Voluntary Church parade and Holy Communion service held during the morning. Relieved the 1st Bn. the West Reg. in Right Support Group: 1 platoon at "Kay" and B Coy in CANAL BANK and LANCASHIRE FARM and DAWSON CITY. A Coy in one platoon at Château du Coq at Château du TROIS TOURS.	

WAR DIARY

14th (S) Battalion Royal Welsh Fusiliers

Army Form C. 2118

Place	Date	Hour	Summary of Events and Information	Remarks and references to Appendices
September	19/5 1916		2nd in Command and OC Coys went over to front line, right sector. Relieved 11th Batt. Royal Welsh Fusiliers in front line in trenches. Coys in order from right A B C D. Relieved by 13th R.W.F. (two coys and 1 platoon) on CANAL BANK, LANCASHIRE FARM & DAWSON CITY, and (one coy, one platoon) at Chateau des TROIS TOURS. Enemy quiet. Heavy rain during night hampered work - working parties mainly occupied repairing breaks in parapet and drainage.	
September 18/19 1916			OPERATIONS. A patrol was led by 2 Lt. Seymour went out from the right of E.25 with the object of capturing an enemy patrol which was reported working on his support trench. None were found but Lewis gun fire was heard. This was reported to the Artillery who bombarded the support line as this patrol. Enemy front line apparently empty, held and his wires & materials damaged. Intelligence Enemy Quiet. Work interrupted by bad weather - mainly repairing & cleaning EALING and COFFEE TRENCHES. Our Artillery active. A Raiding party of the 13th R.W.F. attempted to parade the enemy trench in front of E.25 but did not succeed. Our artillery co-operated with intense fire from 2.10 am to 2.15 am. Enemy retaliations inconsiderable and Evening during night quiet. Work owing to wet weather work mainly due was drainage	

Army Form C. 2118

WAR DIARY
or
INTELLIGENCE SUMMARY
(Erase heading not required.)

14th (S) Battalion
Royal Welsh Division

Instructions regarding War Diaries and Intelligence Summaries are contained in F.S. Regs., Part II. and the Staff Manual respectively. Title Pages will be prepared in manuscript.

Place	Date	Hour	Summary of Events and Information	Remarks and references to Appendices
Sept 19/20			dramof and clearing falls and repairing came in front line and communication trenches	
Sept.	20/21 1916		Enemy light trench mortars active between 3 am & 4 am on left of Battalion front apparently making for our Tr. B at SKIPTON ROAD. Our retaliation stopped this. Rifle grenades registered in gap cut in enemy wire previous to raid on 19th & 20th about 3 enemy half hour fired between midnight and 4.0 am. A patrol went out under 2nd Lt SEYMOUR from C.14 c 9.5½ to ascertain state of wire as Sap C.14 Sept 2.17 and found it well wired. Work clearing falls in EALING and parapet. Wet day.	
September	21/22 1916		Operation. A patrol under 2nd Lt D.C. Morris went out from Tr. B to reconnoitre approach to Sap C.14 & Tr.14. Owing to heavy rain the going was very bad but one was found an approach to enemy line about the wire. A listening patrol went out from the 13th R.W.F. but found no enemy patrol. Enemy fairly quiet, some Tr. B. Welday	
September	22/23 1916		Relieved by 13th R.W.F. in front line with exception of Day in left centre which had to stay in become the 13th R.W.F. had insufficient troops to hold the front line. Brewy moved to LANCASHIRE FARM - DAWSON CITY - MAY & CANAL BANK	

WAR DIARY
INTELLIGENCE SUMMARY

Army Form C. 2118

1st (S) Battalion Royal Welsh Fusiliers

Place	Date	Hour	Summary of Events and Information	Remarks and references to Appendices
			CANAL BANK	
	Sept 22/23 1916		"A" and "C" Coy. to CHATEAU des TROIS TOURS. Alexander men on fatigues after relief snipers.	
	Sept 23/24 1916		D Coy relieved by B Coy in centre left front. D Coy moved to CANAL BANK. All men engaged on working parties. Enemy quiet except a fine day.	
	Sept 24/25 1916		A Coy relieved on left centre front by "C" Coy. 13th R.W. Fus. and A Coy. moved to CANAL BANK. All men employed on working parties. Relieved 13th R.W.F. C Coy (right) D Coy (centre) B Coy (left) 16th R.W.F. Cookers F26. Reserve of "A" Coy apparels (a B Coy. and a/c 6 D Coy. to make up for men who were left at TROIS TOURS CHATEAU. Remainder of "A" Coy in reserve Bank R. (left)	
	Sept 25/26/6 to 27/1916		Receiving party of H & O R's + B officer (St Seymour, Dennis + Wynn) carried out training in CHATEAU.	
	Sept 29 1916		Quiet day. New drain emerging from EALING to post FUSILIER FARM (EALING TRENCH is extremely wet.) Raiding party of 13th R.W.Fus. went out from E.25 at 11.30 pm, enemy wire without opposition, after effective scare gun barrage. Only 6 of the enemy were met, and (all these) their papers were handed and to ALL BACK as well as time fuses found in the trench. The party	

WAR DIARY
INTELLIGENCE SUMMARY
(Erase heading not required.)

Army Form C. 2118

14th (S) Battalion
Royal Welsh Fusiliers

Place	Date	Hour	Summary of Events and Information	Remarks and references to Appendices
	Sept 29.9.16		Returned leaving 2/Lt Lack missing and eight casualties returned. Unfortunately about the officer being missing no identification were obtained. Enemy retaliation was fair, but no damage was done. Section of sappers relieve from working parties and work is entering on wire entanglements by us, but all the new wire is on our side. Post the enemy was unable and heard bombs began to be laid to Posts 6 & 6 HUDDERSFIELD ROAD. This way is extremely bad. Drains from ealing deepened. Enemy trench mortars are now concentrated on his support line, day officer also report many lights coming from his support line. Daylight patrol of 2Lt De Mouris & 28 O.R's left C148 9.0 to reconnoitre ground between C148 7.6 & C148 9.0 C148 7.6. Captured enemy wiring parties repair. Reported from point C148 7.6 a 9 a.d. after what seemed to be upward slope for 50 yrs turn left from cut a 9 a.d. after what seemed to be short slope twenty wide. A much erased crater which was thought not to be falall and lands date thrown at them but in chance was noticed. The enemy took as change. Patrol returned 12/25 am.
	Sept 30.9.16		Day work on trench boards towards HUDDERSFIELD R. from Bay 6. 2 men sewers put up on own wire.

N.G. Wheeler
Major
14th (S) Batt. Royal Welsh Fusiliers

11.C.
8 sheets

Vol II

WAR DIARY.
of
14th Battalion.
ROYAL WELSH FUSILIERS.
October 1916.

WAR DIARY Army Form C. 2118

or

INTELLIGENCE SUMMARY

(Erase heading not required.)

14th (S) Battalion
Royal Welsh Fusiliers

Instructions regarding War Diaries and Intelligence Summaries are contained in F. S. Regs., Part II. and the Staff Manual respectively. Title Pages will be prepared in manuscript.

Place	Date	Hour	Summary of Events and Information	Remarks and references to Appendices
Hebuterne	1st	1916	Day work on trench boards towards HUDDERSFIELD Rd from BRIDGE 6. Two new saluts put up in same sector. A fighting patrol of ten men under 2nd Lieut Seymour went out and encountered an enemy patrol. Our party attacked with Bombs and rifle fire and inflicted losses but the enemy retaliated with T.M.B and the Lieut L. Seymour was wounded and our party had to withdraw.	
October	2nd	1916	Relieved by 13th Battn R. W. Fus. in front line but owing to desertion of Raiding Party from 13th R.W.Fus "C" Coy were left in front line to hold the Right Bank front and "D" Coy after relief moved to TROIS TOURS CHATEAU. "A" Company & CANAL BANK EAST and LANCASHIRE FARM and "B" Company & CANAL BANK WEST. Relief complete 8.50 P.M.	
October	2/3	1916	All men employed on working parties during the day and night. "D" Coy and Headquarters bathed.	
October	3rd	1916	"D" Coy relieved "C" Coy on right. whereto "B" Coy moved back to TROIS TOURS CHATEAU and "C" Coy moved to CANAL BANK WEST.	
October	4th	1916	"A" Bay completed trench board laying from BRIDGE 6 to head of HUDDERSFIELD ROAD. Scallops were also put up. The Burgoin trench was improving approval of runda.	
October	5th	1916	"C" Coy relieved left Coy 13 R.W.Fus in the afternoon and "B" Coy the centre Coy after dark. "A" Coy was thereafter arranged the other 3 companies.	
October	5/6	1916	A new 5' drain F was cut from EALING (C.I.N.E.3.7) to click running parallel to EALING from the NILE (at C.I.N.C.0.2). This ditch about 2' of water was carried down. was also deepened.	

WAR DIARY
or
INTELLIGENCE SUMMARY 14(S) Battalion Royal Welsh Fusiliers

Army Form C. 2118

(Erase heading not required.)

Place	Date	Hour	Summary of Events and Information	Remarks and references to Appendices
October	5/6	cont.	Bosch also commenced a drain parallel to & about 10 yards behind parados, commencing from Fusilier LANE and working to left. Fusilier LANE was also cleaned out.	
October	6/7	19.6	Revetment of CANAL DEFENCES. Enemy very active with T.M's one of which dropped 300 yards behind the N.L.G.	
October	6/7	19.6	Drainage work continued. Enemy were active behind parados in last night. New work behind parados in night returns getting on very quickly. Move my knife.	
October	7.	19.6	Revetment of CANAL DEFENCES continued. Enemy artillery regularly miles T.M's & artillery which fired on working parties near KRUPP SALIENT frequently every morning. EALING is improving on regards when last week. 19th Division Ban. Welsh Regt. are working on a communication trench 10 yds to the left.	
October	7/8	19.6	A very clear moonlight night (particularly Fusilier) and firing in new parapets on night extremely quiet at night.	
October	8.	19.6	About noon "C" Coy were heavily shelled by enemy. This we failed to get observation on and it was reported to Brigade. No material damage was done and no casualties. One heavy Bosch however landed on head of EALING in afternoon, Brig. and Bay report some of an heavy shell dropping shortly his	

1875 Wt. W593/826 1,000,000 4/15 J.B.C. & A. A.D.S.S./Forms/C.2118.

Army Form C. 2118

WAR DIARY
or
INTELLIGENCE SUMMARY

14th (S) Battn. Royal Welsh Fusiliers

(Erase heading not required.)

Instructions regarding War Diaries and Intelligence Summaries are contained in F.S. Regs., Part II. and the Staff Manual respectively. Title Pages will be prepared in manuscript.

Place	Date	Hour	Summary of Events and Information	Remarks and references to Appendices
Béthune	4th		Weekly hot bath and parades. Show was reported. Work on Canal Bank front continued.	
Béthune	8/9	1916	Training work continued as usual. Bayonet - Bomb and advanced parades as usual in the company.	
Béthune	9th	1916	Relieved by 13th R.W.F. Owing to demand of rations party by 13th R.W.F. enemy innominée was late, it was anticipated we would reach the Camps cantoned on CANAL BANK. Half men B.Hqrs moved to TROIS TOURS CHATEAU.	
Béthune	10th	1916	Two Companies commenced working parties for the 13th Rose. Ruyfusiliers. "B"-Coy reported things quiet. Rifles are very buggy.	
Béthune	11th	1916	"C" Coy relieves "B" Coy in trenches on 7 of June 16. Coy came to CANAL BANK (left) and provided ration parties for the 13th and Ruyfusiliers.	
Béthune	12th	1916	Supplied 13th R.W.F. noise every ends myself working and ration parties. 13th R.W.F. exchanged enemy's trench = 1 prisoner, 1 m gun.	
Béthune	13th	1916	Working parties supplied 15th R.W.Fus. road. 4 prisoners secured.	
Béthune	14th	1916	Returned to support by the 17th R.W.Fus. Relief complete 9.0 p.m. "C" Coy relieved by 13th R.W.F. moved from the TROIS TOURS CHATEAU.	

1875 Wt. W593/826 1,000,000 4/15 J.B.C. & A. A.D.S.S./Forms/C. 2118.

WAR DIARY or **INTELLIGENCE SUMMARY**
(Erase heading not required.)

Army Form C. 2118

1st (S) Battalion Royal Welsh Fusiliers

Place	Date	Hour	Summary of Events and Information	Remarks and references to Appendices
October 14th 1916			Above many shells dropped in the CHATEAU GROUNDS killing one 19th Pioneer wounding two others. Lieut. ORMSBY, Lt. T.N. PRINGLE & D.C. MORRIS with the raiders moved to "E" camp. The remainder of the Battalion came to "P" camp.	
October 15th 1916			Battalion has been reduced to the size of two ordinary company, so nearly all the officers on our units attended the training for details, and 3 an remainder for a training school and Bombing School (about 3 platoons in all).	
—	16 1916		The Bat less the raiders and other details about formed into a Coy. to training and ordinary company training continued working parties at night. Battalion inspected by Army Commander.	
—	17 1916		Company training carried on and working parties formed	
—	18 1916		Orders received that Bath. was to relieve 16th Batt. R.W.F. Right Support Batt. in Right (11th) Bde Sector, and Support and Draw Lines reconnoitred by 2nd in Command & O.C. Coys. Company training morning	
—	19 1916		Inspection of men Relies and all equipment preparatory to going into the line. Battalion paraded at 4.0 p.m. and entrained at 4.45 pm at PESELHOEK for YPRES Asylum. Relief of 16th RWFus. complete at 8.30 pm in Right Support "A" Coy. finding garrison for FRASCATI & IRISH FARM Posts.	

WAR DIARY
INTELLIGENCE SUMMARY

14(S) Batt. Royal Welsh Fusiliers

Place	Date	Hour	Summary of Events and Information	Remarks and references to Appendices
Oblr.	20th 1916		Relieved 13th Batt. The Welsh Regiment on right. B Coy right centre, A Coy on RIGHT, A/C combined in CENTRE and D on LEFT. Line is very wet particularly in centre where the trench is composed of 6 inch to 1 ft. water, knee deep between Batt. H.Q. at IRISH FARM. Trench very quiet as enemy is about 600 yds. away.	
	21st 1916		Nothing to report. Work is purely maintenance. Line is chiefly held. Enemy have guns, is extremely quiet. Lykring patrol went out to find whether CANADIAN DUGOUTS are occupied, Farmer that day were not.	
	22nd 1916		The past 3 days were particularly fine and there was considerable aeroplane activity. Enemy quiet. Gas alarm went off about 7.30 pm. well to our Right, known parts was not affected.	
	23rd 1916		Line quiet. Some desultory artillery turn up on CROSS ROADS TURN which did no damage.	
	24 1916		Wet day and the tracks to and from line were muddy and difficult. Damage to upkeep of trench head of FINCH ST and the town have to be made in hand. The first casualty of the tour happened about 10 pm when a man of CENTRE Coy was hit in the head by M.G. bullet.	

WAR DIARY
INTELLIGENCE SUMMARY 14th (S) Bat. Royal Welsh Fusiliers

Place	Date	Hour	Summary of Events and Information	Remarks and references to Appendices
October	25. 1916		Relieved by the 13th Batt. The Welsh Regiment in the Line and IRISH FARM. Relief complete at 9.30 p.m. Relieved 13th R.W.Fus. in CANAL BANK (our E.Dup) and 2 platoons of B Coy. relieved the 16th Welsh at LANCASHIRE FARM with the acting platoon in CANAL BANK (E). Relief complete 12.30 p.m. Raiders have been ordered to return to their Coys, and were moved up from E Camp to join "A" Coy. at TROIS TOURS CHATEAU	
"	26 27 1916		All the men from CANAL BANK and CHATEAU working R.E. fatigues. Was supervision of 15th R.W.Fusiliers. Work on CANAL BANK (new dugouts) and thickening parapet E23 & E27 most of the front. The work is done between the hours of 1.0 A.M. and 10.0 A.M.	
"	28 1916		Same day and night. Fatigues and 13th R.W. without suitables under orders from 13th R.W. with out relief from CHATEAU by brigade. all men were out all day the chateau men cleared the mud away from near the huts. Wooden boards are to have thought worked for two days ago.	
"	29 1916		Same day and night. Fatigues.	
"	29/30 1916		Berloof had a successful raid in which 3 prisoners were taken & (One with IRON CROSS) and many few slight casualties on our part.	

Army Form C. 2118

14th (S) Battalion,
Royal Welsh Fusiliers

WAR DIARY
or
INTELLIGENCE SUMMARY
(Erase heading not required.)

Instructions regarding War Diaries and Intelligence Summaries are contained in F.S. Regs., Part II. and the Staff Manual respectively. Title Pages will be prepared in manuscript.

Place	Date	Hour	Summary of Events and Information	Remarks and references to Appendices
October	30	1916	Relieved 13th R.W.F. in front line. D. Coy on Right, B. Coy in Centre, A Coy (consisting of raiding party) on left. A will be providing party to thoroughly patrol no man's land, where the raid will be carried on. Relief complete 7.30 p.m.	
	30/31	1916	An officer's patrol of 20 men under Lieut. Ornsby went out from E.26 with object to reconnoitre, capture or kill enemy, about 100 yds in front of our wire they came upon a ditch which ran parallel with our line and which was impossible to cross. They moved to a block feature but owing to recent rains they could not cross the ditch, which in its left sector swollen out into a lake. Right returned, attempted to help behind parados drilling in new work E.22. Centre filling in new work E.22. Cleaning pailes in WE new entrance to Ealing. Left cleaning NILE near head of Skipton. Weekly army arriving from line. 13 R.W.F. supplied wkg parties of 1 off. 50 O.R. for work on E.22 and 1 off. 25 men on E.26. Work from 11.0 am to 10.0 am.	
	31/		Bombs dropped near dugout - flew back compressed and spare for new officers kitchen dugout. Enemy shell dropped near left coy head qs at 1.30 p.m. and caught new working work. Right: 2 killed; 6 wounded. Sleepers not arriving continuing R.E. work on E.22. Centre: new Coy's kitchen at Lancs. fm. left. Left cleaning R.E. spoil from new dugout in Lanc. fm. Left cleaned work & falks in NILE & Fraudserie - Left continuing NILE along Huddleston Road	
	31/10			H. Horton Lt Col 14th Rwf
Capt & Adj
Capt & 2/Lt Major
14 (S) Battalion Royal Welsh Fus

WAR DIARY

FOR

NOVEMBER 1916

14th BATTALION

ROYAL WELSH FUSILIERS

Vol 12

12.C.
9 sheets

WAR DIARY or INTELLIGENCE SUMMARY

Army Form C. 2118

14TH BATTN. ROYAL WELSH FUSILIERS.

Place	Date	Hour	Summary of Events and Information	Remarks and references to Appendices
Thiepval	30•31/10/1916		Quiet night. Corps reports large numbers of trains making for this front. Work RIGHT training which parades winning in front of E.22 (2 counters) CENTRE. Labs in front sub and NIKE. Dump. Kitchen at LANCASHIRE Fm. LEFT. Renewing NIKE, draining behind parados in E.26. 13" RWF parties worked as usual on E.26 but the E.23 party of 50 O.R. owing to EALING being blocked worked on spaces for dugouts in LANCASHIRE Fm. & clearing tramway. C.O. Boy. LG. and training LANCASHIRE Fm dumps.	
Nov.	1. 1916		Rast Wickrane than usual for a rather heavier enemy bombardment and 6pm. That also dropped "MINNIES" in E.27 for which we got prompt and effective retaliation. The "MINNIES" did no amount of work. CANAL BANK. Renewing officers mess arrest near Bridge H.A. clearing for new officers' kitchen and new shell dugout near Brid'g 6. RIGHT Coy. Continuation of work in E.23 - filling in CENTRE Coy. Concrete posts for new Sunken. Renewing front clearing labs in front - using re-arrangement of dumps at Retailed and laying of R.E. works E.26 and realignment of NIKE Continuation of R.E. work. (left)	
Nov.	1-2. 1916		Patrol of 1 NCO. 3 men went out from E.24 at 11.0pm Cr. Failed to see any exceptional movements in enemy lines - returned at 1.0 hrs reporting no man's land very weak and occupied on enemy front.	

WAR DIARY
INTELLIGENCE SUMMARY
34th BATTN. ROYAL WELSH FUSILIERS.

Army Form C. 2118

(Erase heading not required.)

Place	Date	Hour	Summary of Events and Information	Remarks and references to Appendices
N.	2.	19.16	**Work** RIGHT Coy. Filling in E.2.3. CENTRE wiring. 5 concertinas put out in E.2.d. LEFT Filling in new bays in E.26.	
		19.16	**Work** CANAL BANK. Officers Kitchen wrecker and floor sewn. 20 yards of Trench Boards re-laid on proper piles. Latrines dug out near Bridge 6. RIGHT Coy Shelters Roads and Rd erected at LANCASHIRE Fm. Construction of New work in E.2.3. CENTRE Dump Kitchen, chimney of which made and top and beyond. Construction of R.E. work in E.2.3. 30ft. LEFT Coy new work in NILE (Left) wiring. Dance return. Work in NILE (Left)	
"	3.	19.16	Enemy is extremely quiet at night 15 and 3 am enemy's active dying of any movement at his part if 1 N6 MINS LANG RIGHT Coy sent out a listening Patrol of 1 NCO and 3 men from E.2.3 to listen for movement in enemy lines and at HEENACKS in fighting patrols, everything was reported quiet and NO TRANS LAND activity met. They returned after 2 hours. CENTRE Coy relined them with a similar patrol which brought back some report. Work CANAL BANK. New Back an dugout near Bdge. 6. New Mens Kitchen floors and Pant vaulted. RIGHT Coy Entering works in trenches drain behind parades with R.E. located in E.2.3. 50 yds Tramway at LANCASHIRE FARM raised and theres' 6 concertina put out opposite E.2.3.	

WAR DIARY or INTELLIGENCE SUMMARY

Army Form C. 2118

14th BATTN. ROYAL WELSH FUSILIERS.

Place	Date	Hour	Summary of Events and Information	Remarks and references to Appendices
	Nov 14, 1916		CENTRE Coy front line, and covered floor to support trenches open to dugout trenches. Continued work in E24. perfect. LEFT Coy. Bd. movement in NIKE (left) pulled down. SKIPTON RD. Main dispersed. Continued R.E. work on E26. LEFT Coy front line covered by shell & were about 100yds wide and passage impossible. At 10.0 pm were shelled "MINNIE" EALING. retaliation which was effective. No damage was done. On CANAL BANK. the new kitchen was manned and the whole was ready for use before relief. Can visit the Soup Kitchen at LANCASHIRE Fm. Battns relieved us in front line. Relief completed 6.50 p.m. Companies are now as follows:- A+B CANAL BANK WEST. X Coy. 2 Platoons at LANCASHIRE FARM and 2 platoons on CANAL BANK EAST. C+D Coys and Hdqrs at TROIS TOURS CHATEAU. After relief we employed as following working parties:- (1) 1 Off. 1 Sgt. and 50 O.R. to work from 6.0 pm - 10.0 pm on E23 (2) 1 Off. 25 O.R. to work from 6.0 am - 10.0 am on E26 (3) 12 O.R. from LANCASHIRE FARM to carry R.E. material from AUSTERLITZ to new work on NIKE. (Right). (4) 16 Off. & 400 O.R. from TROIS TOURS CHATEAU to carry from AUSTERLITZ to E23.	

WAR DIARY or INTELLIGENCE SUMMARY

Army Form C. 2118

14TH BATTN. ROYAL WELSH FUSILIERS.

Place	Date	Hour	Summary of Events and Information	Remarks and references to Appendices
Ypres.	5th 1916		CHATEAU COYS. supplied 13th R.W.F. with 2 N.C.Os and 20 men for all day work in CANAL BANK dugouts. Carried night working parties ao H.X. 16 but in addition two dugout training parties under R.E. Every available man was out.	
"	6th/7th 1916		Provided the same working parties for CANAL BANK and CHATEAU TROIS TOURS	
"	9th 1916		Relieved 13th R.W.F. in front line C-D on RIGHT A-B in CENTRE X Coy on left. Relief complete 7.30 p.m.	
"	10th 1916.		Quiet night. During morning enemy dropped three "minnies" on CENTRE Coy. for which we took quick & effective retaliation WORK. RIGHT. — Back post strengthened: Large party dug a new wide drain on a length of 50 yards from 2us. LIER DRAIN Coy HQ. CENTRE — dugouts LANCASHIRE Fm. completed on left. — work on NINE (Ledge) LEFT COY. — patrol of 1 officer and 1 man left E2 & 6 Coy examined ditch in no mans LAND. Enemy was out from 10.0 P.M. — 11.0 P.M. but bright moonlight prevented them going more than 150 yds. which was for France, consequently division found it seemed the same. Our Artillery + TM. stop on extreme left of Onpcole front at 11.0 P.M. French Belgian took part.	

WAR DIARY
or
INTELLIGENCE SUMMARY

(Erase heading not required.)

Army Form C. 2118

BATTN. ROYAL WELSH FUSILIERS.

Place	Date	Hour	Summary of Events and Information	Remarks and references to Appendices
Nov	11.11.1916		For the enemy retaliated weakly in no about 3.0 am but did no damage. WORK. RIGHT. maintenance. 30 yds. of drainage done behind parados. CENTRE. LANCASHIRE Fm. Dugouts on) construction of new R.E. parapet work to E.23. LEFT. construction of new trenches in NILE Right Cay, also put 5 crenelles and some trip wires out in right of Div. CANAL BK. excavating for 3 new dugouts for newsupport barrier NILE. Relaying of duckboards.	
Nov	12th 1916		Day was quiet. Night work on New Trench between E.22. Right Cay under 30 yds. Work CANAL BK. trench Bolo. (double row) completed to Bolo. S. 2 new dugout frames put up and dugout spaces continued. RIGHT. 30 yards running on right of D.22. maintenance of each post. Drainage behind parados, 30 yds. 4' wide completed. CENTRE continued quiet. Rifles for drainage. 2 trench elephants fixed at LANCASHIRE FARM. LEFT - Work on NILE (north) revetment and new parapet in E.26 under 19th PIONEERS.	
Nov	13th 1916		Work carried out on same lines. Drainage work on RIGHT carried out on another 30 yds. During the afternoon artillery strafe CAESAR'S NOSE wirecut. marked at 1.0 hrs. 14.20.16 and TM's retaliated by enemy steps. retaliation for night 10 u.	

1875 Wt. W593/826 1,000,000 4/16 J.B.C. & A. A.D.S.S./Forms/C.2118.

WAR DIARY or INTELLIGENCE SUMMARY

Army Form C. 2118

14th BATTN. ROYAL WELSH FUSILIERS

(Erase heading not required.)

Place	Date	Hour	Summary of Events and Information	Remarks and references to Appendices
New.	14.7.16		We fired 1500 round on CAESERS NOSE. enemy retaliation was very weak. Hostility patrol of 12 O.R. under Lieut H.S. ORMSBY went out from E.26 and got within 10 yards of enemy wire, reported going good and thing quiet. Work on bomb line, 2 seats for bombs and 8 AA cupolas at LANCASHIRE FARM officers shelter & new one finished on CANAL BANK excavating for 2 dug outs completed. From 2pm - 2.45pm and 12" howitzers fired on KOHN FARM with good effect. Enemy retaliation was negligible. At 9 pm. an officers fighting patrol 12.O.R. under 2nd Lt. D. Jones went out from E.26. but bright moonlight prevented their getting very close to enemy line. Reported work going on which many chains, on which an 18 pounder fired.	
New.	15.7.1916		Relieved by 14th RWF. at 8.50pm and Bivouced near by Forum Lé "P" Camp.	
"	16.7.1916		Training at "P" camp and Working Parties from each Bay, attached to Railway Company. Working Parties found at night.	
"	17.7.1916		Training in morning and Working parties found at night. Drawing of Railway Company.	
"	18.7.1916		Training in morning and Working parties at night. Drawing of Railway Company continued.	
"	19.7.1916		Church Parade. Battery Battalion. Working Parties at night. Drawing of Railway Party continued.	

WAR DIARY
or
INTELLIGENCE SUMMARY

(Erase heading not required.)

14TH BATTN. ROYAL WELSH FUSILIERS

Army Form C. 2118

Place	Date	Hour	Summary of Events and Information	Remarks and references to Appendices
Nowa	20th 1916		Training in morning - working parties at night. Training of the Raiding Party continued.	
"	21st 1916		Training in morning. Brigadier-General visited camp and saw Raiders Coy. at work and inspected camp. Working parties at night. Test alarm carried out.	
"	22 1916		Training in morning. Working Parties at night. Raiders Training continued. Tactical scheme of Brigade (Gaspers)	
"	23 1916		Training in morning. Inspection by Divisional Commander. Raiding Party and Camp. Brigade Competitions at night in which our Party was winning competition.	
"	24 1916		Training in morning - Raiding Party left for "E" Camp under Capt. G. Jones. Demin Offices went front line.	
"	25th 1916		Batt. entrained at 3.45pm. for the front line. relieved the 16th Batt. The Welsh Regt. - relief complete at 9.40 pm. Fighting Patrol under Lieut. H.S. Ormsby went out but encountered no enemy. Front line to the Right of Bolton Trench held by him composed Boys of the Battalion - on Row. 13th R.W.F. ac LANCASHIRE Fm. Two Boys two Platoons of 13th R.W.F. on CANAL BANK EAST & WEST. - Left Boy. Trenches held by one Boy. of 16th R.W.F.m.	
"	26 1916		Battalion in front line. Fighting Patrol under 2nd Lieut. H.N. Jones went out but encountered no enemy. Enemy shelled LANCASHIRE Fm.	

Army Form C. 2118

WAR DIARY
or
INTELLIGENCE SUMMARY
(Erase heading not required.)

14TH BATTN. ROYAL WELSH FUSILIERS

Instructions regarding War Diaries and Intelligence Summaries are contained in F. S. Regs., Part II. and the Staff Manual respectively. Title Pages will be prepared in manuscript.

Place	Date	Hour	Summary of Events and Information	Remarks and references to Appendices
	Nov 27.1916		About 1.0pm advanced a unit. Work done excluding front line. Drainage, timing and connecting up. HEADINGLY LANE with the NILE. Battalion in line two Raiders Boulogne. Our support trench heavily bombarded between 7.0pm — 9.30pm. with T.M.B. S-9 and G.2. Our retaliation particularly after the S.O.S. rang very effective and enemy quiet for rest of night. Casualties nil. Night work intensified during bombardment but continued later. Parapet, dummy and drainage.	
	28.1916		Relieved in front line at 6.40pm by the 13th R.W.F. Right Boy swing to CANAL BANK WEST. Right Centre Boy. 2 platoons Canal Bank West and 2 platoons CHATEAU TROIS TOURS.	
	29.1916		Work done — connecting HEADINGLY LANE and NILE — drainage. Working parties found per night from Osoveren and Raiders at "E" Camp inspected by G.O.C. 39th Division.	
	30.1916		Working parties found per night from Boesinghe and to Potijzer.	

3rd XI.1916

[signature]
Lieut. Col. Commanding
14th R.W. Fusiliers

14th BATTN. ROYAL WELSH FUSILIERS
Vol 13

WAR DIARY
FOR
DECEMBER 1916

13.C.
8 sheets

Army Form C. 2118.

14TH (S) BATTALION,
ROYAL WELSH
FUSILIERS.

No............
Date............

WAR DIARY
or
INTELLIGENCE SUMMARY.
(Erase heading not required.)

Instructions regarding War Diaries and Intelligence Summaries are contained in F. S. Regs., Part II. and the Staff Manual respectively. Title pages will be prepared in manuscript.

Place	Date	Hour	Summary of Events and Information	Remarks and references to Appendices
Dec.	1-19.16		Relieved 13th R.W.F. with two coys. (composite) in the Right and Right Centre Front line. Relief complete at 4.40 p.m. Work on front line parapet. Enemy raided left Batt. Front line but were repulsed. Considerable rifle & M.G. firing over our front line but none yielded. Own activity Nil.	
do	2-19.16		Front line held by two composite coys. Large wiring party found by Raider Bay. Right Brigade were wired. Work on front line parapet C.14.d.7. and C.13.b.1. between Right Bay and the Canal Bank. Lightly patrolled under 2Lt W. Jones. Of 12 men went out from C.14.5 but encountered no enemy.	
do	3-19.16		Front line held as before. Raiders Bay again continued wiring — strengthening wire made previous night and completing 175 yards of strong wire from C.14.d.6 to b.14.6. Work on front line parapet and dugouts in support and Canal Bank as before. Drainage. Lightly patrolled under 2Lt W. Jones, went out from C.14.6 but encountered no enemy.	

2353 Wt. W2544/1451 700,000 5/15 D. D. & L. A.D.S.S./Forms/C. 2118.

14TH (S.) BATTALION, ROYAL WELSH FUSILIERS.

No............
Date............

Army Form C. 2118.

WAR DIARY
or
INTELLIGENCE SUMMARY.
(Erase heading not required.)

Instructions regarding War Diaries and Intelligence Summaries are contained in F.S. Regs., Part II. and the Staff Manual respectively. Title pages will be prepared in manuscript.

Place	Date	Hour	Summary of Events and Information	Remarks and references to Appendices
Dec.	4th 1916		Relieved by 13th R.W.F. in Right & Right Centre Bays. Front line at 6.0 p.m. - Drainage, clearing up and augmenting embrasures during the day. Working parties found at night for front line Batt.	
do	5th 1916		Battalion in Support. Working parties improving running parties found to front line.	
do	6th 1916		Battalion in Support. Working parties to front line and running parties found.	
do	7th 1916		Relieved 13th R.W.F. in front line and LANCASHIRE FARM at 5.0 p.m. C+D Coys Right Bay, A+B Coys Right Centre. - Detachment of 50 men from Raiders Bay, under Lieut. W.S. ORMSBY, on left hand, and Capt. F.S. JONES and remainder of Raiding Bay at LANCASHIRE FARM. Fighting patrol of 10 men under Lieut. R. WILLIAMS, went out from B.H.L. but encountered no enemy. Enemy quiet. Went - Brrr BANK and Support Line augment. Front line - enemy quiet. A fighting patrol	
do	8th 1916.		Battalion in front line - enemy quiet. A fighting patrol under 2/Lt H.H. TONET went out from C.H.7. but encountered	

2353 Wt. W2544/1454 700,000 5/15 D. D. & L. A.D.S.S./Forms/C. 2118.

WAR DIARY
INTELLIGENCE SUMMARY

Place	Date	Hour	Summary of Events and Information	Remarks and references to Appendices
			execution	
			No enemy - work on CANAL BANK & Support Line dugouts, some mining.	
Dec 9th 1916			Battalion in front line. A minor offensive operation was carried out by Capt T.G. TONET in conjunction with the TMB. After a recent TMB bombardment of CAESER'S NOSE, Capt. T.G. TONET and his party of 15 men went out from C.H.1. with a Bangalore torpedo to be put under the enemy wire and if possible effect an entry. The torpedo was however extremely defective and broke in several places and Mr Onsley had to be drawn before reaching the wire. The enemy was quiet and no retaliation was made. No casualties. Work on CANAL BANK and Support Line dug-outs, mining - drainage.	
10 Oct 1916			Relieved by 13th R.W.F. at 6.0 p.m. Enemy artillery active particularly during relief time. Working parties found for front line.	
11 Oct 1916			Battalion in support - working parties found for front line.	
12 Oct 1916			Battalion relieved in support line by the 16th SHERWOOD FORESTERS and entrained at 9.30 p.m. at YPRES Asylum. to POPERINGHE and bivouac there for the night.	

14TH (S) BATTALION, ROYAL WELSH FUSILIERS.

No.............. Date..............

WAR DIARY
or
INTELLIGENCE SUMMARY
(Erase heading not required.)

Army Form C. 2118.

Place	Date	Hour	Summary of Events and Information	Remarks and references to Appendices
Sec.	13.2.1916		Battalion entrained at 9.50 a.m. at CHEESE MARKET STATION, POPERINGHE for BOLLEZEELE and marched from there to billets in the training area at MERCKEGHEM.	
"	14.2.1916		Day devoted to cleaning up clothes, equipment and billets.	
"	15.2.1916		Parties: training of all cups. The remainder of the day being devoted to Baths at BOLLEZEELE.	
"	16.2.1916		Battalion and Company training during the day in the TRAINING AREA.	
"	17.2.1916		Burns of England and nonconformist parades. - the day otherwise spent as a holiday. Football match with 15 R.W.F. which we won 3-2.	
"	18.2.1916		Battalion and company training in the morning and afternoon devoted to a practice of the Coup-de-Main preparatory to a surprise Com____de Commander-in-Chief.	
"	19.2.1916		The Batt. as a unit in the 113th Infantry Brigade was inspected by Gen. Douglas D/A/G - the Commander-in-Chief. Bay. Training carried on the the afternoon.	

WAR DIARY
or
INTELLIGENCE SUMMARY.
(Erase heading not required.)

Army Form C. 2118.

14TH (S) BATTALION,
ROYAL WELSH
FUSILIERS.

Place	Date	Hour	Summary of Events and Information	Remarks and references to Appendices
Locre	20.12.16.		Company training carried on in the morning, and a Battalion Route March in the afternoon.	
	21.12.16		Company training carried on in the morning. Route march in the afternoon.	
	22.12.16.		Battalion & company training in the morning — Afternoon devoted to preliminary practise of proposed attack scheme and organisation of company for attack.	
	23.12.16		Battalion drill and company training in the morning. Company training in the afternoon and football comp. in which used a batch at BAILLEUL in the morning.	
	24.12.16		Church and recreational parade, in the morning, remainder of day spent as holiday. Defeated 15th West at football 2 goals to 1.	
	25.12.16		Xmas day spent as a holiday — Football competition in which A Coy. was successful. Boxing competitions and concert in the evening. Aftern dinner was provided.	
	26.12.16		The Battalion took part in a Brigade Route March and was inspected by G.O.C. 38th Division at the route. The men were turned out.	

WAR DIARY
or
INTELLIGENCE SUMMARY

(Erase heading not required.)

14TH (S) BATTALION, ROYAL WELSH FUSILIERS.

Army Form C. 2118.

Place	Date	Hour	Summary of Events and Information	Remarks and references to Appendices
Sea	27. 1916.		The Battalion found parties to act as enemy & in the Bouffes schools for 13.15 R.W.F. and to work on trenches at LEDRING HEM — the remainder carried on with Coy. training.	
	28. 1916.		The Battalion with the 16 R.W.F. took part in a Brigade attack scheme, on a line of enemy trenches — particular attention being paid to organising all men to definite duties in particular section of the captured trench. The afternoon was devoted to Company training.	
	29 1916.		Company training carried on in the morning, the afternoon being devoted to cleaning up and inspection preparatory to move.	
	30 1916.		The B Coy and the act Qr Mr paraded at 8.45 am to embark in lorries and proceed to MOULLE C Coys. left at MERCHEGHEM to carry on training area and form dumps of our RE material. B Coys. arrived at MOULLE at noon and relieved 13th Bn. the Welsh Regt. due in their duties inside, including Musketry School.	

WAR DIARY
or
INTELLIGENCE SUMMARY.

(Erase heading not required.)

Place	Date	Hour	Summary of Events and Information	Remarks and references to Appendices
Dec.	31.12.1916		A Coy. and dead Q.K. Coy. employed as markers range squads under Divisional musketry school. C & D Coys. entrained in lorries at MERCHEGHEM at 9.0.a.m (their billets being taken over by the 16th Welch Regt.) and arrived at MOULLE at 10.45 a.m. and took up their new billets there.	

W. P. Wren
Major.
Commanding 14th (S) Battalion,
Royal Welsh Fusiliers.

31.12.1916.

WAR DIARY
FOR
JANUARY 1917.

Vol 14

14TH Batt: ROYAL WELSH FUSILIERS

14TH (S) BATTALION, ROYAL WELSH FUSILIERS.

Army Form C. 2118.

No..........
Date.........

WAR DIARY
or
INTELLIGENCE SUMMARY.
(Erase heading not required.)

Instructions regarding War Diaries and Intelligence Summaries are contained in F. S. Regs., Part II. and the Staff Manual respectively. Title pages will be prepared in manuscript.

Place	Date	Hour	Summary of Events and Information	Remarks and references to Appendices
January	1st 1917		Party of 8 Officers, 16 NCO's and 140 men found for Musketry school as markers, range parties, range finders, were parties making up the remainder of the Batt. found to assist R.E. in construction of ranges.	
"	2nd 1917		Parties found as on previous day. - Reserve Lewis Gunners kept back for training.	
"	3rd 1917		Parties found as on previous day for Musketry school. - Training of Reserve Lewis Gunners.	
"	4th 1917		Parties found as on previous day for Musketry school. - Training of Reserve Lewis Gunners.	
"	5th 1917		No parties found for Musketry at huts but all available men detailed to assist in range construction.	
"	6th 1917		All available men working on range construction under R.E. supervision.	
"	7th 1917		All available men working on range construction under R.E. supervision.	
"	8th 1917		All available men working on range construction under R.E. supervision.	
"	9th 1917		The Batt. relieved of work under 2nd Army Musketry School at MOULLE by 5th K.INGS (55th Division) The Batt. paraded at learn	

2353 Wt. W3514/1454 700,000 5/15 D. D. & L. A.D.S.S./Forms/C. 2118.

14TH (S) BATTALION, ROYAL WELSH FUSILIERS.   Army Form C. 2118.

WAR DIARY
or
INTELLIGENCE SUMMARY.
(Erase heading not required.)

Place	Date	Hour	Summary of Events and Information	Remarks and references to Appendices
	Jan 10th 1917		Alarm. Bent at 10.0 a.m. and marched to St. MEMOLIN station and there entrained at 1.0 p.m. for CHEESEMARKET STATION, POPERINGHE, arriving there at 5.30 p.m. and from there marched to G Camp to take up new quarters. Transport came on by road resting the night at ZEGGERS CAPEL.	
	11th 1917		Morning devoted to cleaning up billets, ammunition and equipment, and all men bathed in the afternoon. Company training carried on morning and afternoon and a commencement made in divisional sports competition in football, boxing, musketry. B.O, O'Coys, and Sgt Major Mardle f&s line, night inspection with a view to taking over the line night 14/15 ?? Jany.	
	12th 1917		Coy. training and lectures morning and afternoon - very wet weather interfered with training - progress made with competition in divisional sports.	
	13th 1917		The Batt. relieved the 16 "Sherwood Foresters in reserve to the Front Line. H. Qrs. & A Coy. At Q.5 at TROISTOURS CHATEAU and B-Coy on Canal Bank West.	

WAR DIARY or INTELLIGENCE SUMMARY.

(Erase heading not required.)

Army Form C. 2118.

14TH (S) BATTALION, ROYAL WELSH FUSILIERS.

Place	Date	Hour	Summary of Events and Information	Remarks and references to Appendices
Jany	14.	1917.	The Battalion relieved the 17th Warwick Fusiliers in the front line from the night to COFFEE TRENCH and the 17th Rifle Brigade at SKIPTON, relief being complete at 7.0 pm. A fighting patrol under 2Lt MORRIS went out from C14.5 but encountered no enemy.	
"	15	1917.	Battalion in front line. A Coy Right, B Coy Centre, C Coy Left and D Coy Support. Nening quiet. A patrol under Lieut N.H. EDWARDS of 10 men went out from the Centre Coy but met no enemy. Work done in Support Line. Canal Bank Dugouts. Clearance of rubbish.	
"	16	1917.	Battalion in front line. Enemy quiet. A patrol of 10 men under Lieut Powell went out from left Coy but met no enemy. Work done on dugouts in Support Line and Canal Bank and wiring in east Company front.	
"	17	1917.	Battalion relieved in front line at 5.30 pm by 13th R.W. Fus. and went into Support Lin dugouts in CANAL BANK EAST and 6.15-9.1L at TROIS TOURS CHATEAU. Enemy quiet. Work done during the day on Support Line Canal Bank. Working parties found for front line	

WAR DIARY
or
INTELLIGENCE SUMMARY.
(Erase heading not required.)

Army Form C. 2118.

Place	Date	Hour	Summary of Events and Information	Remarks and references to Appendices
Canny	18.	1917.	Battalion sent a party to wire the support line. Battalion in support. Working parties found for front line Batt. and wiring parties for support line.	
"	19	1917	Battalion in support - working parties found for front line Batt. and wiring party for support line. Considerable hostile artillery activity.	
"	20	1917	Battalion relieved 13th R.W.F. in front line at 5.15 p.m. A Coy. Right, B Coy in Centre, D Coy on Left and C Coy in support. Enemy "shrapnelled" intermittently. Company on Left of sector. No damage reported. Hostile m.g. active during the night. A patrol made up of 10 men went out from the Left Coy. They were detected from the German parapet. The enemy opened rapid fire which resulted in our suffering 3 casualties. Work done on dug-outs. Wiring in each company front.	
"	21	1917.	Battalion in front line. Enemy quiet. A patrol under Lieut. R. WILLIAMS. left the Right Coy. front, but found no enemy. Work cont'd.	

WAR DIARY or INTELLIGENCE SUMMARY

Army Form C. 2118

14th (S) BATTALION, ROYAL WELSH FUSILIERS.

Instructions regarding War Diaries and Intelligence Summaries are contained in F.S. Regs, Part II. and the Staff Manual respectively. Title Pages will be prepared in manuscript.

(Erase heading not required.)

Place	Date	Hour	Summary of Events and Information	Remarks and references to Appendices
			continued	
			on dugouts in the support and on the Canal Bank. Wiring on each Coy. front also the supports.	
	Jany 22 1917		Batt. in front line. in trenches activity. own artillery fired about 50 L.T.M.s during the day. Fighting patrol of 10 men under Lieut Evans left C No.10 at 10.6pm but encountered no enemy. Work on the dugouts—	
	Jany 23 1917		Batt. in front line. own artillery fired at intervals during the day. Hostile shewn fairly active. A fighting patrol under Lieut. Brock left the Breakaway front at 10.6 pm. They were out for two hours but saw no signs of the enemy. Work continued on dugouts in supports and on Canal Bank. Wiring on each Coy front and supports.	
	Jany 24 1917		Batt. relieved in front line at 6 pm by the 13 W.Rs. & moved into support C & D. Coy. CANAL BANK B TROIS TOURS CHATEAU. and A to POPERINGHE for two days rest. Artillery on both sides considerable. Aeroplane activity in the afternoon. Work on dugouts continued in support and on the CANAL BANK. The usual parties carried on with the wiring of front line and supports.	
	Jany 25 1917		Battalion in support. Working parties found for the support and front line. At night a party of 1 Offr and 3 men entered the wiring in front of the Hostile Frontway.	

1875. Wt. W503/826. 1,000,000. 11/16 J.P.C & A. A.D.S.S./Forms/C. 2118.

Army Form C. 2118.

14th (S) Battalion,
Royal Welsh Fusiliers

WAR DIARY
or
INTELLIGENCE SUMMARY.
(Erase heading not required.)

Instructions regarding War Diaries and Intelligence Summaries are contained in F. S. Regs., Part II. and the Staff Manual respectively. Title pages will be prepared in manuscript.

Place	Date	Hour	Summary of Events and Information	Remarks and references to Appendices
Camp	26.	1917	Battalion in support. Working parties as on the 25th inst. wiring in front of the outposts continued. "A" Coy returns from POPERINGHE and occupy dugouts on CANAL BK WEST close to Bejaria Bridge. Artillery on both sides quiet at intervals during the day.	
Camp	27	1917	Battalion in support. Working and wiring parties furnace on 26th inst.	
Camp	28	1917	Batt. relieved the 13 Rwf. in front line. A&B on the right and C&D on the left. A fighting patrol went out from the left but. returned with nothing to report. Quiet day.	
"	29	1917	Battalion in front line. Work on dugouts in support and on Canal Bank line strengthened in front sides & double MG nose lively than usual.	
	30.		Special left the right company front at 10.0 p.m. was out for two hours but met no enemy.	
	30.	1917	Battalion in front line. Work continued as on the	

Army Form C. 2118.

WAR DIARY
or
INTELLIGENCE SUMMARY.
(Erase heading not required.)

14th (S) Battalion
Royal Welsh Fusiliers

Place	Date	Hour	Summary of Events and Information	Remarks and references to Appendices
	29		29th inst. At 1.30 a.m. in the morning the enemy heavily bombarded the trenches to our Right & left. Our artillery carried out reciprocal fire with some effect. ~~Enemy~~ A fighting patrol under 2/Lt W. H. Edwards left the front line C147 but encountered no enemy.	
	30	1917	Battalion in front line. Artillery fairly quiet on both sides. Work continued on the dug outs in the Support and on Canal Bank. A patrol under Lieut P. G. Williams left C.13.d. and were out for 2 hours. They saw no signs of any hostile patrols. Warm continues in front of supports.	

Sherbourne Capt
for Major
Comdg 14th R.W. Fusiliers

T2134. Wt. W708—776. 500000. 4/15. Sir J. C. & S.

WAR DIARY
14th Battn RWF
FEBRUARY 1917.

Army Form C. 2118.

WAR DIARY
or
INTELLIGENCE SUMMARY.
(Erase heading not required.)

14th (S) Battalion
Royal Welsh Fusiliers

Place	Date	Hour	Summary of Events and Information	Remarks and references to Appendices
Feby	1.1917		Battalion returned to the front line at 6.30pm by the 13th R.W.F. and went into support, A&B on Canal Bank, D to the TROIS TOURS Chateau and "C" to POPERINGHE in two companies. Working party on the 31 Jany 1917. Artillery quiet on both sides.	
Feby	2.1917		Battalion in support. Working parties found for supports and Canal Bank. Wiring in front of supports continued. Agincoray.	
Feby	3.1917		Battalion in support. Working parties as on 2nd instant. Wiring party found for the supports. "B" Coy returned from POPERINGHE and take up quarters on the CANAL BANK WEST. A little artillery fire during the day.	
Feby	4.1917		Battalion in support. Work as on the 3rd instant. Enemy very quiet. The Battalion relieved the 13th R.W.F. in front line at 6.30 P.M.	
Feby	5.1917		A & B Coys (Front line and supports respectively) on the Right and C & D (Front line and supports respectively) on the left. Front line held by 13 Posts - 12 Lewis Gun posts of 3 gunners and 3 rifle men and a post of riflemen and bombers as per attached sketch.	

PILKEM RD.

1 L.G.
2 A.C.C. Infantry
3 L.G
4 L.G
FUSILIER TR.
5 L.G
6 L.G
OLD EALING
NEW EALING
7 L.G
8 L.G
9 L.G
10 L.G
11 L.G
SKIPTON
12 L.G
13 L.G

N

Army Form C. 2118.

14th (S) Battalion.
Royal Welsh Fusiliers

WAR DIARY
or
INTELLIGENCE SUMMARY.
(Erase heading not required.)

Instructions regarding War Diaries and Intelligence Summaries are contained in F.S. Regs., Part II. and the Staff Manual respectively. Title pages will be prepared in manuscript.

Place	Date	Hour	Summary of Events and Information	Remarks and references to Appendices
July	6.1917		Major A.P. O'Kelly took over command of the Battalion from the return of Colonel HODSON. Battalion in front line. Enemy's artillery bombarded the front line system actively and our front line was evacuated from 8.30pm to 10.0pm and again from 9.0pm to 10.0pm. A fighting patrol of 10 men under Lieut D.Y. DAWES went out from the left subsector but encountered no enemy. Work done on bays, herOts at HEADINGLY, LANCASHIRE Fm and MILE and accommodation for men in the same places. Winning line.	
"	7.1917		Battalion in front line. Enemy quiet but increased artillery activity on our part. A fighting patrol of 10 men under Lieut D.C. MORRIS went out from the Right subsector but met no enemy. Work as on previous day.	
"	8.1917		Battalion in front line. A fighting patrol of 10 men under Lt. JAMES went out from the Right subsector but met no enemy. Progress made with my HeadQrs and dugouts in the Support line. Winning line and erection of material	

T2134. Wt. W708—776. 500000. 4/15. Sir J. C. & S.

WAR DIARY
or
INTELLIGENCE SUMMARY.
(Erase heading not required.)

Army Form C. 2118.

14½ (S) Battalion
Royal West Surreys

Place	Date	Hour	Summary of Events and Information	Remarks and references to Appendices
July	9. 1917		in emergency dumps. Enemy quiet.	
			Batt. relieved by 13thRB.F. in Gas line at 7.30 p.m. and went into support. Training party of 5 officers and 15 o.rs. taken out of the Batt. and sent to Camp for training - their places taken by 5 offr. & 190 men from the 55th Division (L'pool territorials) under Captain WATT. B'Coy. and 1/2 POPERINGHE for recreation.	
"	10. 1917		Battalion in support - working parties formed for front line. Battalion reorganised so as to form four Coys. out of the reserve left (after L'pool Raiding party) and the L'pool recruits.	
	11. 1917		Battalion in support. Working parties found for front line.	
	12. 1917		Battalion in support. Working parties found for front line. 9. O.C. 113 Infantry Brigade inspects Raiding Party.	
	13. 1917		Battalion relieved 13th Rifle B. in Front Line. During the relief a raid of the Raiding party the Battalion was made up with 5 officers and 1700 O.R from the L'pool Branch (55th Division) the Right Subsector being Nearly 120 L'pool recruits under the command of Capt Watt and the Left held being held by the details of the Batt. under Lieut. Jack with 50 L'pool recruits attached.	

Army Form C. 2118.

14th (S) Battery,
Royal Welsh Fusiliers.

WAR DIARY
or
INTELLIGENCE SUMMARY.
(Erase heading not required.)

Instructions regarding War Diaries and Intelligence Summaries are contained in F.S. Regs., Part II. and the Staff Manual respectively. Title pages will be prepared in manuscript.

Place	Date	Hour	Summary of Events and Information	Remarks and references to Appendices
July	14.7.1917		Battalion in front line, enemy wired and our artillery bombarded the German front line system all day, our front line being evacuated. Work carried on on Coy. Head Qrs in HEADINGLY - LANCASHIRE Fm and NILE and on dugouts. Reconnaissance for the raid carried out by patrols.	
do	15.7.1917		Battalion in front line. The Lonsport Serveach being relieved by 5 Officers and 170 OR of the 17th Bn Sherwood Foresters (39th Div). Our artillery again bombarded the German 3C line system and front line being evacuated. We carried on ordy Head Qrs and dugouts in support line. Enemy quiet except for some artillery and rifle-fire. Enemy Reconnaissance to the river returned, supposed grenading.	
do	16.7.1917		Battalion in front line, our artillery again bombarded German front line system opposite our left subsection and that subsection evacuated. Enemy retaliated with trench Mortars in the evening and inflicted some casualties at SKIPTON. Fighting reconnoitering patrols and a following	

T2134. Wt. W708—776. 500000. 4/15. Sir J. C. & B.

WAR DIARY
or
INTELLIGENCE SUMMARY

(Erase heading not required.)

Army Form C. 2118

14½ (8) Battalion
Royal Irish Fusiliers

Place	Date	Hour	Summary of Events and Information	Remarks and references to Appendices
February	17. 1917		post throughout the night, kept watch on the gap in the enemy's wire at the points of entry for the Raiding Party. Work as before. At 3.19 am. 17/2/13 Battn. in which at 8.0 pm by the 13th Bn. R.I.F. advanced into support and entered the Raiding Party under Lieut. H.S. ORMSBY attached as a Raid as an B.H.Q.'s a B.H.Q. a 3.H. Capt. J.C. Ellis acted as O.C. Raid in and trenches and kept liaison with the Artillery. the Party of Lt. ORMSBY consisted of two other officers Lieuts. E.F. YORK, R. WILLIAMS, C.T. LLOYD and (E.L. JAMES and 145 O.R. effected an entry but were met in the enemy front line by a heavy guard. Parties of Artillery barrage. Bombers were heavy and met with fierce resistance none of the Raiding Party were able to progress beyond the front line wire. The enemy supervision and support trench. ORMSBY was wounded early but he displayed the greatest gallantry in encouraging his men forward and the whole party not their utmost to break through the barrage but without success. The party withdrew after being 15 minutes in the enemy trench and again suffered loss through M.G. and B fire in retirement. Lieut. E.L. JAMES was reported killed and did not return. Lieut. R. WILLIAMS was wounded & Lt. ORMSBY who was wounded however a second time succeeded to his injuries the following day.	
Valey	18. 1917		Battalion in support. The Raiding party returned to B camp and then to POPERINGHE.	

Army Form C. 2118.

4th (S) Battalion
Royal Welsh Fusiliers

WAR DIARY
or
INTELLIGENCE SUMMARY.
(Erase heading not required.)

Instructions regarding War Diaries and Intelligence Summaries are contained in F.S. Regs., Part II. and the Staff Manual respectively. Title pages will be prepared in manuscript.

Place	Date	Hour	Summary of Events and Information	Remarks and references to Appendices
July	1.9.1917		Battalion in support. Railway Party came to CANAL BK. by train from POPERINGHE and enquired their dump.	
do	20-1917		Battalion in Support - working parties found in trenches.	
do	21-1917		Battalion relieved 13th R. Welsh Fus. in front line at 6.30 PM — "A" Coy in front line right, "B" Coy in Support. "D" Coy front line left, "C" Coy in Support. Wiring front line Prot. all round.	
do	22 1917		Batt. in front line. Enemy quiet. Work so some artillery work done on own Rifts. and dugouts in Support line and wiring of front line and front line posts. A fighting Patrol went out from left subsection but met no enemy.	
do	23 1917		Batt. in front line. Work as on previous day. Enemy quiet. Work for some artillery in LANCASHIRE Fm area.	
do	24 1917		Battalion in front line. W.R. as on previous day. Enemy quiet till 3.0 am. (24/25) when he opened an intense barrage on EALING - LANCASHIRE Fm and FUSILIER trenches and also at the trench junction at SKIPTON. At the same time a	

T2134. W1. W708—776. 500000. 4/15. Sir J.C. & S.

Army Form C. 2118

WAR DIARY
or
INTELLIGENCE SUMMARY

14th (S) Bn. R.W. Fus

(Erase heading not required.)

Instructions regarding War Diaries and Intelligence Summaries are contained in F.S. Regs., Part II and the Staff Manual respectively. Title Pages will be prepared in manuscript.

Place	Date	Hour	Summary of Events and Information	Remarks and references to Appendices
	Feby 25. 1917		A raiding party of the enemy estimated at 50 men entered our Front line 40 yds to the right of EALING and captured a prisoner (Sgt JONES) "A" Coy. and a Lewis Gun in No. 6. Post. The hostile artillery BARRAGE caused somewhat heavy casualties, both in the working parties of the 19th WELSH (Pioneers) and to our own Unit inflicting three officers:- Captain P.F. CRADDOCK, 2nd Lieut W.T. WILLIAMS and Sergt STANLEY JONES. Our Artillery retaliation was not as effective as usual.	
do	26. 1917		The Batt. was relieved at 6.35 p.m. in the Front line by the B.R.W.F. and went into Support. Work on as on previous days. Trench & wiring.	
do	27. 1917		Battalion supported A.B. & C. Coys in CANAL BANK and Coy TROIS TOURS Chateau. Working parties and wiring parties from Coys. Line Batt. on support line and also on parapet work in 2nd Line.	
do	28. 1917		Batt. relieved in support by 10th Bn. The WELSH Regt. Working parties found from the late Batt. to work in support lines morning and afternoon and after relief Batt. marched to E Camp. and went into huts there	
28th Feby 1917.			The Batt. in "E" Camp. The day spent in cleaning up and refitting and re-equipping the men	

A.L. Hodson Lieut-Colonel
Comdg. 14th (S) Battalion
Royal Welch Fus.

1875 Wt. W503/826 1,000,000 4/15 J.B.C. & A. A.D.S.S./Forms/C. 2118.

SECRET   38th Division No. G.S. 4123

VIII Corps
———————

              REPORT ON RAID OF THE 14TH BATTALION
              ROYAL WELSH FUSILIERS ON THE NIGHT
              17/18TH FEBRUARY 1917.
              ————————————————————————————————————

        The orders for the raiding party, together with the
Artillery scheme for the same, have already been forwarded
to you.

        The raiding party consisting of 5 Officers and 122
men moved into "NO MAN'S LAND" and were in position at the
Assembly Point by 3.15 a.m. opposite their objective, the
German trenches about C.14.a.,3.4.

        All the arrangements up to this point worked very
well, the discs by which the advance of the raiding party
was to be guided were placed successfully in position by
Lieut. STORK and his party, who got up to the German wire
without any difficulty.

        The Artillery barrage opened punctually at 3.19 a.m.
on the 18th instant, and the raiders promptly advanced so as
to get as close as possible to the barrage before it lifted
at 3.22 a.m.   The moment the barrage opened, heavy fire
from 7.7 cm. guns was opened by the Germans on their own
front line.   The raiding party, however, advanced through
the gap that had been previously made in the wire, and
successfully entered the front line where, however, they
found no Germans.

        The various parties detailed for the front trench,
supervision trench and the main communication trench leading
back from the German support line, after entering the front
line, started to move towards their objectives, but the
enfilade fire of the German Artillery, combined with the

Page 2

throwing of hand grenades from the German support line and from the flanks, caused a good many casualties, unfortunately, especially amongst the leaders. The parties became somewhat mixed, but were sorted out by Captain ORMSBY the leader of the raid, Lieut. JAMES, Lieut. LLOYD and 2nd Lieut. WILLIS.

The fire, however, was found so heavy that the men were unable to advance, and eventually the retirement was ordered.

Captain ORMSBY, although mortally wounded (died some 7 hours later), set a fine example of coolness standing on the parapet and directing operations, and effected an orderly withdrawal.

The raiders re-entered our trenches after being some ¼ of an hour in the enemy's front line.

The German trenches were found very much knocked about, so much so that they were hardly recognisable, but were still intact. They appeared to about 6 ft. deep and revetted with brushwood. No dugouts or Germans were found in the front line, and no identifications were obtained.

Our total losses were four killed, eleven missing (all probably killed) and 25 wounded.

It was evident that on account of the frequent raids which had taken place in the YPRES Salient, the enemy had decided on a definite policy of withdrawing his troops from possible points of entry, and making arrangements for bringing Artillery fire on to his own front line.

H.E. Pryce Lt-Cl

Major General,
Commanding 38th (Welsh) Divn.

22/2/1917.

16.C
6 sheets

14th Batt. Royal Welsh Fusiliers.
Vol 16

WAR DIARY

for

MARCH 1917.

Army Form C. 2118

WAR DIARY
or
INTELLIGENCE SUMMARY

(Erase heading not required.)

1/4th (5) Battalion Royal Fusiliers

Instructions regarding War Diaries and Intelligence Summaries are contained in F. S. Regs., Part II. and the Staff Manual respectively. Title Pages will be prepared in manuscript.

Place	Date	Hour	Summary of Events and Information	Remarks and references to Appendices
March	1st. 1917		Battalion in "E" Camp. Training carried on in the morning and afternoon. A large party found for the R.E.	
	2nd. 1917		Bay. training and lectures morning and afternoon. Heavy Infan interfered with the usual training. A.B.C companies Bay. visit the Baths at POPERINGHE.	
	3rd. 1917		Battalion in E Camp. Company training in the morning and inter-company football matches in the afternoon.	
	4th. 1917		Battalion in E Camp. Church Parade and route march. "B" Bay. baths at POPERINGHE	
	5th. 1917		Battalion in "E" Camp. Training morning and afternoon. A large party engaged on Camp improvements.	
	6th. 1917		Battalion in E Camp. Heavy snow interfered with the day's work. Heavy snowstorm in the morning also afternoon. An effort made to carry out the Recreation Training Programme.	
	7th. 1917		Battalion in E Camp. Snow Cavoricked work. Recreational training carried out. Concert in the evening.	
	8th. 1917		Battalion in E Camp. Bay and training carried on morning and afternoon. Battn. inspected by G. O. C. 113 Bde. and complimented on its appearance.	

WAR DIARY
INTELLIGENCE SUMMARY

(Erase heading not required.) 1/4th Bn Royal Welsh Fus[iliers]

Army Form C. 2118

Place	Date	Hour	Summary of Events and Information	Remarks and references to Appendices
March	9th 1917		Battalion at Camp. Bayonet training in the morning. Route march.	
"	10th 1917.		The Batt. relieved the 10th Bn. The West Rgt. in the front line at 3 p.m. A & B Coys (front line and supports respectively) on the right, C & D Coys. (front line and supports respectively) on the left. The distribution was as on previous tour. Front line held by 13 Lewis Gunposts of 2 gunners and 3 riflemen and one post of riflemen and bombers.	
"	11th 1917.		Battalion in front line. Front quiet. Kept lowering Artillery work done on Bay Vee Ox and dugouts in Subsidy Line. Wiring of Butt Line. A fighting patrol went out from the left Coys but encountered no enemy.	
"	12th 1917.		Battalion in front line. Work on Bay Vee Ox, at LANCASHIRE FARM and HEADINGLY. Wiring of Butt line continued. A little hostile Artillery activity during the day. A fighting patrol left Right sector but without result.	
"	13th 1917		Battalion in front line. Considerable Artillery activity with many snipers fairly busy opposite PILKEM Rd. Kennel Fartles. Patrol left our front at the head of EALING but saw no enemy.	
"	14th 1917.		Batt. in front line. Hostile day work continued on dugouts in the Subsidy Line and wiring of Butt and front line strengthened.	

1875 Wt. W.593/826 1,000,000 4/15 I.B.C. & A. A.D.S.S./Forgs/C. 2118/

WARY DIARY
or
INTELLIGENCE SUMMARY of 1st (S) Battalion. Royal Welsh Fusiliers

Army Form C. 2118

(Erase heading not required.)

Place	Date	Hour	Summary of Events and Information	Remarks and references to Appendices
	March 14th 1917		Relieved in Front Line by the 13th Bn Glouster Regt.	
	15th 1917		Battalion in support. Small R.E. carrying parties and R.E. carrying parties at night. Wiring to the right and left of Halifax Rd. commenced. Work on Coney St. continued.	
	16th 1917		Battalion in Support. Large Wiring Parties found for work on HIGHLAND FM and HALIFAX Rd. Wire carrying parties at night. Training for Storm on CANAL BANK during the afternoon.	
	17th 1917		Battalion in Support. Wiring and carrying parties as on 16th instant. Physical training in the afternoon.	
	19th 1917		The Battn relieved the 13th Welch at 6.0 p.m. Wiring of the front line. Enemy opened a heavy bombardment on our front line trench at 4.15 am. Our artillery replied promptly and with good effect.	
	19th 1917		Battalion in Front line and enemy quiet. Work done wiring X line and each side of HALIFAX RD.	
	20. 1917		Battalion relieved in front line by 10th Bn The Welsh Regt. at 10.45 P.M. and moved to B Camp - all in billets by 1.20 am	
	21 1917		Batt. informed to ESQUELBECK at BRANDHOEK at noon and marched from ESQUELBECK to MERCKEGHEM and billets at 6.0 p.m.	
	22 1917		Day devoted to cleaning up and baths at BOKLEZEELE	

WAR DIARY
or
INTELLIGENCE SUMMARY

(Erase heading not required.)

Army Form C. 2118

Instructions regarding War Diaries and Intelligence Summaries are contained in F. S. Regs., Part II. and the Staff Manual respectively. Title Pages will be prepared in manuscript.

Place	Date	Hour	Summary of Events and Information	Remarks and references to Appendices
Met.	23-	1917	Training carried out on new basis of Platoon organisation as to S.S.143 - Musketry - Lewis Gun - Bombing - Special training of specialists - rumours and bayonet fighting.	
"	24	1917	Training as before and a Battalion Route March.	
"	25	1917	C of E and Nonconformist Church Parades and recreational training in the afternoon. General line adopted the day.	
"	26	1917	Training as before. Particular formation of Platoons in new organisation in attack. Brigade transport Route March.	
"	27	1917	Training as before and Battalion Route March.	
"	28	1917	Training as before, particulars made tactical exercises for platoons. "Dieuxcouple Battalion Concert" held in the evening.	
"	29	1917	Sudden training interfered with by bad weather but Boys carried on with indoor training during the morning and went for Route March by Coys. in the afternoon streets being too wet to train by. training and forging bayonet.	
"	30	1917	Battalion inspected whilst training by the Bn.tn Commander who expressed himself as pleased as what he saw - particular attention being paid to correct formation in the new Platoon organisation. The afternoon devoted to preparing for the move tomorrow.	

Army Form C. 2118

WAR DIARY
or
INTELLIGENCE SUMMARY
(Erase heading not required.)

Instructions regarding War Diaries and Intelligence Summaries are contained in F.S. Regs., Part II. and the Staff Manual respectively. Title Pages will be prepared in manuscript.

Place	Date	Hour	Summary of Events and Information	Remarks and references to Appendices
March	31/1917		Morning devoted to cleaning up billets and handing over to incoming unit (10th WELSH) Battalion paraded at 2.0 pm on Battalion Parade Post and march class entraining for YPRES to ESQUELBECQ and Asylum at 5.30 pm. The Battalion then marched to the Canal Bank and relieved the 15th R.W.F. in support in the TURCO Sector at 11.30 pm.	

1st April 1917

H. Hodson Lieut.-Colonel.
Commanding 14th (S.) Battalion
Royal Welsh Fusiliers.

17.C.
10 sheets

14th BATTN. ROYAL WELSH FUSILIERS. Vol 17

WAR DIARY

FOR

APRIL 1917.

Army Form C. 2118

WAR DIARY
or
INTELLIGENCE SUMMARY

14(S) Battalion
Royal Welsh Fusiliers

(Erase heading not required.)

Instructions regarding War Diaries and Intelligence Summaries are contained in F. S. Regs, Part II. and the Staff Manual respectively. Title Pages will be prepared in manuscript.

Place	Date	Hour	Summary of Events and Information	Remarks and references to Appendices
April	1st	1917	Batt. in support in CANAL BANK and supplying a garrison of 1 Officer and 37 other ranks (from D Coy) to HILLTOP FARM Strong Point. The feelers being new to their unit reconnaissances by officers and NCOs were carried out. Training continued on CANAL BANK and working parties supplied to RE	
	2	1917	Batt. in support on CANAL BANK. Training carried out by Coys in CANAL BANK and reconnaissances of forward area. Working parties supplied to RE.	
	3	1917	Batt. in support on CANAL BANK, and training carried on. Working parties supplied to RE from line Back a Beau Blun and interfered with work.	
	4	1917	Training carried on and working parties found to RE during the day. In the evening the Batt. relieved the 15th Bn. R.W.F. in the Right Sector. (HILLTOP – TURCO – SEALS). C Coy Right Subsector, A Coy in support. D Coy left Subsector, B Coy in support. The front line is held in posts averaging 1 NCO and 6 men in strength and the Right Sup. Batt. find a garrison of 1 NCO + 18 men to TURCO FARM. Batt. Sup. Coys find men for helping Pioneers ready to deliver counter attack up to the front line in case of attack. The details so near to this unit and the front line posts are held to be attached sketch.	

1875 Wt. W593/826 1,000,000 4/15 J.B.C. & A. A.D.S.S./Forms/C. 2118.

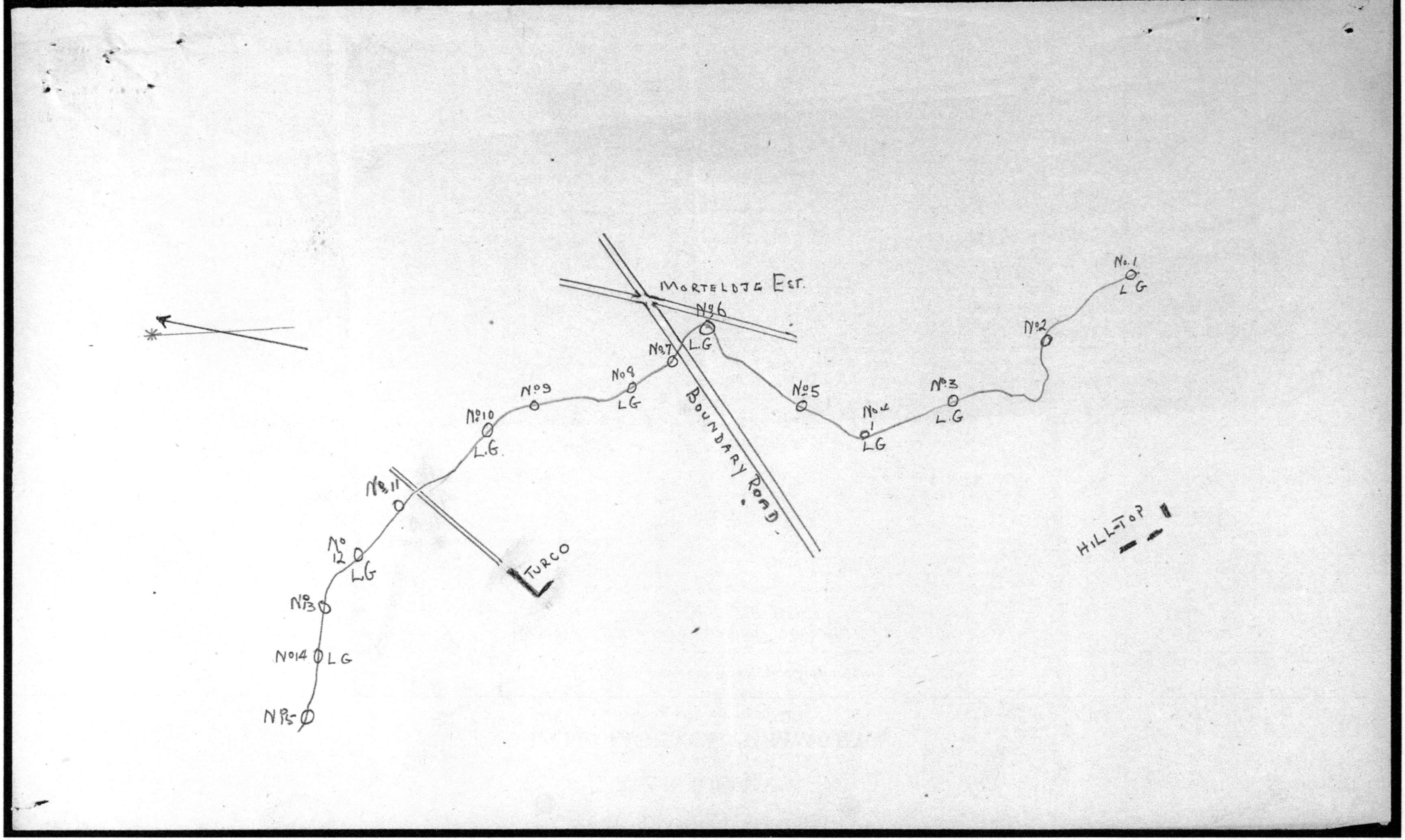

MORTELDJE EST.
BOUNDARY ROAD
TURCO
HILL-TOP
No. 1 LG
No 2
No 3 LG
No 4 LG
No 5
No 6 LG
No 7
No 8 LG
No 9
No 10 LG
No 11
No 12 LG
No 13
No 14 LG
No 15

WAR DIARY
INTELLIGENCE SUMMARY

Army Form C. 2118

14th (S) Batt. Royal Welsh Fus.

Place	Date	Hour	Summary of Events and Information	Remarks and references to Appendices
Aponne	5	1917	Batt. in front line. Our artillery quiet but enemy active and shelled Batt. H.Q. 1915 at LA BELLE ALLIANCE freely in the afternoon inflicting some wounded and after dark the enemy was very active with M.G. and Rifle fire particularly to the left of MORTELDJE. Thing at HILL TOP and TURCO and front line posts. A fighting patrol went out from the left but encountered no enemy.	
	6	1917	Artillery activity. Patrouwear in the morning, but enemy subsequently quieter except for M.G. and Rifle fire in the morning at "stand to" in the Rifle fire after dark. Int: Coy relieved "B" Coy. in the Right "B" Bay. "D" Coy. relieving Coy. in the left. A fighting patrol went out from the night "B" Bay but encountered no enemy.	
	7	1917	Enemy quiet except for M.G. and Rifle fire. 2nd Lt. ——— & party went out from the left but encountered no enemy. Work continued - wiring HILL TOP and TURCO - camouflage and parapet work and maintenance.	
	8	1917	Enemy quiet but for some artillery activity at 10.15 p.m. the Batt. was relieved by the 15th R.W.F. and went into support at CANAL BK. 10 Officers and 371 men furnishing a garrison for HILL TOP. Work continued - wiring HILL TOP and ——— & line at PICKEM ROAD.	
	9	1917	Batt. in support; Bodies arranged to sleep in ELVERDINCHE working parties found to wire HILL TOP and PICKEM ROAD (X line) and carrying parties.	
	10	1917	Batt. in support during day and in the evening relieved the 10th R.S.F. South Wales Borderers in the CENTRE Bde. sector (FARGATE and ...)	

WAR DIARY or INTELLIGENCE SUMMARY

Army Form C. 2118

11th (S) Battalion
Royal Welsh Fusiliers

Place	Date	Hour	Summary of Events and Information	Remarks and references to Appendices
April	11	1917	and SKIPTON) relief being complete at 10.25 P.M. D Coy Right F.C. Line Lubricolin. B Coy. left St Lugie Lubricolin. A Coy. left support in the Butt Line and C Coy. in support on CANAL BANK. No enemy activity. Batt. in front line — enemy quiet — No day inventive. Work done by Support Coys. in BUTT Line was — Revetment, Work done by support of the present front line — strewing abatis and hyperois parties in front of INKERMAN in the rear to by special a fighting patrol went to HUDDLESTON Cross Roads but met no enemy.	
	12	1917	Battalion in front line — enemy quiet — A fighting patrol from the left Lubricolin again went to HUDDLESTON Rd Cross Roads but met no enemy. Work continued as in previous day.	
	13	1917	Batt in f.c. line. Enemy quiet. A fighting patrol went out from the Butt Bay below in the direction of CEDAR'S MISSE but met no enemy. Work continued as before. A Coy. received B Coy in the left Batt. Sub.	
	14	1917	The Bn. was relieved by the 15th R.W.F. in the front line, relief complete at 10.55 p.m. and came into support on the CANAL BANK. The day uneventful and the enemy quiet.	
	15	1917	Batt in support in CANAL BANK. Wkg. parties arranged as follows: A Coy — two tunnelled French S of BAIRD TRENCH, B Coy Menin and Right TMB emplacements, C Coy. new cemetery French N of HARKNESS, D Coy. Cable Burying.	
	16	1917	Batt. in support — Work carried out as before.	

Army Form C. 2118.

WAR DIARY
or
INTELLIGENCE SUMMARY.
(Erase heading not required.)

Instructions regarding War Diaries and Intelligence Summaries are contained in F. S. Regs., Part II. and the Staff Manual respectively. Title pages will be prepared in manuscript.

Place	Date	Hour	Summary of Events and Information	Remarks and references to Appendices
Shrul	19/4/1917		Battalion relieved in support by the 13th Bn. the Welch Regt. at 4.55 a.m. and marched to "D" & "E" Camps. (A37 b.1.0.0.) which camps were shared with the 13th & 16th Batt R.W.F. having no rations now accommodation.	
"	19/4/1917		Day devoted to cleaning - baths and disinfesting clothes.	
"	19/4/1917		Company having carried out under new Platoon organisation - also some items in the Divisional Recreation Programme arranged for, but owing to bad weather could not all be completed. The Batt. arranged for & had rather successful Boxing carried on. The Batt. put through various Box tests which proved satisfactory and useful. In the Brit. Recreation we ---- won the tug of war. (B Coy.) and drew with the 15th R.W.F. in Rugby football.	
"	21/4/1917		Coy. training continued and recreational training. Afternoon advanced a lecture in the evening upon "Liason with Artillery".	
"	22nd 1917		Left and arrangements parades in the morning. At 7.45 p.m. the Coy. paraded accompanied by and march in to the front line relieving the 13th Bn. the Welch Regt. at 1.15 a.m. in the ZWAARTHOF Fm. Sector. A fighting patrol under Mr. Poulson went out at 10.0 p.m. to the HUDDLESTONE Cros Roads but encountered no enemy. The experience	

A6945 Wt. W14422/M1160 350,000 12/16 D. D. & L. Forms/C/2118/14.

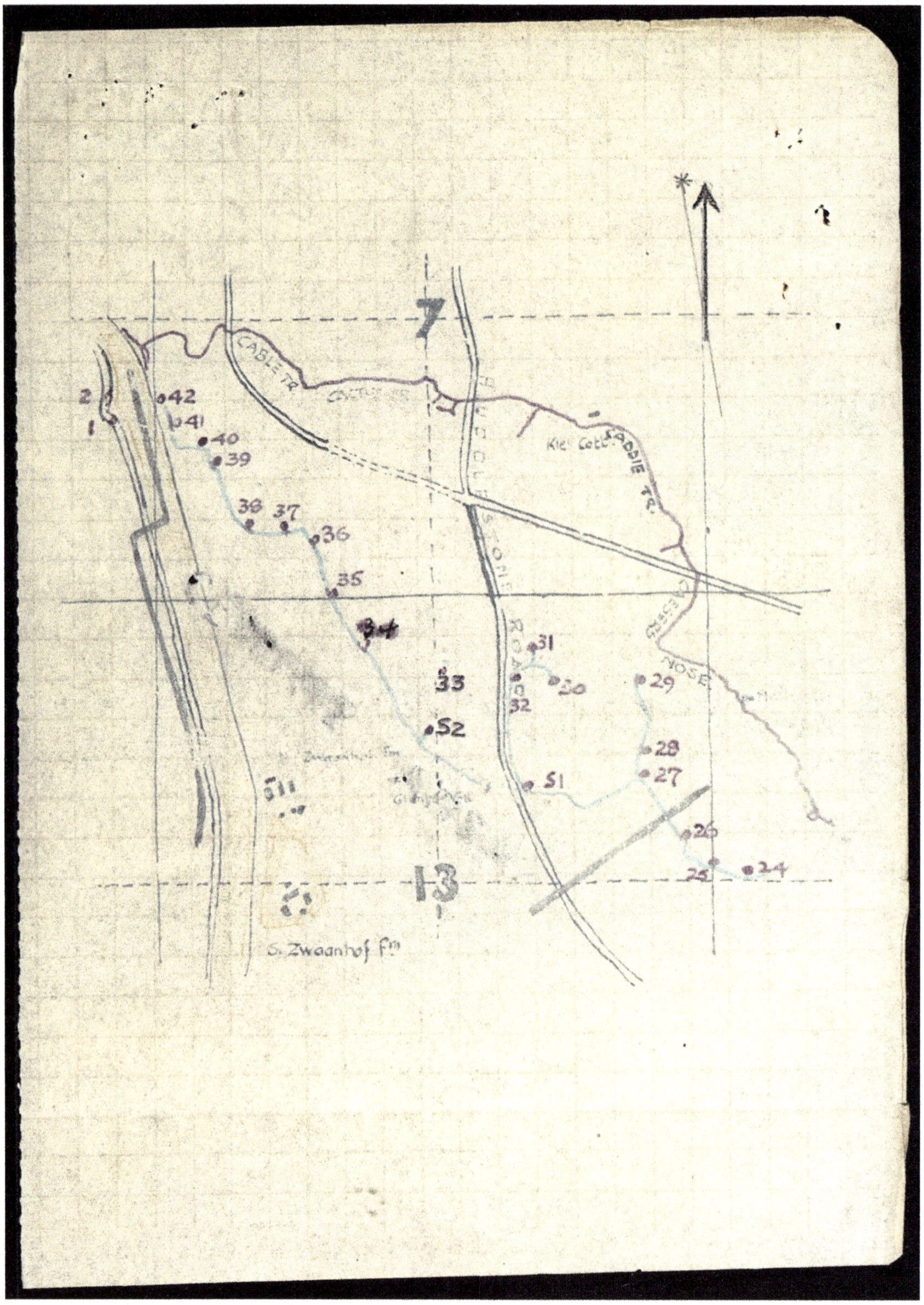

7
CABLE TR.
Kiel Cott.
SADDIE TR.
NOSE
2
1
42
41
40
39
38
37
36
35
34
33
52
31
30
32
29
28
27
51
26
25
24
13
S. Zwaanhof Fm

WAR DIARY
or
INTELLIGENCE SUMMARY.
(Erase heading not required.)

Army Form C. 2118.

Place	Date	Hour	Summary of Events and Information	Remarks and references to Appendices
	April 22nd 1917		Dispositions were taken up as follows:- "B" Coy. RIGHT 2/Lt. Leebester - "A" Coy LEFT 2/Lt. Lubrook. "C" Coy. BUTT Line and D Coy in support a Barut BANK. Batalion in Ft. Line - enemy quiet throughout wcxgronce wire Artillery activity. A fighting patrol went out under 2/Lt (?) LLOYD but met no enemy. Working parties supplied by support companies in construction of new trench leading forward from junction of HARKNESS & YORKSHIRE and on Sap No. 2. Work done also on BARNSLEY RD (chopped) BUTT LINE and wiring tons a pros. He attacked Skeeket shows an present disposition in pros	
	April 24th 1917		Batt. in Ft. Line. enemy quiet during the day. but about 9.45pm an active artillery duel commenced on the Right and spread to the sector. The offices on watch in Right subsector being heavily shelled held up the RED "S.O.S." Rocket and for about 1 hour (till 10.20pm) there was an intense artillery bombardment on our service. but no supposed no casualties. work continued as before.	

A6945 Wt. W11422/M1160 350,000 12/16 D. D. & L. Forms/C/2118/14.

WAR DIARY
or
INTELLIGENCE SUMMARY.
(Erase heading not required.)

Army Form C. 2118.

Place	Date	Hour	Summary of Events and Information	Remarks and references to Appendices
April	25. 1917		Batt. in front line - enemy quiet throughout the day - much aeroplane activity. Work continued as usual and good progress made.	
"	26th 1917		Enemy quiet and work continued. The line inspected by the G.O.C. 113th Inf. Bde. who expressed himself pleased with the work done and elaboration of the same. At 9.30 pm the Batt. was relieved in the front line by 15th R.W.F. and came into Support on CANAL BANK.	
	27th 1917		Batt. in Support on CANAL BANK. Training carried on by Coys. and working parties found for R.E. and Pioneers when available men being available.	
	28th 1917		Battalion in Support on CANAL BANK. Training and working parties found for R.E. and Pioneers, as before and training continued. Some artillery activity on and from at night.	
	29th 1917		Battalion in Support - Work and training continued. Considerable artillery activity in this sector C1.	

Army Form C. 2118.

WAR DIARY
or
INTELLIGENCE SUMMARY.
(Erase heading not required.)

Place	Date	Hour	Summary of Events and Information	Remarks and references to Appendices
April	30-19.17	at 9.30 p.m. and 12.30 a.m. (29th/30th)	— a raid being successfully made on the enemy trenches at TURCO trench about 12.30 a.m. Battalion relieved the 15th R.W.F. in front line at 9.10 p.m. D.Coy - RIGHT Subsector. B.Coy - Left Subsector. "C" Coy - Right Support (on CANAL BANK.) and "A"Coy in BUTTs line and FARGATE Group Point.	
	30-4-17			

W. Hobson Lieut. Colonel
Comdg. 16 (S) Bn. Royal Welsh Fusiliers

Vol 18

14th ROYAL WELSH FUSILIERS

WAR DIARY

FOR

MAY 1917

18.C
9 sheets

WAR DIARY
or
INTELLIGENCE SUMMARY.
(Erase heading not required.)

14TH (S) BATTALION, ROYAL WELSH FUSILIERS. Army Form C. 2118.

Place	Date	Hour	Summary of Events and Information	Remarks and references to Appendices
Ap 30/May 1st.17			A successful raid was made by the 13th Bn the Welch Regt. from the TURCO Salient on KRUPP SALIENT at 10 A.M. About H.Q. AM the enemy retaliated with heavy shelling on the whole Divisional Front but no casualties were suffered in this sector.	
May 1-17			Battalion in front line. Enemy quiet during the day except for desultory shelling. A fighting patrol under Lt C. W.B.C. HUNKIN went out from Pot 36 but not no enemy work done in repair of hob- and particularly repair of Cabré Valley where broken in by the bombardment. Also making Coy. Head Qrs at WELSH HARP and BUTT 22 shellproof.	
May 2-17			Battalion in front line - enemy quiet but for some casual shelling in the morning which done damage. A fighting patrol went out from 9R132 under Lt L. J. C. BROMAGE but met no enemy. Work continued as before	
May 3rd 17			Battalion in front line. Enemy quiet. A fighting patrol went out under Lt C. E. W. EVANS from Pot 36 but met no enemy. Work continued as before	

A6945 Wt. W1142/M1160 350,000 12/16 D.D.&L. Forms/C./2118/14.

Army Form C. 2118.

14TH (S) BATTALION,
ROYAL WELSH
FUSILIERS.

No..................
Date.................

WAR DIARY
OR
INTELLIGENCE SUMMARY.
(Erase heading not required.)

Instructions regarding War Diaries and Intelligence Summaries are contained in F. S. Regs., Part II. and the Staff Manual respectively. Title pages will be prepared in manuscript.

Place	Date	Hour	Summary of Events and Information	Remarks and references to Appendices
	May 4th 1917		Battalion relieved in Front Line at 9.30 p.m. by the 15th Batt. Royal Welsh Fusiliers, and came into support on CANAL BANK. One platoon of "B" Coy. on relief march to Roussel Farm to take part in the training of the new Platoon organisation in the Brigade School under Lieut-Colonel C.C NORMAN.	
	May 5th 1917		Battalion in support on Canal Bank - working parties supplied for R.E. and Pioneers engaged upon construction of new trenches in Front Line (BAIRD to HARKNESS and HARKNESS to ALMA) New Dugouts East & West CANAL BANK and new T.M. Emplacements. Men also trained in relays at ELVERDINGHE, and training carried on. The Battalion in front line was relieved by the enemy at Pos 128 - This unit ready to move during bombardment.	
	May 6th 1917 " 7 1917		Battalion in support, work, training and Battalion in Support. work, training and bathing entrained on as in the previous day.	

A6945 Wt. W14424/M160 350,000 12/16 D. D. & L. Forms/C/2118/14.

Army Form C. 2118.

14TH (S) BATTALION,
ROYAL WELSH
FUSILIERS.

WAR DIARY
or
INTELLIGENCE SUMMARY.
(Erase heading not required.)

Instructions regarding War Diaries and Intelligence Summaries are contained in F. S. Regs. Part II. and the Staff Manual respectively. Title pages will be prepared in manuscript.

Place	Date	Hour	Summary of Events and Information	Remarks and references to Appendices
May	9-1917		The Batt relieved the 15th R.F. in the Front line at 11.40 pm "C Coy Right Subsector "A" Coy Left Subsector, "B" Coy in the Butt line and "D" Coy in Support on CANAL BANK. A fighting Patrol under Lieut J. Jones Iiwanto went out from Post 36 and except to the German wire which is reported good.	
May	9.1917		Battalion in Front line. went quiet but for some desultory shelling. A Fighting Patrol under Lieut Dy DAVIES went out from POST 32 to the HUDDLESTONE Cross Roads but met no enemy. Camouflage put up above HUDDLESTONE ROAD, COLNE VALLEY and SAP 42. Wiring at SKIPTON BAY and work done in NEW YORKSHIRE and NEW ALMA.	
May	10.1917		Batt in Front line. Quiet day but for some desultory shelling. A Wiring Patrol under Lieut C.J. Lloyd went out at 10 AM. from Post 35. towards HUDDLESTONE Cross Roads. No enemy encountered.	

WAR DIARY or INTELLIGENCE SUMMARY

14TH (S) BATTALION, ROYAL WELSH FUSILIERS.

Army Form C. 2118.

Place	Date	Hour	Summary of Events and Information	Remarks and references to Appendices
	May 11. 1917		1 Batt. in front line. Wiring patrol under 2nd in C. O.M Jones left our lines at 11.30 P.M. from Post 32. and worked towards HUDDLESTONE CROSS ROADS and thence to C.7.d.2.5½. No enemy met. Lt. Col. H.V.R. HODSON proceeded to Wounded ENGLAND. and Major W.R WITHERDEN assumed command.	
	May 12. 1917		Batt. relieved by the 15th Bn. R.W.F. in front line. Relief complete 9.45 p.m. Batt. then moved to support on CANAL BANK. Work and training continued.	
	May 13 1917		Batt. in support on CANAL BANK. Batt. stood to arms at 3.6 A.M. 13th/14 May 1917 during heavy bombardment of the front line and support trenches of the 13th Bn. R.W.F. in the LANCASHIRE Fm sector. Our artillery opened and quickly and effectively made the 13th Bn. R.W.F. dispose of a party of Germans who attempted to raid one of the posts in the front line. 13 Bn. R.W.F. captured 1 German prisoner	

Army Form C. 2118.

14TH (S) BATTALION.
ROYAL WELSH FUSILIERS.

WAR DIARY
or
INTELLIGENCE SUMMARY.
(Erase heading not required.)

Instructions regarding War Diaries and Intelligence Summaries are contained in F. S. Regs., Part II. and the Staff Manual respectively. Title pages will be prepared in manuscript.

Place	Date	Hour	Summary of Events and Information	Remarks and references to Appendices
May	14th 1917		Batt. in Support on Canal Bank. Work & training continued	
May	15th 1917		Batt. in Support on Canal Bank. Work and training continued	
May	16th 1917		Battalion relieves the 15th R.W.F. in the Front Line. A Coy left Support Bay (Buff Line), B Coy left Front Bay, B Bay, Right Support Bay, Canal Bank and D Coy Right Front Bay. A flying Patrol under 2Lt. A.K.S. Evans, went out but encountered no enemy.	
May	17th 1917		Batt. in Front Line. Enemy Quiet. Patrol went out under 2Lt C.J. Shardlow up Huddlestone Road as far as Cross Roads. No enemy seen.	
"	18th 1917		Battalion in Front Line. Patrol went out under 2Lt H.P. Jones. No enemy seen.	
"	19th 1917		Battalion relieved & proceeded to back area under canvas.	

A6945 Wt. W11422/M1160 350,000 12/16 D. D. & L. Forms/C./2118/14.

WAR DIARY
or
INTELLIGENCE SUMMARY.
(Erase heading not required.)

Army Form C. 2118.

14TH (S) BATTALION,
ROYAL WELSH
FUSILIERS.

Place	Date	Hour	Summary of Events and Information	Remarks and references to Appendices
May	19ᵗʰ 1917		Batt. relieved in trenches line by 13ᵗʰ Batt. The Welch Regt. Relief complete 10.0 p.m.	
"	20ᵗʰ 1917		Batt. marched from Canal Bank 12.50 a.m. night of 19/20 May and marched to YPRES ASYLUM STATION and went to POPERINGHE by train arriving at about 3.15 a.m. Batt. then marched to Z Camp. F.25 & 33.32 arriving about 4.10 a.m. Batt. left Z Camp at 2.30 p.m. and marched to HERZEELE arriving at 5.30 p.m. The billets were as follows:-	
			Dickebusch being as follows:-	Sheet 27
			Battalion Headquarters.	D.9.a.1.7.
			A Company.	D.11.c.0.2.
			B Company and Transport Lines.	D.4 a 9½.5
			C Company	D.12 a 4.5
			D Company.	D.17 c 3.5.
May 21.			Day devoted to cleaning up.	

Army Form C. 2118.

**14TH (S) BATTALION.
ROYAL WELSH
FUSILIERS.**

WAR DIARY
or
INTELLIGENCE SUMMARY.
(Erase heading not required.)

Instructions regarding War Diaries and Intelligence Summaries are contained in F.S. Regs., Part II. and the Staff Manual respectively. Title pages will be prepared in manuscript.

Place	Date	Hour	Summary of Events and Information	Remarks and references to Appendices
May	22nd 17.		Drel morning and companies did motor learning until 12.30 p.m. Day. Route marches and judging distances 2.0–4.0 p.m.	
	23rd 19.7		Platoon training 9.0 to 12.15 p.m. The remainder of the day devoted to mechanical training	
	24th 19.7.		Platoon training by Coy. Bays in the morning on No.1 area. A.B.Bays practiced in the morning C.D. Bays bathed in the afternoon. A.B.Bays carried on with platoon training	
	26th 19.7		Training continued in the morning. Day in the camp and on the Bays. Platoon training - the transport went for a march. The afternoon devoted to Brigade Sports.	
	24th 19.7		Coy. E. and Transport. Church parades in the morning. The Coy. E. parade was a Brigade parade and the G.O.C. gave medals to men recently awarded.	
	25th 19.7		All Coys. engaged in platoon training and route marches	

WAR DIARY
or
INTELLIGENCE SUMMARY.
(Erase heading not required.)

Army Form C. 2118.

Place	Date	Hour	Summary of Events and Information	Remarks and references to Appendices
May	28th 1917		Battalion training continued along on range and other days in area No.1. two parades were provided in No 20 general instruction in the Bayonet by the Bayonet Running Officer.	
"	29th 1917		Bay on Peaton. Arrangements by all Companies	
"	30th 1917		The Batt. paraded at 5.15 am and marched to BUYSSCHEURE and during the day a resting place arriving there about noon.	
"	31st 1917		The Battalion paraded at 5.30 am at BUYSSCHEURE and marched via St. Omer to ESQUERDES where billets were taken over from the 2nd Aucklands (New Zealand). The training area was resumed by the C.O. 2nd Cond. and O.C. Coys.	

W Horton Lieut. Colonel
Comdg 14th (S) Battalion
Royal Welsh Fusiliers

1/6/1917

Vol 19

19.C.
11 sheets

14th BATT ROYAL WELSH FUSILIERS

WAR DIARY

FOR

JUNE 1917

WAR DIARY
or
INTELLIGENCE SUMMARY

Army Form C. 2118.

14TH (S) BATTALION,
ROYAL WELSH
FUSILIERS.

Place	Date	Hour	Summary of Events and Information	Remarks and references to Appendices
June	1st 1917		All companies spent the day in the new training area, situated approximately North West of the village of KEULINGHEM - Platoon training being carried on.	
	2nd 1917		The morning was spent on the training area in Platoon training and the afternoon spent as a holiday. At night the Battalion paraded at 8.0 p.m. and marched to the training area to carry out a Brigade exercise in digging running advanced trenches - each working party being only protected. The Battalion returned to Billets at 3.0 A.M.	
	3rd 1917		Church of England and nonconformist parades. The remainder of the day being a holiday.	
	4th 1917		The day spent on "C" Rifle Range (635) and was fired thro': - (1) Application 260 yds. (3) Rapid fire 5 rds. 300 yds 25 secs (2) Rapid fire (5 rounds) 200 yds 1 minute (15 rounds)	
	5th 1917		Morning devoted to Kit Inspection and bathing parade.	

WAR DIARY
or
INTELLIGENCE SUMMARY.
(Erase heading not required.)

Army Form C. 2118.

14TH (S) BATTALION
ROYAL WELSH
FUSILIERS

Place	Date	Hour	Summary of Events and Information	Remarks and references to Appendices
June	6.6.17		The afternoon spent in field firing exercise under the Officers of a line South of St Quelmes. At night the Battalion paraded at 8.0 p.m. and marched to the training area to carry out a practice exercise in advancing in darkness on to the front line to a tape's line forward of the unit in No Mans Land and onward of that from under a barrage and on to the second line advancing from the front line trench 50ˣ behind the first line. Each line organised in two waves as in new platoon organisation.	
	7.6.1917		The morning spent in the new platoon training and the afternoon spent in rest and recreation. The Battalion paraded in fighting order and proceeded to the training line & practised and carried out a Battalion attack scheme.	

WAR DIARY
OR
INTELLIGENCE SUMMARY.
(Erase heading not required.)

Army Form C. 2118.

Instructions regarding War Diaries and Intelligence Summaries are contained in F.S. Regs., Part II. and the Staff Manual respectively. Title pages will be prepared in manuscript.

Place	Date	Hour	Summary of Events and Information	Remarks and references to Appendices
June	8th 1917		The Battalion paraded in fighting order and marched to the area allotted for field firing practice	
"	9th 1917		The Battalion was through a successful gas test on the training area and afterwards carried on training, special attention being had to musketry	
"	10th 1917		The Batt. paraded in full marching order at 1.0 pm to march to ST OMER and there entrained with the 16th R.W.F. at 4.40 pm for POPERINGHE and from there marched to "Y" Camp, arriving there at 9.0 pm.	
"	11th 1917		The Battalion in "Y" Camp - close order drill by Companies in the morning and inspection in the afternoon. MAJOR WHELDON and Ocup. proceeded to the trenches (ZWAANHOF SECTOR) with the 15th R.W.F. to take over the trenches line	
"	12th 1917		The Battalion paraded at 8.15 pm and marched to POPERINGHE and there entrained for a spot	

WAR DIARY
or
INTELLIGENCE SUMMARY.
(Erase heading not required.)

Army Form C. 2118.

Place	Date	Hour	Summary of Events and Information	Remarks and references to Appendices
			ot ot	
			adjacent to VLAMERTINGHE where the Battalion was met by Guides from the 14th Batt. the Welsh Regiment, the Battalion then marched into the CANAL BANK	
June	13th D.17		relieving the 14th Batt. the Welsh Regt. in support relief being complete at 1.40 AM (12th/13th).	
			Batt. in support on CANAL BK, and engaged in digging a new trench from Pot. 27 to Pot. 30 and in deepening a 2'x 2' trench from Pot 31 to Pot 40. Heavy hostile shelling of communication trenches by day and night, and quiet aerial activity.	
	14th 19.17		Batt. in support on CANAL Bank. Digging and deepening of new trench as on previous night. Heavy hostile shelling of communication trenches and CANAL BANK, and much aerial activity	
	15th 19.7		Batt. in support on CANAL BK. hostile shelling and aerial activity as on previous days.	

Army Form C. 2118.

WAR DIARY
or
INTELLIGENCE SUMMARY.
(Erase heading not required.)

Instructions regarding War Diaries and Intelligence Summaries are contained in F. S. Regs., Part II. and the Staff Manual respectively. Title pages will be prepared in manuscript.

14TH (S) BATTALION. ROYAL WELSH FUSILIERS.

Place	Date	Hour	Summary of Events and Information	Remarks and references to Appendices
June	16th 1917		The Batt. relieved the 18th Batt. R.W.F. in the front line, relief complete 5.0pm. Shelling and aerial activity seen previous day. Lt-Col. H.V.R HODSON went to "A" Coy H.Q. to be i/c of the Proposed School for Platoon Officers. Major W.P. WHELDON assumed command of the Battalion. A Lystning Patrol went under 2Lt W.B.C. HUNKIN from Post 38 - no enemy seen.	
	17th 1917		Batt. in front Line. A patrol went out from Post 36 under 2Lt W.B.C. HUNKIN, working in the direction of C7a.12.7. Two posts were observed in the enemy lines about 50-100 yards apart. No enemy encountered.	
	18th 1917		Batt. in front Line A Patrol went out under 2nd Lt. R.T. EVANS from Post 31 working towards C7d 23.7. No enemy encountered.	
	19th 1917		Batt in front Line. A Patrol went out from 36 Post under 2 Lt. G.S. WILLIAMS, and worked towards C7c 93c 8. No enemy have have been. There is no gap in the wire.	

Army Form C. 2118.

14TH (S) BATTALION.
ROYAL WELSH
FUSILIERS.

No. ....
Date. ....

WAR DIARY
or
INTELLIGENCE SUMMARY.
(Erase heading not required.)

Instructions regarding War Diaries and Intelligence Summaries are contained in F. S. Regs., Part II. and the Staff Manual respectively. Title pages will be prepared in manuscript.

Place	Date	Hour	Summary of Events and Information	Remarks and references to Appendices
June	19/19.7		Another hot morning at C7.c.63.8. Owing to of what proved a wide shallow crater having been filled with wire, the wire being connected to the grenade syphons on either side. Between crater and post the wire was broken down for a space wide enough to take three men walking abreast. No hostile patrol was seen.	
	20/19.7		The Batt. was relieved by the 15th R.W.F. and three Coys went to the dugouts in CANAL BANK whilst the other Coy. bivouacked in a field 300 yds west of CANAL BANK. Working parties supplied for the new front line between Posts 40 and 48 and Posts 32 and 43.	
	21/19.7		Battalion in support. Working parties formed as before in New Front Line but work continued during to a raid which was carried out in the Batt. front by the 15th R.W.F.	
	22/19.7		Battalion in support. Work continued on new F.L. line as before - considerable hostile artillery activity.	

A6945 Wt. W17422/M1160 350,000 12/16 D. D. & L. Forms/C./2118/14.

Army Form C. 2118.

WAR DIARY
or
INTELLIGENCE SUMMARY.
(Erase heading not required.)

Instructions regarding War Diaries and Intelligence Summaries are contained in F. S. Regs., Part II. and the Staff Manual respectively. Title pages will be prepared in manuscript.

Place	Date	Hour	Summary of Events and Information	Remarks and references to Appendices
June	23/1/7		Batt. in Support, work continued on new I.C. Line as before - usual considerable artillery activity during the night and morning of 23/24th. particularly on CANAL BANK and bridges.	
	24/1/7		Intense hostile artillery bombardment all morning and until 2.0 pm, and then ceased. In the afternoon the Battalion relieved the 13th RWF in the I.C. Line at 5.15 PM	
	25/1/7		Batt. in front line holding posts as before appeared quiet. A Coy. left front subsector, B Coy right front subsector, C Coy. in Support. Considerable hostile artillery activity particularly in CANAL BANK and bridges	
	26/1/7		Batt. in I.C. Line. Operation from B Coy. under 2nd Lt. H.P. Jones raided the German trench at C.7.c.95.75. The zero hour was 10 PM. and the raiders were assisted by all our Barrage of Artillery and the Stokes Mortar guns. An entry was effected	

N
GERMAN LINE
CABLE
CACTUS TRENCH
CADDIE TRENCH
CAESERS NOSE
HUDDLESTONE ROAD
CANAL
BAIRD
YORKSHIRE
FARGATE S P
HARKNESS AV
ALMA TRENCH
INKERMAN
BARNSLEY
COLNE VALLEY
Wash Harp
S. ZWAANHOF FARM
42
41
40
47
39
38
37
36
46
45
44
35
33
31
30
32
43
26
27
52
51
65

WAR DIARY
or
INTELLIGENCE SUMMARY
(Erase heading not required.)

Army Form C. 2118.

14TH (S) BATTALION
ROYAL WELSH
FUSILIERS

Place	Date	Hour	Summary of Events and Information	Remarks and references to Appendices
			and the Right and Left Clearing Parties penetrated the enemy line for 30 yards on each side but did not meet any. The party stayed in the enemy trench for five minutes and then returned to our own line without a casualty. The enemy wire was well broken and his trench considerably damaged. Enemy retaliation feeble.	
June	27/17		Batt. in Front Line – the hostile bombardment of the Canal Bank continued.	
June	28/17	At 5.15pm	the Battalion was relieved in the front line by the 1st Batt. Border Regt. and came into Support on the Canal Bk. (3mm. 25/27) and was later that night relieved by the 1st Bn. K.O.S.B. and marched to the Newport Lines where they bivouacked for the remainder of the night.	
June	29/17		Lt. Col. N.T.R. Hodson, left the Batt. to take up duties as instructor in the Senior Officers School at Aldershot and Major E.W.P. Uniacke DSO 7/6th Royal Welsh Regt. assumed command. A/c G.O.A.M.	

WAR DIARY
or
INTELLIGENCE SUMMARY
(Erase heading not required.)

Army Form C. 2118.

Place	Date	Hour	Summary of Events and Information	Remarks and references to Appendices
	June 30.17		the Battalion paraded and proceeded in buses to BORRE where it was billeted for the night. At 6.30 a.m. the Battalion paraded at BORRE and marched to the Entraining N. of HAZEBROUCK and from there proceeded in buses to LIGNY LES AIRE which was reached at 10.30 a.m. where the Battalion was billeted.	
	June 30/9/17			

J.P. Thurocke
Lt. Colonel
Commanding
14th (S) Battalion
Royal Welsh Fusiliers

Vol 20

20.C
10 sheets

14TH BN. ROYAL WELSH FUSILIERS

WAR DIARY

JULY — 1917

WAR DIARY
or
INTELLIGENCE SUMMARY.
(Erase heading not required.)

Army Form C. 2118.

14th (S.) BATTALION
ROYAL WELSH
FUSILIERS.

Place	Date	Hour	Summary of Events and Information	Remarks and references to Appendices
July	1st 1917		The day devoted to cleaning up and improvement of billets – Voluntary C of E + nonconformist services.	
"	2nd 1917		Platoon training in 2 areas adjacent to billets and CO's Inspection of all companies and billets.	
"	3rd 1917		The Batt. marched to the training area at M28 (close to ERVUIN) and there completed a section of the reptiles of the PILKEM RIDGE to be used later for practice purposes.	
"	4th 1917		Platoon training carried out in training area and also Company training	
"	5th 1917		The Batt. paraded at 10.0 A.M. to march to the TRAINING AREA where Coy. training was carried out, and awaited a visit of Inspection by the Corps Commander, who however did not arrive	
"	6th 1917		Reveillage marched to the training area at different times arranged to fit in with Bath arrangements provided for the whole Battalion at the Coal mines FLECHINELLE.	

WAR DIARY
or
INTELLIGENCE SUMMARY.
(Erase heading not required.)

Army Form C. 2118.

Place	Date	Hour	Summary of Events and Information	Remarks and references to Appendices
	July 7 1917	7.15am	The Batt. paraded at 7.15am and marched to the training area to take part in a Brigade exercise near the PILKEM Ridge - the unit being in Reserve and providing a carrying party to attacking units.	
	July 8 1917		Church of E. and Nonconformists services at 10.30am in the morning and a lecture by the C.O. to all officers and sergeants at 11.30am in ARTILLERY BARRACKS. In the evening a service of GYMANFA GANU in the village schoolroom.	
	July 9 1917	8.30am	Divisional exercise on the training area near the PILKEM replica. The Batt. reached the assembly point on the TRAINING AREA at 8.30am and Bays & Boy (less 3 platoons) were detailed as carrying parties and the men were instructed in the use of YUKON packs. The remainder of the Batt. moved by band in artillery formation by stages to C 7 Central - YKLA - GRETCHEN and IRON CROSS ridge.	

WAR DIARY
INTELLIGENCE SUMMARY
(Erase heading not required.)

Army Form C. 2118.

Place	Date	Hour	Summary of Events and Information	Remarks and references to Appendices
	July 10/19.17		A Coy. proceeded to the training area and carried on training there. B & C Coys. proceeded to the Range & spent day at L.G.N.Y. and received instruction in musketry and Lewis Gun Training.	
	July 11/9.17		B & C Coys proceeded to the training area and carried out Coy training there. A Coys. and Lewis Gun Provisional Coy. to the Range for musketry instruction.	
"	12/9.17		Divisional Exercise on the training area. The Batt. reached the assembly point at 8.30AM. As between Bdays. 77 Platoon of B Coy. practised the duties of carrying parties, whilst the remainder of the Batt. in Brigade Reserve moved forward to the IRON CROSS RIDGE.	
"	13/9.17		The day spent as a complete holiday, divine service being applied to the men and the afternoon spent in sports games etc.	

WAR DIARY
or
INTELLIGENCE SUMMARY.
(Erase heading not required.)

Army Form C. 2118.

17th Bn. BATTALION.
ROYAL WELSH
FUSILIERS.

Place	Date	Hour	Summary of Events and Information	Remarks and references to Appendices
July	14th 1917		"B.C." Coys. carried out training were all ser officers were taken for instruction in (Tactical situation by the C.O. At Noon, went to the Range for Musketry Instruction.	
—	15th 1917		The Batt. paraded at LIGNY and dance marched to REtY, from where it proceeded in Buses to CAESTRE, arriving close in billets at 1.0 pm.	
—	16 1917		Coy. training particularly restrained undertaken carried out in the morning. At 7.30 p.m the Battalion paraded at the RAILWAY Crossing at CAESTRE and proceeded (t PROVEN arriving into Camp P.I. at 11.0 p.m (about F8b).	
—	17 1917		The Battalion in P.I. Camp. Heavy rain all day prevented any outdoor training - but indoor training was carried on.	
—	18 1917		Coy training carried on in the fields adjoining the Camp - special attention being paid to Physical Exercises and musketry.	
—	19 1917		Company training as before.	

WAR DIARY
or
INTELLIGENCE SUMMARY.
(Erase heading not required.)

Army Form C. 2118.

Place	Date	Hour	Summary of Events and Information	Remarks and references to Appendices
July	20.17		The Batt. paraded at 9.45am and marched to a field at A5c and stayed in that field till 8.30pm when the Batt. again paraded and marched to INTERNATIONAL CORNER STATION where it entrained at 11.15 pm for ELVERDINGHE. from where it marched in Artillery formation to the CANAL BANK (ZWAANHOF Section) there relieving the 1st Batt. SOUTH LANCASHIRE REGT. as battalion in support - relief being complete at 2.0AM. Three officers and seventy men of "B"Coy did not accompany the Batt. but proceeded to the transport lines.	
July	21.1917		Battalion in Support on CANAL BANK - considerable artillery activity particularly on the part of our Artillery - Working parties found and large carrying parties supplied for creation of dumps.	
	22.1917		In the morning the working and carrying parties continued. In the afternoon the Battalion retuned	

WAR DIARY or INTELLIGENCE SUMMARY

Army Form C. 2118.

(Erase heading not required.)

Place	Date	Hour	Summary of Events and Information	Remarks and references to Appendices

| | July 23/1917 | | relieved the 16th Batt. R.W.Fus. in the front line relief being complete at 6.30pm. Disp – Right Front Coy. – A Coy. – Left Ft Coy. "C" Coy. which have attached men of "B Coy formed the Garrison for FARGATE – the BUTT Line and were Coy in Support. During the night the enemy sent over a considerable number of Gas shells – respirators being worn extensively from 11.0pm to 5.0 AM – work much interrupted but casualties few. A reconnoitring patrol (Lieut. G Powell & 2 min) patrolled the German wire in front of CACTUS TRENCH and found it were broken. Battalion in front Line – considerable artillery activity on both sides during the day and in the night the enemy again sent many gas shells both on the CANAL BK and front Line, and there were a number of casualties – the action of the Gas being delayed for some hours. A patrol under 2/Lt. W.G | |

Army Form C. 2118.

WAR DIARY
or
INTELLIGENCE SUMMARY.
(Erase heading not required.)

Instructions regarding War Diaries and Intelligence Summaries are contained in F. S. Regs., Part II. and the Staff Manual respectively. Title pages will be prepared in manuscript.

Place	Date	Hour	Summary of Events and Information	Remarks and references to Appendices
		N.O	ROBERTS entered the German trench but found no Garrison. Work interrupted by gas - but carried on mainly of clearance and maintenance and construction of Strong Points in front line by wiring.	
	July 24/17		Batt. in front line - again considerable artillery activity though less on part of the enemy and fewer gas shells. WELSH HARP shelled heavily - work carried on as before. The Batt. relieved in front line at 2.30am by the 13th R.W.F. and marched to "H" Camp. All men reported in camp at 7am. Several casualties reported owing to gas shelling on previous day	
	25/9/17		Battalion in "H" Camp and day devoted to cleaning up and re-organisation after casualties. Inspection of camp by G.O.C. 113 Inf Bde/20	

A6945 Wt. W11422/N1160 350,000 12/16 D. D. & L. Forms/C.2118/14.

WAR DIARY
or
INTELLIGENCE SUMMARY.
(Erase heading not required.)

Army Form C. 2118.

Place	Date	Hour	Summary of Events and Information	Remarks and references to Appendices
July	26.17		Batt. in "Hamp". Training carried on underlay arrangements during the day. At midnight a platoon of "D" coy. under 2Lt. J.C. Bromage raided the enemy trench in front of 40 × 6 66 E. on night of 25th junction of CABLE and CACTUS trench. They found the trench unoccupied and one sergeant and 9 men lost direction in returning and probably wandered into CABLE TRENCH and are at present missing. The artillery co-operation was good.	
"	27.17.		The Batt. in "Hamp" but stood by during the day in receipt of orders from Divisions held @ 5 to be ready to march to CANAL BANK within one hour - the enemy heavy reported to be evacuating his line. No further order was received.	
"	28.17		Battalion in "Hamp". Training carried out in the morning and the Batt. paraded in full fighting equipment in the afternoon the Batt. was allotted Back for all men	

WAR DIARY
or
~~INTELLIGENCE SUMMARY.~~
(Erase heading not required.)

Army Form C. 2118.

Place	Date	Hour	Summary of Events and Information	Remarks and references to Appendices
	July 29-17		Col. C. and non-commissioned arrived in the morning. After 1 parade of the Batt. the charge of the Battalion was had and an outside detail of the Batt. was had at 3.0 pm. At 7.0 pm the Battalion paraded and marched to CARDOEN Farm to rec. there the night under Major WHELDOY.	
	30/7/17		Battalion remained at CARDOEN Fm. were reported by 83 tank cutlife gases of whom 39 were sent back to the transport lines to refit. to fit up. 2 women of those missing on the Raid returned in hospital. brought in by the Guards Division wounded. At 8.30 pm Batt. marched up to the line under Major Wheldon. Lt.-Col. Uniacke remained C.W. at the transport lines. Brigade orders under together with 10 officers and 40 men	S.N. Uniacke Lt. Col. R.W. Johnston Comdg. 14th R.W. Johnston

WAR DIARY
~~INTELLIGENCE~~ SUMMARY

Army Form C. 2118.

Place	Date	Hour	Summary of Events and Information	Remarks and references to Appendices
	July 30-1917		The Batt. paraded to move to the Bramby/Trenches as follows:-	
			HeadQrs- consisting mainly of runners and signallers under Lieut. A.T. APSIMON	
			Lewis Gunners under 2nd Lieut. G.E.J. EVANS.	
			"A" Carrying Party, being a party of 30 men detailed to go and report to and carry for the 13? Batt. R.W.F. under 2nd Lieut. G. Powell	
			"B" Carrying Party of similar strength detailed to carry for the 16 Batt. R.W.F. under 2nd Lt. J.C. BROMMAGE	
			"C" Carrying Party of similar strength to report to and carry for the 15? Batt. R.W.F. under Lt.Col. D. JENKINS.	
			"D" Carrying Party of similar strength to report to and carry for the 113" T.M. Batty. under Lt. E. ROBERTS	
			"T" Carrying Party of similar strength, being a water carrying party - detailed to carry water for all parts, under the direction of the Scoff Officer.	

WAR DIARY
or
INTELLIGENCE SUMMARY.
(Erase heading not required.)

Army Form C. 2118.

Place	Date	Hour	Summary of Events and Information	Remarks and references to Appendices
Curs.	July 30/17		— 32 Stretcher Bearers under the M.O. In this order the Batt. moves off from CARDEN FARM at 8.30 p.m. in Artillery formation following the prescribed route – namely TRACK 10. The Batt. came under heavy shell fire while passing through the Battalion but arrived without any casualties at their Assembly Quarters at B.24.b.5.9½ by HULL'S FARM at 10.30 p.m. Shortly before midnight the Carrying Parties – "A", "B" & "C" moved forward from their Assembly Quarters and assembled in CORRIDOR TRENCH between BRIDGE 6z and BRIDGE 6N, from there to move independently at ZERO and attach themselves to the Unit for which they were carrying. "D" Carrying Party reported direct to the 113th T.M. Batty. at FARGATE at manipl. In the meantime rations were issued – hot tea and rum were prepared to be drunk before ZERO.	

WAR DIARY
or
INTELLIGENCE SUMMARY.
(Erase heading not required.)

Army Form C. 2118.

Place	Date	Hour	Summary of Events and Information	Remarks and references to Appendices
	July 31/1917		ZERO which was fixed at 3.50 AM. For one hour and fifty five minutes after ZERO the remainder of the Batt. not on carrying duties remained in the assembly trenches until the time it was presumed that the BLACK LINE had been captured (just behind PILKEM) At 5.40 am information was received that the 15" R.W.F. was moving forward and the rise Lewis had been detailed under 2nd Lt. G.E.J. Evans to attack themselves to the unit and he for the remainder of the day with the command of Lt. Col. C.E. NORMAN, D.S.O. Headquarters moved forward at the same time in rear and arrived at VILLA GRETCHEN about 6.30 am and at once obtained touch with the Brigade forward station. Up to this time there had been very little hostile shelling	

WAR DIARY

(Erase heading not required.)

Army Form C. 2118.

Place	Date	Hour	Summary of Events and Information	Remarks and references to Appendices
			About 8.0 AM the enemy opened a vigorous barrage and kept it up throughout the day, alternating between PILKEM - the VILLA GRETCHEN LINE and CACTUS RESERVE Line. From all reports the Carrying Parties did their work extremely well and quickly and each party less a few stragglers reported back to Batt. H.Q.R. at VILLA GRETCHEN by 5.0 pm. 2nd Lt. D. JENKINS & S.Lt. GWILYM POWELL were wounded whilst carrying. About 6.0 pm Major W. P. WHELDON received orders to report to the G.O.C. 113th Inf. Bde. at C PERISCOPE HOUSE - on arrival there the G.O.C. ordered Major W. P. WHELDON to send back orders to the Batt. to move to BARLEY COPSE in artillery formation at once. Apparently the 15th R.W.F. had not consolidated on the GREEN LINE but had dug themselves about 150 yds. to the rear and the rear of BRIERLEY ROAD and this unit was therefore	

ordered to make two STRONG POINTS on the GREEN Line and dig in a line of Posts to connect up with the 11th Inf Bde on the Right and the GUARDS Division on the left. The General and Major. W.P. WHELDON reconnoitred the position for the STRONG Points and fixed them approximately at U.27.c.8.3 and U.27.a.1½.1. The Batt. by that time (about 7.45pm) had arrived at BATTERY Copse and was divided up into three parties — one party under Lieuting J.C. BROMMAGE to hold STRONG Pt at U.27.a.1½.1 and link up by posts with the 11th Inf Bde — one party under 2nd Lt E. ROBERTS to hold STRONG POINT at U.27.c.8.3 and 2 Lt. L STEPHENS with his party to put out a line of Posts to link up with the GUARDS Division on the left. Batt. H.Q. Orb. was at NORMAN JUNCTION. By 11.30 pm the Strong Points and Posts were all dug to a sufficient depth although the rain had by then commenced to fall heavily and there was much hostile shelling at the same time.

14th Battn. Royal Welsh Fusiliers.

War Diary.

August 1917

WAR DIARY
or
INTELLIGENCE SUMMARY.

Army Form C. 2118.

Place	Date	Hour	Summary of Events and Information	Remarks and references to Appendices
			Communication Connection was established with the GUARDS but the nearest post of the 114th Bde. was not found till about 1.0 pm. During the day 2nd Lt. H.P.JONES, Bde. Liaison Officer was wounded, and Lieut. CHISHOLM JONES our Transport Officer was killed at VLAMERTINGHE bringing up rations.	
August 1-1917			Livingstone morning and the afternoon, the position in the GREEN LINE indicated above were held by the Batt. Rain fell heavily throughout the day and there was heavy hostile shelling on our own lines and particularly on the front (STEENBEEK) line which was held by the 17th R.W.F. to our front and by the 11½ S.W.B.S. to our Right. Between 3.0 – 5.0 pm many wounded men from the 115th Bde. began to come through our lines. About 4.0 pm Major WHELDON received orders from the 113th Inf. Bde. to relieve the 17th R.W.F. in the front line.	

An order was immediately sent to 2nd Lt G.E.T. Dans and 2nd Lt Lewis Brown who was with the 15th R.W.F. to report back to the Unit at once and arrangements were made with the 115 Inf Bde. to reconnoitre the front line Fouchwick.

Whilst these things were being done and intelligence 5.0 pm it became clear that a certain amount of demoralisation had set in the front line Battalion. Cuisencie. Parties of unwounded men belonging to the 17th R.W.F. were seen retreating to our lines. Orders were then given for every man, with the exception of 2 runners and 2 signallers attached to Head Q.s, to stand to on the Green Line - hold up all stragglers and defend the line at all costs. There were every indication at the time that the enemy was either preparing or had launched an counter attack and the bombardment was intense. The measures taken were reported to the G.O.C. 115 Bde. who approved and ordered us

WAR DIARY
or
INTELLIGENCE SUMMARY
(Erase heading not required.)

Army Form C. 2118.

Place	Date	Hour	Summary of Events and Information	Remarks and references to Appendices
			with any available men to reinforce the 17th R.W.F. on the left about 6.0pm.	
			2nd Lt. G.E.T Evans with his crew Lewis Gun Team reported back to the Unit and he was ordered forthwith to take up his guns and reinforce the 17th R.W.F. which he did at 6.0pm. 2nd Lt. E. ROBERTS and his men were retired in STRONG Pt. U.27.c.8.3 by Lieut. A.T APSIMON and the 4th OBS decided and 2Lt. ROBERTS and his men were ordered to follow the Lewis Gun Teams and also reinforce the 17th R.W.F. and they moved up about 6.30pm. During the time considerable difficulty was experienced in copying with the numbers of stragglers retreating from the front line and no information could be obtained as to what really was happening. Major JESSE WILLIAMS therefore took out a patrol consisting of himself, S/6908 Lance/Sgt THOMAS. E. and	

A6945 Wt. W14432/M1160 350,000 12/16 D.D. & L. Forms/C/2118/14

WAR DIARY
or
INTELLIGENCE SUMMARY.
(Erase heading not required.)

Army Form C. 2118.

Place	Date	Hour	Summary of Events and Information	Remarks and references to Appendices
			3rd 8.5.2 Pte. S.F. CHATER and went forward about 300 yds. from the GREEN LINE to ascertain whether an enemy counter-attack was in progress.	
			About 8.15 pm Major T. WILLIAMS returned and reported that there was no counter-attack, no any evidence of the enemy massing for counter-attack. This was reported to the 115th Bde. by Major WHELDON, and the O.C. ordered Major LIST to move all the men under his command nice in the GREEN LINE forward. At the same time the mile was informed that the 115 Bde. front-line was abandoned and that we constituted the front-line.	
			At 8.30pm the whole of the GREEN LINE moved forward in extended order to a line just ever left of U.27.d.7.5. and by 10.pm the front-line had be reconstituted with a series of posts on the point linking up with the GUARDS on the left. but there was a considerable gap	

Army Form C. 2118.

WAR DIARY
or
INTELLIGENCE SUMMARY.
(Erase heading not required.)

Place	Date	Hour	Summary of Events and Information	Remarks and references to Appendices
	August 2nd 17		between us and the 11th Hfs. Bde. which was practically fallen up by remnants of the 115th Inf. Bde.	
		About 1 a.m.	Capt. VAUGHAN of the 13th R.W.F. reported at B.H.Qrs. at NORMAN JUNCTION he would at this time from BRIERLEY RD at U.27 A.7.5 to the right and take over from the 11th Hfs. Bde. our men in that sector were to be relieved and were to hold the front line between BRIERLEY RD at that point and the Railway.	
		About 1.30pm	He produced a guide for Capt. VAUGHAN to the future and marked Bay of the 13th R.W.F. reported at NORMAN JUNCTION and 20102 Pte. GEORGE VARLEY (armourer) who had guided up Capt. Vaughan also guided up the Bay to the front line and we held the line thence forward from BRIERLEY RD to the Railway. The line was held throughout the day in heavy rain and unimportant shelling, extending in the afternoon, owing to the difficulty of getting up rations to the advanced	

WAR DIARY
INTELLIGENCE SUMMARY
(Erase heading not required.)

Army Form C. 2118.

Place	Date	Hour	Summary of Events and Information	Remarks and references to Appendices
			Strict orders were given that the IRON RATIONS were to be eaten. Our own wounded were collected together which wounded men of the 115th Inf Bde. and 1st Bn. - 15th R.W.F. was of the greatest assistance in this work.

About 4.30pm we received orders from the 113th Inf Bde that event march of the 114th & 115th Inf Bdes are remaining in the front line were to be relieved and ordered to march back to the CANAL BK. and that the 113th Inf Bde was to hold the horseshoe front - the 15th & 16th R.W.F. on the right and the 13th & 14th R.W.F. on the left.

By arrangements with Lt. Col. R. CAMPBELL. DSO. 13th R.W.F. the 13th R.W.F. took over the forward posts by the STEENBECK the front line at U.27.a.7.8 and the STRONG PTS. in the GREEN LINE. This unit took over the line hitherto held by the 15th R.W.F. from BATTERY COPSE to the PILKEM Rd at IRON CROSS - the line being in rear of the TRAMWAY and BRIERLEY ROAD.

By 9.0 PM our men in the front line had been relieved | |

WAR DIARY
or
INTELLIGENCE SUMMARY.
(Erase heading not required.)

Army Form C. 2118.

Place	Date	Hour	Summary of Events and Information	Remarks and references to Appendices
			by the 13th Batt. R.W. Fus. the relief being carried out under an actively intense bombardment. By 10.0pm the whole was taken over the BATTERY COPSE to IRON CROSS line in a series of nine posts of 1 NCO & 6 men each, four of the posts being Lewis Gun Posts.	
			While fixing these posts the A.T. APSIMON was mortally wounded and 2nd Lieuts. G.E. T. EVANS & L STEPHENS were wounded. his toll were no casualties amongst the men.	
			Connection was immediately established with the Guards on the left, but the 16th R.W.F. on the right were not found until the following morning.	
Hugras	2nd 3/1917		The line taken over the previous night was held throughout the day and the advancement night. During the day severe hand to hand hand to hand fighting and doing gains of ground and a lot drink. This was largely due to the energetic activities of RSM TUCKER.	

WAR DIARY

(Erase heading not required.)

Army Form C. 2118.

Place	Date	Hour	Summary of Events and Information	Remarks and references to Appendices
	August 4 1917		Weather conditions were also bad and the trenches were full of water. At intervals during the day there was a considerable amount of hostile shelling and our artillery was, as on previous days, extremely active. The main enemy and machine gun fire became slightly better. There was the usual hostile bombardment at intervals throughout the day. At 9.0 pm we were relieved by the 114th Bde (14th Welsh) and the men marched back to ELVERDINGHE CHATEAU independently by Pls, guns, & coys, under to the right of PERISCOPE HOUSE, thence proceeding alongside Railway for 100 yards, and from thence proceeding along a track marked by the 113 TM Bty to CACTUS Piston and across the CANAL to ELVERDINGHE CHATEAU each man was given a complete set of dry clothing & a hot meal at finish. All the Battn was in before 2.0 am. On arrival at the	

WAR DIARY or INTELLIGENCE SUMMARY.

Army Form C. 2118.

Place	Date	Hour	Summary of Events and Information	Remarks and references to Appendices
Dupont	5th 1917	At 9.0 am	the Batt. paraded at the CHATEAU grounds and marched to the train and entrained for PROVEN and reached PALMA Camp at PROVEN about 1.0 pm.	
"	6 Aug 17		Complete rest to all ranks.	
"	7.8.1917		Cleaning up - reorganisation and re-equipment. Visit from the Earl of CAVAN (Corps Commander) the Brigade General who all expressed themselves as pleased with the excellent work done by the unit and the Division in the recent operations.	
	8.8.1917		In the morning by Training carried on, particular attention being paid to close order drill. In the afternoon successful sports were carried out.	
	9.8.1917		Coy Training continued and lectures to Platoon Commanders and N.C.O.s.	
	10.8.1917		Coy Training continued special attention devoted to the organisation of the platoon in battle formation and patrols.	

WAR DIARY
or
INTELLIGENCE SUMMARY.
(Erase heading not required.)

Army Form C. 2118.

Place	Date	Hour	Summary of Events and Information	Remarks and references to Appendices
	August 11/17		Coy training continued in the morning and route march in the afternoon. 26628 Sgt Qureshi H. 36890 Sgt Nash H.J. 49063 Sgt Thewlidge and 36968 Sgt E Thomas awarded the MILITARY MEDAL	
	August 12th/17		Church parade service in Camp at 9.30 am. Col E. Bolchowie at 11.30 am R.C. Service in PROVEN Church.	
	August 13/17		Coy training and special training in L.G - grenades and rifle grenades.	
	August 14/1917		The Batt. paraded in fighting order at 10 am and marched to the training area at Fr.W. to carry out a Battalion exercise involving attacks in strong points and wood fighting.	
	August 15/17		A Coy. paraded at 6.45 am and marched to HERZEELE to do their RANGE firing (5 rounds application and 10 rounds Rapid) and the Lewis Gun Section also did their firing. C+D Coys. carried on with Coy. training near Buicht.	

WAR DIARY
or
INTELLIGENCE SUMMARY.
(Erase heading not required.)

Army Form C. 2118.

Place	Date	Hour	Summary of Events and Information	Remarks and references to Appendices
	August 16 1917.		A successful concert held in the evening. Inspection of all Box Respirators in the Batt. at 8.30 A.m. At 10. Am. C/B Coy proceeded to Zillebeke and marched to HERZEELE to carry out Firing practice on the range. A/B Coys. carried on with Coy. training. A successful concert was held in the evening.	
	August 17 1917		All were bathed at CHATEAU COUTHOVE and Company training continued for rest of the day.	
	August 18 1917		Coys carried on with Box Respirator Drill and Physical training till 10.0am & afterwards prepared for the move. The Battalion paraded at 3 pm & marched to PROVEN STATION & there entrained for ELVERDINGHE. On arrival at ELVERDINGHE the Companies marched independently to a camp in MACKHOFF FARM Area (close to DAWSONS CORNER) all the unit being in camp by 7.30 p.m.	
	August 19 1917		C of E. & non-conformist Church Services & the morning devoted to tidying up & the arrangement of camp & construction of	

WAR DIARY
or
INTELLIGENCE SUMMARY.
(Erase heading not required.)

Army Form C. 2118.

Place	Date	Hour	Summary of Events and Information	Remarks and references to Appendices
August	20 1917		range close by SARAGOSSA FARM. Coy. by Coy. fired on range including Lewis Gunners B, C & D Coys. occupied in Company training. Special attention being paid to the solution of problems including the taking of strong points.	
August	21 1917		B. Coy. including Lewis Gunners on range and other B. Coys. occupied with Company training as before. Major José Williams awarded the D.S.O. R.S.M. S. Tucker awarded the M.C. #20569 Cpl Elias Jones and 22587 L. Cpl R. Williams awarded the D.C.M.	
August	22 1917		C. Coy. including Lewis Gunners on range. Two other Coys. occupied with Company training as before. At 7 p.m. Coys. moved independently out of the Camp & relieved the 10 S.W.B. in CANDLE TRENCH & CHENIN DRIVE being in support to the 115 Bde. Working parties found for road & tramway construction. Enemy quiet save for some shelling.	
August	23 1917		Battalion in support in CANDLE TRENCH - working parties again found for road tramway construction. Enemy quiet save for some	

WAR DIARY
or
~~INTELLIGENCE~~ SUMMARY.
(Erase heading not required.)

Army Form C. 2118.

Instructions regarding War Diaries and Intelligence Summaries are contained in F. S. Regs., Part II. and the Staff Manual respectively. Title pages will be prepared in manuscript.

Place	Date	Hour	Summary of Events and Information	Remarks and references to Appendices
Shelling	August 24th 1917		The Battalion relieved at 2 p.m. by the 13 R.W.F. and marched to bivouacs by HULLS FARM - all the Battalion in Camp by 4 p.m.	
	August 25th 1917		The Battalion paraded at 11.0 a.m. and the G.O.C. 113th Bde. presented ribbons to men who had been awarded honours in the recent offensive. All new draft men were put through a gas chamber by the Divisional Gas Officer. Company training in afternoon.	
	August 26th 1917		Company training in morning. In the afternoon the Battalion practiced assembling on a taped line moving forward thence to an attack. Reconnaissance of the line had carried forward of LANGEMARCK carried out during the day by Major Wakelam, 2 Lieut. Johan Capt Stott and some N.C.O's.	
	Aug. 27th 1917.		'B' Company on the Range, Company training of Officers training under specialist Officers, Battalion practices forming on a taped line	

A6945 Wt. W14122/M1160 350,000 12/16 D. D. & L. Forms/C./2118/14.

WAR DIARY
or
INTELLIGENCE SUMMARY.
(Erase heading not required.)

Army Form C. 2118.

Place	Date	Hour	Summary of Events and Information	Remarks and references to Appendices
August	28th 1917		Battalion parade in fighting Order and practised an attack over the Replica. - Specialist having much Specialist officers in the afternoon. - Reconnaissances of the Front Line and Country forward of LANGEMARCK, carried out by Company Commanders.	
August	29th 1917		2nd Lieut R.J Evans and 6 O.R. carried out reconnaissance of the Routes to the Front Line forward of LANGEMARCK. "A" & "B" Coys on Range - "C" & "D" Coys - "PROBLEMS". The Battalion relieved 11th Battn R.W.F'rs in the Front Line. Left Sector of the Divisional Front - relief being completed at 2.22 am (29/30). 2nd Lt John and 2nd Lt Shaw took out reconnoitring patrols on the left & right respectively. - Dispositions "A" Coy Front line in 9 Posts. "B" Coy Right Support. "D" Coy Left Support. + "B" Coy divides - One platoon in right Support with "C" Coy + two platoons in left Support with "A" Coy.	
Do.	30	?	Battalion in Front Line: 2/Lt John + 2nd Lt Edwards carried out patrol reconnaissances on left + right respectively. Enemy fairly quiet but at times put down his barrage of Langemarck - Wurf Farm	

WAR DIARY
or
INTELLIGENCE SUMMARY.
(Erase heading not required.)

Army Form C. 2118.

Place	Date	Hour	Summary of Events and Information	Remarks and references to Appendices
	31/8/17		Line commenced, both on Right & Left & almost 60 yards completes	
August	31	19.7.	Battalion in front line. Her troops took out fighting Patrol with intent to capture nearest enemy post on the left - but did not locate them. Wiring continued on front line and 100 yards put out. Enemy fairly quiet but occasional bombardment on LANGEMARCK and some sniping in front line.	

Sept: 1st 1917

Carleton
Major for Lt.-Col. Comdg
1st (S) Battalion Royal Welsh Fus.

14th Batt: ROYAL WELSH FUSILIERS
Vol 22

WAR DIARY

FOR

SEPTEMBER 1917.

22.C
11 sheets

WAR DIARY
or
INTELLIGENCE SUMMARY.
(Erase heading not required.)

Army Form C. 2118.

Place	Date	Hour	Summary of Events and Information	Remarks and references to Appendices
	September 1st 1917		About 5.0 a.m. Battalion Forward Command Post was struck by a shell, and the woodwork ignited. Post was evacuated, but an hour later about 23 Officers, N.C.O.'s and men returned to it's A.C. that moment Bombs in the building exploded and the centre of the building collapsed burying all three Officers (all who were in) were brought out. Capt. Higham - wounded. 2/Lt R. Evans - killed. 2/Lt. Toulson - wounded. Seven men were brought out. Of these five were taken to the dressing station, and one died immediately. It is believed 13, including 9 Signallers were buried. It was impossible to get at him to satisfy. Lt Col Uniacke D.S.O. returned from leave. Battalion was relieved by the 15th R.W.F.S. Relief completed at 2.22 a.m. Battalion moved back into Reserve to a house about 300 S of Iron Cross.	
	September 2nd 1917		Salvage party of 1 N.C.O. + 10 O.R. worked during the day	

WAR DIARY or INTELLIGENCE SUMMARY

Army Form C. 2118.

Place	Date	Hour	Summary of Events and Information	Remarks and references to Appendices
	Sept. 2nd (cont'd)		and other parties worked for Brigade. At night the whole Battalion was out on Salvage and carrying work.	
	Sept. 3rd 1917		Heavy shelling during the day but no casualties. Salvage and small working parties for Brigade. At night 90 men wired on the Green Line in front of LANGEMARK. 70 men carried men and stakes. "D" Coy found 1 Off. + 50 men for carrying under Brigade arrangements.	
	Sept. 4th 1917		Salvage party as usual. Battalion was relieved by 13th Welsh Regt. (relief completed 11.45 p.m.) and moved to the MALAKOFF FARM area getting in at 2.30 a.m. — 4 slight casualties.	
	Sept. 5th 1917		Rested and cleaned up, after a short parade in the morning. Working party 1 Off. 130 O.R. fuching ammunition from the dump to Candle Trench.	

WAR DIARY
or
INTELLIGENCE SUMMARY.
(Erase heading not required.)

Army Form C. 2118.

Place	Date	Hour	Summary of Events and Information	Remarks and references to Appendices
	September 6th 1917		"Drill and Tactics" (as per orders). Working party as on the previous night.	
	Sept 7-9-17		Parade of Battalion at 9.20 a.m. for the G.O.C. Brigade to present Ribands to Major Grose Williams — D.S.O. — R.S.M. S. Inches — M.C. Musketry drill, wiring, tactics. Sentence of 70 days F.P. No 1. for using insubordinate language awarded to No. 241786 Pte Pascoe E. "S" Coy. promulgated to Battalion — paraded.	
	Sept 8th 1917		Divine Service for all denominations.	
	Sept 9th 1917		Musketry Drill, Wiring, Tactics. One man slightly wounded whilst in his home.	
	Sept 5th and 9th/9/17		During whole stay in this camp heavy shelling during night and bombs dropping.	
	Sept 10-1917		Battalion was relieved by the 12th R.B. Took in 9.30 am and marched to Elverdinghe Station where it entrained	

A6945 Wt. W14422/M160 350,000 12/16 D. D. & L. Forms/C./2118/14.

WAR DIARY
or
INTELLIGENCE SUMMARY
(Erase heading not required.)

Army Form C. 2118.

Place	Date	Hour	Summary of Events and Information	Remarks and references to Appendices
	Sept 10th (contd)		Marched to INTERNATIONAL CORNER arriving at 11-30 a.m. for SARAWAK CAMP in the S.L. area, arriving at 1. p.m.	
	Sept 11th 1917		Company training by all Coys - Route march in the morning and tactical exercise in the afternoon.	
	Sept 12th 1917		Company training - Route march in the morning, under Coy arrangements, followed by specialist training. "A" Coy on the range.	
	Sept 13th 1917		Company training as before - Route march and tactical exercise. Baths for the men.	
	Sept 14th 1917		Battalion paraded in Shell-marching order at 10-0 am and marched to EECKE, and arrived there at 5 pm and were there billeted for the night.	
	Sept 15th 1917		Battalion paraded in Shell-marching order at 9-0 am and marched to MORBECQUE arriving there at 1-0 pm and were there billeted for the night.	

WAR DIARY
or
INTELLIGENCE SUMMARY.
(Erase heading not required.)

Army Form C. 2118.

Place	Date	Hour	Summary of Events and Information	Remarks and references to Appendices
	Sept. 16th 1917		Battalion paraded in full-marching order at 8-45 am. and marched to SAILLY-SUR-LA-LYS and arrived there at 4-30 pm. and were billeted there for the night.	
	Sept 17th 1917.		In the morning the men of the unit had baths at SAILLY. Reconnoitring parties of Officers and N.C.O.s from each Coy. had been sent forward on previous days to view the new Battalion front. At 5-0 pm the Battalion paraded by Coys and marched to the front line, there relieving the 2/9th Kings Liverpool Batt. of the 57th Division, relief being complete at 9.45 pm. Dispositions were taken over from the relieved unit, the front and support lines being held on orts from the right by "D" Coy. "A" Coy. & "B" Coy respectively "C" Coy being in Reserve in the subsidiary line, together with "D" Coy of the 15th KRWF. Appended is a sketch showing the disposition of the Battalion in the new front	

Place	Date	Hour	Summary of Events and Information	Remarks and references to Appendices
	Sept 17th (cont)		The 114 Brigade hold the line on our right and the 16th Battn R.W.F. of our Brigade hold the line on the left. The 115th Brigade being to the left of the 16th R.W.F.	
and not South of ARMENTIERES.				
	Sept 18th 1917		Battalion in front line – enemy inactive. Work commenced in Company sectors consisting of wiring the parts damaged and trench maintenance. Two Russian prisoners escaped from the German lines and came into our lines.	
	Sept 19th 1917		Battalion in front line – little activity until about 7.30 p.m. when the enemy bombarded the Left Battalion sector heavily with T.M.B. and Shell and inflicted casualties but our Left Coy did not suffer and casualties.	
	Sept 20th 1917		Battalion in front line – quiet day, and work continued – wiring, drainage, and trench board repairs also progress made with the construction of a new Orderly Room	

Army Form C. 2118.

WAR DIARY
or
INTELLIGENCE SUMMARY
(Erase heading not required.)

Instructions regarding War Diaries and Intelligence Summaries are contained in F. S. Regs., Part II. and the Staff Manual respectively. Title pages will be prepared in manuscript.

Place	Date	Hour	Summary of Events and Information	Remarks and references to Appendices
	Sept 21st 1914		Battalion in front line — Quiet day, and work continued as before.	
	Sept 22nd 1914		Battalion in front line. Work continued — wiring the subsidiary line, flank defences and in rear of front line post — the object of the front line wiring in rear being to shepherd any enemy attacking to the L.G. positions in the support line. — Enemy quiet.	
	Sept 23rd 1914		Battalion in front line, and work continued as before. Enemy quiet, but for some little T.M.B. in the night.	
	Sept 24th 1914		Battalion in front line. Work continued as before, and parties also detailed to assist the R.E. in drainage. — New Orders room completed.	
	Sept 25th 1914		Battalion in front line, relieved by 15th Bn R.W. Fus., relief being complete at 10.0 pm. "C" & "D" Coy remained in the Subsidiary line as left Coy. "A" Coy were detailed as "abling" occupat. at STEAKY-BACON Farm, and "B" & "D" Coys	

A6945 Wt. W11427/M1160—350,000 12/16 D. D. & L. Forms/C./2118/14.

WAR DIARY
or
INTELLIGENCE SUMMARY
(Erase heading not required.)

Army Form C. 2118.

Place	Date	Hour	Summary of Events and Information	Remarks and references to Appendices
	Sept 25th (contd)		Were in Camp at ROLANDRIE FARM. Battalion H.Q. at ARTILLERY FARM and CANTEEN FARM.	
	Sept 26th 1917.		Battalion in Support. 'A' 'B' & 'D' Coys - Baths and rested. Day own to cleaning up generally.	
	Sept 27th 1917.		Battalion in Support. 'C' Coy to Battalion Baths. Coy parades in the morning and afternoon. Close order Drill, Musketry, and Physical exercises. Working Parties also found to assist R.E's in drainage.	
	Sept 28th 1917.		Battalion in Support. Battalion paraded at 9.30 a.m in ROLANDRIE FARM and the Brigadier General presented Ribands and Certificate as follows:- No. 20589 Cpl E Jones - Bar to Military Medal No. 55333 Pte. H. Elsthellr - Military Medal No. 14282. Pte. J.V. Roberts - Distinguished Conduct Certificate Afterwards Company training was carried on.	

WAR DIARY
or
~~INTELLIGENCE SUMMARY~~

(Erase heading not required.)

Army Form C. 2118.

Place	Date	Hour	Summary of Events and Information	Remarks and references to Appendices
	Sept 29th 1917		Battalion in support. Company training carried on in the morning. In the evening "B" Coy relieved "C" Coy in the Subsidiary line. "C" Coy came to ROLANDRIE FARM, and "B" Coy went into the Subsidiary line to take up the duties of 6th Coy in support in that line, it being now decided that the 6th Coy should live in the Subsidiary line.	
	Sept 30th 1917		Church of England however an R.C. Service in the morning. Recreation in the afternoon.	

W.P. Mea —

Major for Lt Col
Comdg
1st Bn R W Fus

30th Sept 1917

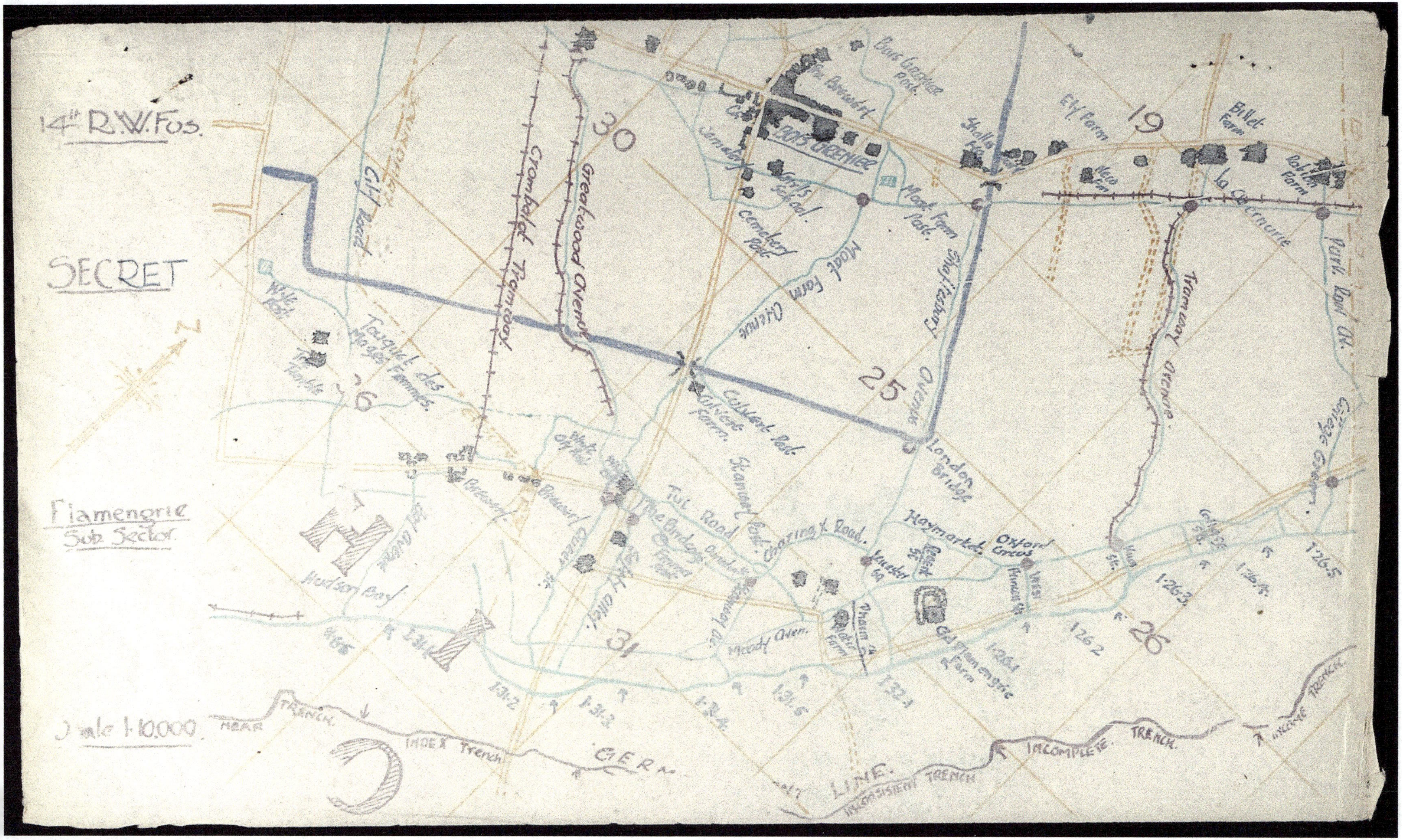
14th R.W.Fus.
SECRET
Flamengrie
Sub Sector
Scale 1:10,000
Park Road Av.
Cottage Green
Robiny Farm
Billet Farm
La Cavernune
Tramway Avenue
19
Ely Farm
Shaftesbury Avenue
London Bridge
25
Moat Farm Post
Moat Farm Avenue
Bois Grenier
Bois Grenier Post
Girls School
Cemetery Post
Cemetery
Culvert Post
Culvert Farm
Stanway Post
Charing X Road
Haymarket
Oxford Circus
Regent St.
Leicester Sq.
Gd Flamengrie Farm
30
Greatwood Avenue
Crombalot Tramway
City Road
Touquet des Mages Femmes
Hudson Bay
31
26
Tui Road
Safety Alley
Moody Aven.
Stanway Av.
I.26.5
I.26.4
I.26.3
I.26.2
I.26.1
I.32.1
I.31.6
I.31.4
I.31.3
I.31.2
I.31.1
H
I
INDEX Trench
GERMAN
LINE.
INCOMPLETE TRENCH.
INCONSISTENT TRENCH
NEAR TRENCH.

14TH BATT ROYAL WELSH FUSILIERS Vol 23.

WAR DIARY

FOR

OCTOBER 1917.

23.C
10 shults

Army Form C. 2118.

WAR DIARY
or
INTELLIGENCE SUMMARY.
(Erase heading not required.)

Instructions regarding War Diaries and Intelligence Summaries are contained in F.S. Regs., Part II. and the Staff Manual respectively. Title pages will be prepared in manuscript.

Place	Date	Hour	Summary of Events and Information	Remarks and references to Appendices
	October 1st 1917		Battalion in Support. "A" + "C" Coys carried out Company training during the day.	
	October 2nd 1917		Lt. Col. E.W.P. Miriam D.S.O. left the Battalion, and took command of the 113th Infantry Bae Schools and Major D.O. Skeldon assumed command of the Battalion.	
	October 3rd 1917		The Battalion relieved the 15th Bn. R.W.F. in the front line. Relief complete 10.00 am. Dispositions from the right. A, B + C Coys and in Subsidiary Line 'A' Coy 15th Bn. R.W.F. (5th Coy) "D" Coy 14th Bn. (4th Coy) and 'B' Coy 15th Bn R.W.F. (6th Coy) 'A' Coy sent out a fighting Patrol 1 Officer + 8 O.R. from 6.1 Oak. No enemy patrols encountered.	
	Oct 4th 1917		Battalion in front line. Wiring, draining, and maintenance of trenches carried on in Company Sectors. Stands to over from the Bay Sap. About 160 men from the Sub sector working daily under supervision of R.E. and 5th Coy wiring GREAT WOOD AVENUE. 'C' Coy found a fighting Patrol which was unable to cross ditch running in a SSW direction	

WAR DIARY
or
INTELLIGENCE SUMMARY.
(Erase heading not required.)

Army Form C. 2118.

Place	Date	Hour	Summary of Events and Information	Remarks and references to Appendices
	Oct 4th (Contd)		From Pound. T.20.a.90.20.	
	Oct 5th 1914		Battalion in front line. "A" Coy Sent out a fighting patrol from T.26.c.40.40. at 8.30 pm Patrol returned 10.35pm having encountered no enemy patrols.	
	Oct 6th 1914		Battalion in front line. Little activity. "B" Coy Sent out a fighting patrol from T.31.6.60.05. at 8.30pm.	
	Oct 7th 1914		Battalion in front line. "D" Coy 1st RWY relieved "A" Coy 15th RWY as 1st Coy. "C" Coy 15th RWY relieved "B" Coy 15th RWY as 6th Coy. "C" Coy Sent out a fighting patrol at 8.30 pm from T.20.d.45.15. to endeavour to cross Stream in No Man's Land. at Suspect Bridge at T.26.c.65.70 and to locate enemy posts about that point. Patrol returned at 10.15pm having failed to find Bridge and having been unable to cross Stream.	
	Oct 8th 1914		Battalion in front line. "E" Coy found fighting patrol as on previous middle. Same result. At 12.15 am night 8/9th the enemy bombarded the Sector on our right and attempted to raid the Left	

Army Form C. 2118.

WAR DIARY
or
INTELLIGENCE SUMMARY.
(Erase heading not required.)

Instructions regarding War Diaries and Intelligence Summaries are contained in F. S. Regs., Part II. and the Staff Manual respectively. Title pages will be prepared in manuscript.

Place	Date	Hour	Summary of Events and Information	Remarks and references to Appendices
	Oct 8th 1917 (cont'd)		Bath of Ret Sectr. Many trench mortars fell on our Right and Centre Company Sectors. No casualties, but considerable damage to trenches.	
	Oct 9th 1917.		Battalion in front line. B Coy found a fighting patrol went out from I.26.c.45.55 at 8.30 a.m. No enemy patrols encountered. Damage done to trenches on previous nights repaired.	
	Oct 10th 1917.		Battalion in front line. At 12.0 midnight a raiding party of 2 Officers and 18 o.r. ranks under the command of 2/Lt R.J. Phillips left I.31.a.20.90. with the object of raiding a sunken enemy post at I.31.d.50.50. Whilst the sentry party was cutting the second Belt Barre the enemy in the post just opposite raised the alarm by blowing a horn. The raiders came under heavy rifle & machine gun fire and 2/Lt R.J. Phillips and five other ranks were wounded. 2/Lt Phillips realizing the impossibility of pressing forward gave the order to withdraw which was done in an orderly manner.	

WAR DIARY
or
INTELLIGENCE SUMMARY.
(Erase heading not required.)

Army Form C. 2118.

Place	Date	Hour	Summary of Events and Information	Remarks and references to Appendices
	Oct 10 (contd).		2nd Lt Oliver came across Corporal Robert "A" Coy near to enemy were badly wounded and exhausted and carried him to our lines though himself wounded. The raiding party got 1st through on crossing ditch running from I 31.a.20.60.6. I 31.a.55.75. which was about 6ft wide and 6ft deep.	
	Oct 11th -1914.		The Battalion was relieved by the 15th Bn R.W.F. Relief complete 8.0.a.m. "A" & "C" Coys remained in the Subsidiary Line, as 5th & 6th Coys respectively. "B" & "D" Companies went to LA ROLANDRIE FARM.	
	Oct 12th 1914.		Day devoted to cleaning up and Kit inspections.	
	Oct 13th -1914.		Battalion in Support. Company training carried on during the day and baths at SAILLY SUR LA LYS allotted to the Battalion	
	Oct 14th -1914.		Battalion in Support. Divine Service for all denominations	
	Oct 15th -1914.		Battalion in Support. "B" & "D" Coys went up to Subsidiary Line as 5th & 6th Coys respectively and "A" & "C" Coys came back to LA ROLANDRIE FARM.	

WAR DIARY
or
INTELLIGENCE SUMMARY.

Army Form C. 2118.

(Erase heading not required.)

Place	Date	Hour	Summary of Events and Information	Remarks and references to Appendices
	Oct 16th 1917		Day devoted to cleaning up. "A" & "C" Coys. Baths at SAILLY SUR	
	Oct 17th 1917		LA LYS allotted to the Battalion.	
			Battalion in Support. Company training 9-0 am to	
			12.15 pm. and 1.30 pm. to 2.30 pm.	
	Oct 18th 1917		Battalion in Support. Company training as on previous day	
	Oct 19th 1917		The Battn. relieved the 15th Bn. R.W.F. in the front line	
			Relief complete 8.45 pm. Dispositions as follows. "B" Coy Right front	
			"C" Coy Centre front. "C" Coy Left front. A Coy 4th Coy at Moat Farm	
			D Coy 15th RWF 4/17 Coy. "B" Coy 13th RWF 6th Coy. D Coy Sent	
			out a fighting patrol which went out from T.20.d.50.30. at 10.0 pm and	
			returned at the same place at 11.30 pm. No hostile patrols encountered	
	Oct 20th 1917		Battalion in front line. Hostile artillery and trench mortars	
			fairly active during the day. 'C' Coy sent out patrol from	
			T.32.a.10.80. consisting of 9 other ranks under 2/Lt. Jas. Y. Young	
			Patrol encountered three hostile parties, trying to surround our	
			patrol. Lt Young gave orders for his patrol to retire about 50 yards	

A6945 Wt. W1422/M160 350,000 12/16 D.D.&L. Forms/C./2118/14.

WAR DIARY
or
INTELLIGENCE SUMMARY.
(Erase heading not required.)

Army Form C. 2118.

Place	Date	Hour	Summary of Events and Information	Remarks and references to Appendices
	Oct 20 (contd)		and from this position the patrol opened fire on the hostile parties, and afterwards withdrew into our trenches unnoticed whilst doing so.	
	Oct 21st	Night	Battalion in front line. Hostile Artillery quiet, but hostile Trench mortars very active. They did considerable damage to SAFETY ALLEY, SHAFTESBURY AVENUE and the front line between Nos 1 & 2 coals. "B" Coy sent out a patrol from I.26.a.90.60 at 7.0.p.m. Patrol returned at I.26.a.90.60 at 9.0.p.m. having encountered no hostile patrol.	
	Oct 22	40	Battalion in front line. Hostile Trench mortars still active firing on heads of Communication trenches, especially SHAFTESBURY AVENUE and SAFETY ALLEY. "C" Coy sent out a patrol from I.26.C.40.45 at 12 midnight. Patrol returned at I.32.a.10.90 at 2.15 a.m. No hostile patrol encountered.	
	Oct 23rd 1914.		Battalion in front line. Hostile Artillery and Trench Mortars quiet. Our Artillery cut the enemy's wire at I.31.a.45.50. at 2.0.p.m.	

WAR DIARY
or
INTELLIGENCE SUMMARY.
(Erase heading not required.)

Army Form C. 2118.

Place	Date	Hour	Summary of Events and Information	Remarks and references to Appendices
	Oct 23rd (Contd)		At 6.0 p.m. a listening patrol was sent out from T 32.a.20.90 under 2 Lt. E.S. Jones with orders to signal back by lamp to the Post at T 32.d.20.90. If the enemy came out to wire a platoon of 20 other ranks under 2 Lt. 13 Lau was at the Post ready to go out to attack the wiring party in conjunction with our Stokes Mortars. The listening patrol saw a fighting patrol coming out at 8.0 pm and 2 Lt. E.S. Jones had to withdraw the listening patrol as they were too near the enemy's wire. 2 Lt. Lau took out his platoon and searched No Mans Land but returned at 9.20 am without having encountered the enemy. The Battalion was relieved by the 15th Bn R.W.F. Relief complete 7.10 p.m. B + D Coys went into billets at ERQUINGHEM two companies of the 13th Bn R.W.F. having occupied LA ROLANDRIE FARM temporarily. C + "A" Coys became the 5th & 6th Coys respectively.	

WAR DIARY
or
INTELLIGENCE SUMMARY.
(Erase heading not required.)

Army Form C. 2118.

Instructions regarding War Diaries and Intelligence Summaries are contained in F. S. Regs., Part II. and the Staff Manual respectively. Title pages will be prepared in manuscript.

Place	Date	Hour	Summary of Events and Information	Remarks and references to Appendices
	Oct 24th 1917		Battalion in Support. Days devoted to cleaning up	
	Oct 25th 1917		Baths and Company training.	
	Oct 26th 1917			
	Oct 27th 1917		The Battalion relieved the 15th Battn R.W.F. in the front line. Dispositions from the right. C. D. & A. Companies. B Coy 14th R.W.F. A Coy 15th Bn. R.W.F. and 'B' Coy 15th Bn R.W.F. & 4th, 5th & 6th Coys respectively. "A' Coy sent out a patrol of 1 Officer + other ranks to select a suitable point to make a trench board bridge across the stream running from T.26.b.65.70. to T.26.b.30.05. Point selected about 200 yards from T.26.b.65.70, where there are two or three stumps across the stream. Map reference T.26.b.50.40.	
	Oct 28th 1917.		Battalion in front line. "B' Coy sent out a patrol of 1 Officer and 4 other ranks from T.26.c.40.40. at 12.0 midnight, and reported enemy wire strong between T.32.a.90.90. and T.32.a.65.65.	

WAR DIARY
or
INTELLIGENCE SUMMARY.

(Erase heading not required.)

Army Form C. 2118.

Place	Date	Hour	Summary of Events and Information	Remarks and references to Appendices
	Oct 29 (cont'd)		and about 50 yards in depth with occasional gaps.	
	Oct 29th 1914		Battalion in front line. The moon was too bright to send out a large patrol. B + D Coys each sent out a small patrol 1 Officer + 3 other ranks to see if the enemy was repairing his wire with the object of bringing Artillery Stokes Mortars and Machine Gun fire to bear on the hostile parties. No hostile parties observed.	
	Oct 30th 1914		Battalion in front line. Small reconnoitring patrol sent by Right + Centre Coys. The Brudeau Salient was reconnoitred. Work continued on drainage, and new trench partly dug between BREWERY POST and BAY AVENUE.	
	Oct 31st 1914		Battalion in front line and were relieved at 7.30 pm by the 15th Bn R.W.F. B + D Coys went into Subsidiary line and A + C Coys to billets at ERQUINGHEM	

W Wilson
Major
Commanding
14th (S) Battalion
Royal Welsh Fusiliers

14th BATT. ROYAL WELSH FUSILIERS

WAR DIARY FOR NOVEMBER 1917

WAR DIARY
or
INTELLIGENCE SUMMARY.
(Erase heading not required.)

Army Form C. 2118.

Volume XXIV

Place	Date	Hour	Summary of Events and Information	Remarks and references to Appendices
Loos	1st 1917		Battalion in Support. Day devoted to clearing out Inspection of Kits and Box-respirators. Baths at Sailly Sur La Lys use allotted to 'A' Coy at 11·30 - 12 noon.	
			" " 'C' Coy at 3·0 - 4 pm.	
Loos	2nd 1917		Battalion in Support. Company training carried out in Erquinghem. Major W.S. Lloyd joined the Battalion for duty.	
Loos	3rd 1917		Battalion in Support. Company training at Erquinghem Lents. Cinema started 5 pm.	
Loos	4th 1917		Church Services at Erquinghem and Transport Lents. Battalion relieved 15th R.W.F. in the Front Line. Relief complete	
		7.30 pm.	Dispositions as follows.	
			'D' Coy Right Sub-sector	
			'A' Coy Centre " "	
			'B' Coy Left " "	
			'C' Coy Subsidiary Line.	
			A recruiting patrol left T.20.d.5.2. at 10 pm. - discovered	

A6945 Wt. W14422/M1160 350,000 12/16 D, D, & L. Forms/C./2118/14.

WAR DIARY
or
INTELLIGENCE SUMMARY.
(Erase heading not required.)

Army Form C. 2118.

Instructions regarding War Diaries and Intelligence Summaries are contained in F. S. Regs., Part II. and the Staff Manual respectively. Title pages will be prepared in manuscript.

Place	Date	Hour	Summary of Events and Information	Remarks and references to Appendices
	Nov. 4th (cont'd).		bridge at T.26.b.65.90, also an enemy O.P. at about T.26.b.75.05. A fighting patrol went out from T.31.c.45.45. at midnight and returned at T.31.c.9.4. at 1.50 a.m. No enemy patrols were encountered.	
	Nov. 5th 1917.		Battalion in front line. Fighting patrol left our lines at T.26.b.8.2. and T.26.d.20.65. Enemy wire found to be thick and continuous. O.P. located at T.26.b.75.05. No enemy patrols met. Patrol returned T.26.b.30.05 at 11.20 p.m. Reconnoitring patrol left our lines at T.32.a.1.9. at 11.50 p.m. returning at 1.45 a.m. at T.31.b.8.5. at 1.45 a.m. Enemy wire found thick and continuous.	
	Nov. 6th 1917.		Battalion in front line. Fighting patrol left our lines at T.31.b.6½.3½. at 10.0 p.m., returned at T.32.a.1½.9. at 12 midnight. No enemy patrols encountered.	
	Nov. 7th 1917.		Battalion in front line. Fighting and reconnoitring patrols sent out from T.31.a.10.50, and T.31.d.30.95. respectively. No enemy patrols encountered.	

WAR DIARY
or
INTELLIGENCE SUMMARY.
(Erase heading not required.)

Army Form C. 2118.

Place	Date	Hour	Summary of Events and Information	Remarks and references to Appendices
	Nov 8th 1917		Battalion was relieved in front line by 15th R.W.F. Relief complete 7.25 pm. After relief Companies took up dispositions as follows	
			A + C Coys Subsidiary line. B + D Coys Engungsm.	
	Nov 9th 1917		Day devoted to cleaning up kit, inspections and baths. Battalion in Support.	
	Nov 10 1917		Battalion in Support. B + D Coys carried on with Company training in the morning, and took over hutments in ROLANDRIE FARM from 13th Bn R.W.F. in the afternoon. A successful Concert held in the Cinema Engungsem in the evening. Divine Services C of E. & Roman Cath. + R.C. in the morning and the remainder of the day given to recreation.	
	Nov 11th 1917			
	Nov 12th 1917		Company training carried on by B + D Coys in the morning. In the evening this Unit relieved the 15th R.W.F in the front line Right Sub sector - relief being complete at 7.20 pm	

WAR DIARY
or
INTELLIGENCE SUMMARY.
(Erase heading not required.)

Army Form C. 2118.

Place	Date	Hour	Summary of Events and Information	Remarks and references to Appendices
	Nov 12th (contd)		Dispositions being 'A' Coy Right. 'B' Coy Centre. 'C' Coy Left and 'D' Coy Subsidiary Line. A fighting patrol went out from Left Coy under Lieut Doris, but met no enemy.	
	Nov 13th 1917		Battalion in front line. Enemy quiet, except for some snipers on the Right Coy front. A fighting patrol went out at 4.0 am to lie in wait for any enemy working party on INCREASE TRENCH at T.32.C.14. No working party found. Working parties found for work on Communication trenches - during the Subsidiary Line, Line and Company Headquarters.	
	Nov 14th 1917		Battalion in front line. Enemy quiet. Centre Coy sent out a patrol at 6 pm to lie in wait for any enemy working party at INCREASE TRENCH, which had been bombarded by our Artillery during the day, but no working party appeared. Work carried on as before.	
	Nov 15th 1917		Battalion in front line. Right Company sent out a fighting patrol to reconnoitre to damage done to INCREASE TRENCH	

WAR DIARY
or
INTELLIGENCE SUMMARY.
(Erase heading not required.)

Army Form C. 2118.

Place	Date	Hour	Summary of Events and Information	Remarks and references to Appendices
Nov 15th (cont).			and attack and enemy working parts on Galool. None front. and damage done to INCREASE TRENCH inconsiderable.	
	Nov. 16th 1917.		Battalion in front line relieved by 15th R.W.F. at 7.30 pm. "A" Coy when relieved went to ROLANDRIE FARM. and B & D Coys remained in Subsidiary Line. Battalion Headquarters went to ARTILLERY FARM. + CANTEEN FARM. Lt Colonel E.H.Q. Uniacke D.S.O. relieved from Brigade Class and resumed Command.	
	Nov 17th 1917.		The Coys at ROLANDRIE FARM. devoted the day to cleaning up and overhauls of Billets and Baths.	
	Nov 18th 1917		Dinner served to Col. E. Nonconformists M.E. Remainder of the day devoted to recreation.	
	Nov 19th 1917.		Rams allotted to Battalion at H.8.d.20.30. a. x Cens. rapid fire practice. C.Coy Ballot.	
	Nov 20: 1917		Conform training by "D" Coys in the morning at FROWN GM EM. Relieved 15th R.W.F. in the front line. Relief complete 6.40 pm.	

WAR DIARY
or
INTELLIGENCE SUMMARY.
(Erase heading not required.)

Army Form C. 2118.

Place	Date	Hour	Summary of Events and Information	Remarks and references to Appendices
Nov 20th	Guduecourt		Dispositions as follows: B Coy Right Sector; A Coy Centre Sector; D Coy left & A Coy in Support line. A Consolidating Patrol left I.31.b.55.25 to reconnoitre ditch from I.31.b.7. to I.31.d.30.85 at 12 midnight. Discovered duckboard across ditch at I.31.b.65.07 supported by sunken duckboard ditch about 3 ft wide at I.31.b.0.0. At I.31.d.4.9 two duckboard bridges about 10 yds apart across the ditch. Both infantry wire and Increase Trench impossible to see owing to Pine authorize and Increase Trench impossible to see owing to our fire on account of bombardment — all were broken by several small shell holes. The patrol left at I.31.d.30.95 at 5.35pm and returned at I.31.d.30.90. at 7.30 pm.	
Nov. 22nd 1917			Both infantry line. A patrol reconnoitred to reconnoitre front line East of junction of ditches at I.32.a.43.62. Enemy wire at I.32.a.55.61 is about 4 ft high & 2 ft deep. Ditch about 5 ft across & width makes about 2 feet deep.	

WAR DIARY or INTELLIGENCE SUMMARY

Army Form C. 2118.

Place	Date	Hour	Summary of Events and Information	Remarks and references to Appendices
	Nov. 22nd 1917		"A" Coy was relieved in dell section by 17 Bn C.E.F. The relief (evening) 1 known (unknown) was complete about 10.30 pm. A patrol (left PETER POST at 5.45 pm to examine effect of shoot on enemy wire in front of INCREASE TRENCH. A considerable amount observed working from left & right in front of enemy wire. Two M.G's been informed of and once opened fire. The patrol went out at I.31.d.30.95. Working parties seen at I.31.a.95.55. A patrol of 1 officer, 3 other ranks and 2 signallers was sent out at I.31.b.60.20 to reconnoitre INCREASE TRENCH and bring artillery fire to bear on any enemy parties found working on wire or parapets. No enemy parties observed.	
	Nov 23rd 1917		Battalion was relieved by 15" Batt. — relief complete at 7.40 pm. Patrol sent out from PENSAM POST at 4.40 pm to listen for movement in INCONSISTENT TRENCH at I.32.a.60.55. No movement heard. C.O. and (signal) was relieved at 4.45 pm from I.31.d.30.95.	

WAR DIARY
or
INTELLIGENCE SUMMARY.
(Erase heading not required.)

Army Form C. 2118.

Place	Date	Hour	Summary of Events and Information	Remarks and references to Appendices
	Nov 25th 1917		6 Inch Artillery put life line on enemy trench workup on wire in front of at INCREASE TRENCH at 1.32.c 15.93". Reports seen of head.	
	Nov 26th 1917		Divine Service. Afternoon to Wl Gration. Bn in Support. On training in morning. Recreation in afternoon.	
	Nov 27th 1917		Bn in Support. On training – Football Competition & boxing.	
	Nov 28th 1917		Continued in morning. Relieved the 15th Battn Royal Scots Regt, accupying new Bn Hdqrs at A.P.M vans. Sent out after relief at 4.30 am to reconnoitre state of enemy wire at 1.32.a.6.3.62. Outer belt of wire very thick about 4 ft high & 2 ft depth. Details about 40 yds from enemy wire were taken. Disposition of Coys : 'C' Coy. Right. 'D' Coy left. 'A' Coy Subordian.	
	Nov 29th 1917		Line MONT FARM and 'B' Coy Subordian. firing GIRLS' SCHOOL. Battn in front line. Two Patrols were sent out one at 6.0pm the other at 4.30 am to observe gaps in Enemy wire at 1.32.Q. 05.00 am to trup artillery & T.M. fire on any enemy working	

Place	Date	Hour	Summary of Events and Information	Remarks
	Nov 30: 1917		Parties - No hostile [illegible] at Not point had working parties located - about J.31.d. 60.50. by first patrol. T.M. officer in PETER Post was informed. T.M. fired 30 rounds. About 11.15 pm a heavy enemy bombardment [of] T.M's on left of Left Coy Post (PATRICK POST) + on Support line between KIWI & COLLEGE GREEN. Enemy raiding party seen a few minutes before bombardment opened. Germans quickly dispersed by L.G. fire + Artillery. Quiet [illegible] in No Man's Land. Battalion in trenches.	

Sgd Alexander
Lieut Col.
Comdg 14 Res Bn.

14th Batt Royal Welsh Fusiliers

Vol 25

War Diary for December 1917

25.C
11 weeks

WAR DIARY
or
INTELLIGENCE SUMMARY.
(Erase heading not required.)

Army Form C. 2118.

Place	Date	Hour	Summary of Events and Information	Remarks and references to Appendices
Field	1/12/17		PATROLS :- (1) One Officer & 8 ORs from I 32 a 15 90 at 2.30 am to reconnoitre and listen at I 32 a 63 62 and attack enemy patrols. No enemy patrol seen but his wire examined and found to be fairly consisting of knife rests bound together and thickly filled in. 'SOS' rocket took from PATRICK POST at 6.0 pm. Artillery opened ent. immediately on breek areas. Enemy heavy T.M. still active at intervals on our Left Support and BURNT FARM areas.	
			PATROLS (2) One Officer 10 ORs from I. 26 a 10 05 at 8.30 pm. to proceed along drain to I. 26 d 05 50 and be in wait for enemy patrols. Returned same point 10.35 pm having seen nothing. Enemy T.M.s and Artillery less active than usual.	
	2.12.17		PATROLS (1) 2nd Lieut J.G. Webb and 8 ORs left PETER POST 8.30 pm to watch gap in enemy wire at I.32 a 65.60 and to report enemy working parties on it. When about I. 31. d. 60 50 found enemy patrol to their right waiting for them. Enemy threw two stick bombs and our patrol attacked. A running fight took place with Bosch police which numbered about 15 men and one prisoner secured. Patrol returned 9.45 pm bringing back prisoner and three men wounded.	
			(2) One Officer and 5 ORs from PETER POST 11.0 pm to search for enemy wounded after their encounter wth (?) One enemy wounded found about I. 31. d. 6. 8 and brought to our	

WAR DIARY
or
INTELLIGENCE SUMMARY

Army Form C. 2118.

(Erase heading not required.)

Place	Date	Hour	Summary of Events and Information	Remarks and references to Appendices
	2/12/17		Line 12.30 A.m. - 3 rifles and 3 Steel bombs were also found. Enemy wounded died in our wire. (3) 1 Officer & O.R. from I 34 b 60.3. at 2.30 A.M. (3.12.17) to watch gap in enemy wire at I. 32 a 25.00 and to bring line to bear on any wiring party seen. Returned same point H. 25 fm having seen nothing of enemy.	
	3/12/17		Enemy TMs were active. Fires at intervals at WATER FARM and PENSAM POST. and on Left Support line. Relieves by 15th R.W.Fus - Completed 7.30 p.m. Dispositions. A & D Coys Subsidiary line - Park Row to left - (A Coy Left. - D Coy Right) B & C Coys Right Subsector Subsidiary ('C'Coy Right. 'B' Coy. Left.) Battalion in Subsidiary line. R.E. working parties found for work in SHAFTESBURY AVENUE, making 7 M.G. Emplacements , O.Ps and drainage.	
	4.12.17			
	5.12.17			
	6.12.17		Relieves 15th R.W.Fus. in front line in order "D" "A" "B" in line & 'C' Coy at Guers School in Support.	
	7.12.17	5. A.m.	Own heavy T.M.s in conjunction with Artillery opened on suspected enemy T.M. emplacement. Enemy retaliated heavy on Left Support and WATER FARM	
	8.12.17		Artillery & T.Ms (enemy) opened on BURNT FARM and TRAMWAY AVENUE about 3. P.m. PATROLS (1) 1 Officer 10 O.Rs from PENSAM Post at 6 O pm to reconnoitre enemy wire at I. 32 a 63. 62. and endeavour to locate enemy M.G. at the point. Returned I.32 a 10.90 at 7.45 pm having	

WAR DIARY
or
INTELLIGENCE SUMMARY.
(Erase heading not required.)

Army Form C. 2118.

Place	Date	Hour	Summary of Events and Information	Remarks and references to Appendices
	8/10/17		Found no trace of enemy.	
			(2) Under Special Brigade Defence Scheme as result of prisoners statement a 6/11/1917 was	
			enemy raid 2 L.G.s were put out near ditches at points I.31.d.50.75 and	
			I.31.b.62.12 - A Vickers gun was also fixed at I.31.b.70.22 and a L.G. at I.31.d.35.95	
			On approach of enemy 1 Officer + 20 men would go out into NO MANS LAND and line ditch between	
			L.G. & Vickers Gun. 3 Red Rockets to be fired and Artillery & T.M.s to open barrage 100 yards	
			in front of ditch.	
	9.12.17		Enemy Artillery active with 5.9's on TRAMLINE AVENUE in afternoon. His heavy T.M.s also	
			active on ~~Tramline Avenue~~ ~~afternoon~~ Violently took out as last night. No enemy seen	
			M.G.s Post given up on relief of Right Brigade by 2nd Dis~~n~~ C.E.F. An international	
			Post being held at the head of HUDSON BAY AVENUE.	
	10-12-17		Enemy Artillery shelled Tramline Avenue and left Coy Hqrs with 5.9s + H.25. Heavy	
			T.M.s also active during afternoon and strafing Jocks Joy and new work in HAYMARKET.	
			Work at BHQ on new track to road and Camouflaging. On the whole a quieter day.	
			L.G.s out as before.	
	11.12.17		6-0 AM Enemy opened heavy bombardment of T.M.s on front & support lines o	

WAR DIARY
or
INTELLIGENCE SUMMARY.
(Erase heading not required.)

Army Form C. 2118.

Place	Date	Hour	Summary of Events and Information	Remarks and references to Appendices
	11/12/17		found PATRICK PAN, KIWI and COLLEGE GREEN, and heavy artillery bombardment of TRAMLINE AVENUE and PARK RDN. - Signal dugout at Left Coy HQ blown in, and entrance to Headquarters blocked. CTs blocked in many places but no damage to posts. Gases at 6.30 A.M. Patrol from PATRICK to PAN found about 30 stick grenades in the trench at 1.20 a.m. 95.55 Enemy has entered the trench but retired quickly as our front & supports line LGs had opened out a steady fire onto the gap. NO-MANS-LAND - own artillery retaliated to S.O.S. PATRICK. Casualties 3 slightly wounded. Rest of day quiet. Relieved by 15th R.W.S Fus at 7.30 p.m. and went back to ERQUINGHEM. 'A' & 'B' Coys and Hdqrs in village and 'C' & 'D' Coys at ROLANDERIE.	
	12/12/17		Working Parties on new range and drainage. Cleaning up and Baths.	
	13/12/17		Company Training in morning and working parties as yesterday. Cross country run and football in afternoon. Boxing in evening.	
	14/12/17		Working parties as before in morning. Company training - football in afternoon between 'A' & 'C' Coys for final Company lead - Divisional Minstrels - gave a Concert in the Cinema in the evening.	
	15/12/17		Relieved 15th R.W.S.Fus. in front line in the order A, B, & C in the line & D Coy in Suffolk. Complete 7.15 pm	

WAR DIARY
or
INTELLIGENCE SUMMARY.
(Erase heading not required.)

Army Form C. 2118.

Instructions regarding War Diaries and Intelligence Summaries are contained in F.S. Regs., Part II. and the Staff Manual respectively. Title pages will be prepared in manuscript.

Place	Date	Hour	Summary of Events and Information	Remarks and references to Appendices
	15/1/7		D' Coy found to usual Brigade working parties for work in SHAFTESBURY C.T. Salvage etc. Night very quiet.	
	16/1/7	3.0 A.m.	A heavy bombardment opened on the Portuguese on our RIGHT and to area of BREWERY ROAD, BIRDCAGE WALK and t/j of GREATWOOD AVENUE to area and Intentional Post at t/j of BAY AVENUE (H 36 d 80 00) Enemy tried to raid Intentional Post at t/j of BAY AVENUE (H 36 d 80 00) but was driven off by rifle fire and did not enter our line although a few reached our parapet. One slightly wounded an officers patrol went out to seek identifications but found none. Liaison officers reported later that the Portuguese in the post retired to the support and then L.G. refused to open fire when asked by our attached N.C.O. This N.C.O. however and 3 men of 'A' Coy remained at their post and drove off enemy. 1 Officer & 8 o.rs left I 31 b 50 30 at 11.50 P.M. to reconnoitre gap at I.32 a 05 00. Returned 1.40 a.m. – No gap located Battalion in front line. Weather frosty. Situation very quiet.	
	17/1/7		Line tracks & between hooks. 1 Officer & 10 o.rs left PAN at 8.0 p.m. to locate enemy post between I 26 b 75 70 and I 26 d 50 90 and attack enemy patrols. Returned 10.0 p.m. reporting wire	

WAR DIARY
or
INTELLIGENCE SUMMARY
(Erase heading not required.)

Army Form C. 2118.

Place	Date	Hour	Summary of Events and Information	Remarks and references to Appendices
	17/2/17		Actively above points to be strong but located no post. M.G. at point I.26.b.89.35 (approx)	
	18/2/17		Quiet day - Enemy Battalion in front line.	
			PATROLS (1) 1 Officer & 4 ORs left PAUL POST 4 a.m. to reconnoitre supposed gap at I.32.a.05.00. Returned 5.45 a.m. having located no gap. No enemy movements seen	
			(2) 1 Sergt. 4 ORs left PATRICK at midnight to report whether enemy sap at I.26.b.4.1 was occupied. Returned 2 a.m. having failed owing to Irish nature of ground to approach sap.	
			Battalion in front line. Day quiet and cold.	
	19/2/17		PATROLS. (1) 1 Officer 9 ORs left PATRICK at 9 o'clock to ascertain if enemy sap head at I.26.b.40.10 was occupied. Returned same point 10.45 p.m. having met no enemy and reports sap head apparently not occupied.	
			(2) 1 Sergt. 3 ORs left PAUL at 2 a.m. to reconnoitre gap in enemy wire at I.32.a.05.00 and to bring fire to bear upon enemy working parties seen. Returned 3.50 a.m. reporting very bad visibility owing to ground mist - saw no enemy.	
	20/2/17		Relieved by 15th AusInf. - two Companies of Brigade with 3 Battalions in the Line (each with two Coys in front line and two in Subsidiary line).	

Army Form C. 2118.

WAR DIARY
or
INTELLIGENCE SUMMARY
(Erase heading not required.)

Instructions regarding War Diaries and Intelligence Summaries are contained in F. S. Regs., Part II. and the Staff Manual respectively. Title pages will be prepared in manuscript.

Place	Date	Hour	Summary of Events and Information	Remarks and references to Appendices
	26/7/17		Battalion settles in front SHAFTESBURY AVENUE to PARK ROW – both inclusive.	
			"B" Coy remains in the line but only mans PENSAM and PERCY front line posts. "A" Coy Headquarters was moved to SHAFTESBURY R.A.P. (I 25 a 95.60) took on connecting this "B" Coy Hdqrs. "D" Coy relieved "E" Coy on left and latter moved to QUATRE CHEMINS.	
			"A" Coy occupied Right Subsidiary line with Coy Hdqrs at ONE ASH.	
	27/7/17		"C" Coy bathed at QUATRE CHEMINS Baths and in evening relieved "A" Coy in Subsidiary line, latter moved back to QUATRE CHEMINS.	
			1 Officer + 4 ORs left PATRICK 12 midnight to ascertain whether hq. at I.26.b.90.10 is occupied. Returned same point 2.0 Am + reported hq. all empty.	
	28/7/17		Battalion in front line, very quiet day. Great air activity. Three planes brought down in flames about 3.0 pm as result of air fight. Shelled about I.32 c. 10 50. "A" Coy relieved "B" Coy on right Subsection and latter moved back to QUATRE CHEMINS.	
			1 Sergt. 6 ORs left I.32 a 85.12 at 10.5 pm to lie in wait for any enemy Patrols + report working parties in enemy line. Returned PATRICK 2.5 Am reporting no enemy seen.	
	29/7/17		Battalion in front line. Work on New Support Kitchen + LOGAN Villa in Subsidiary line.	

A6945 Wt. W1422/M1160 350,000 12/16 D. D. & L. Forms/C./2118/14.

WAR DIARY
or
INTELLIGENCE SUMMARY.

Army Form C. 2118.

Place	Date	Hour	Summary of Events and Information	Remarks and references to Appendices
	23/1/17		Lowing in front of SHAFTESBURY POST. Jocks Joy and LONDON BRIDGE, also left support line. Practice patrols sent out from both Companies.	
	24/1/17		Battalion in front line. 'B' Coy relieved 'A' Coy on right & 'C' Coy relieved 'D' Coy on left. 'A' & 'D' Coys came down to Subsidiary line with Hdqrs. at ONE ASH and LOGAN'S WOOD respectively - living. Left support and Bombing Posts. Have on duty Kitchen and fireships in subsidiary line. Patrol left PATRICK but met no enemy.	
	25/1/17		Battalion in front line - Snow - having continued by night of left support line and around BURNT Farm - Also light Company Bombing Posts - Track from JOCKS JOY to PENSKM continued. 1 Officer & 9 ORs left PATRICK Span to point I 26.d 15.50 and thence to I 26.C 85.05 returned same point 9.40 pm observing any special enemy movements (including Xmas festivities) having heard nothing - Their was bright moon and thick snow.	
	26/1/17		Battalion in front line 'A' & 'C' Coys relieved 'B' & 'D' Coys who came down to Subsidiary line - Day work in lines South Wildow and fireships in Subsidiary line - living in front of Subsidiary line by night. Also front bombing posts - 1 Officer, 1 American Officer & 9 ORs left PATROLLS at 10.30pm to reconnoitre ground in front of our own lines I 26.a 75.05 + I 26.a 97.60 & attack any enemy seen. Returned 11.10pm reporting Moon very bright & snow thick. No enemy patrols seen	

A6945 Wt. W14422/M1160 350,000 12/16 D. D. & L. Forms/C./2118/14.

WAR DIARY
or
INTELLIGENCE SUMMARY.
(Erase heading not required.)

Army Form C. 2118.

Place	Date	Hour	Summary of Events and Information	Remarks and references to Appendices
	29.12.17		Battalion in front line. Day quiet - night spent in continuation of wiring support line fronting both and front of BURNT FARM. Two Chinbury Erie Coys wired from I.25.b.40.95 to I.25.b.15.45 and I.19.d.50 to 6 TRAMLING AVENUE.	
	26.12.17		Battalion relieved by 15th R.W.Fus. after 16 latter had been relieved in Crlin Subsector by 12/R.W.Fus. - Relief Complete 8.0.p.m. - A + C. Coys moved back to FLEURBAIX area. D Coy. Relief complete H.1 10 A.1.1, "A" + "C" Coys Billets at RUE de la DORMIORE Dispositions "D" Coy. Farm H.1 10 A.1.1, "A" + "C" Coys Billets at RUE de la DORMIORE (H.9.c.4.6 to H.15.a.9.0) B. Coy. Battn.HQ at H.21.a.3.2.	
	29.12.17		Hostile shelling near Battalion HQ between 2.0pm + 3.30pm One direct hit with a H.2 shell on D. Coy billets resulting in 11 casualties, 7 of whom died. Officers dinner at B.HQ at 8.0pm	
	30.12.17		Battalion HQ moved to the two farms at H.15.C.45.25. "C" Coy moved to the two farms vacated by B.HQ. Working party of 250 men found during the day. D. + C. Coys had their Christmas dinner at 4.0pm	
	31.12.17		Working party of 200 men during the day. "B". + "A" Coys had their Christmas dinner at 3.0pm and 4.0pm respectively. Entertainment for the Battalion at Cinema ERQUINGHEM	

Army Form C. 2118.

WAR DIARY
or
INTELLIGENCE SUMMARY.
(Erase heading not required.)

Instructions regarding War Diaries and Intelligence Summaries are contained in F. S. Regs., Part II. and the Staff Manual respectively. Title pages will be prepared in manuscript.

Place	Date	Hour	Summary of Events and Information	Remarks and references to Appendices
	31/12/17		by WELSH WALLS at 6.0 pm.	

December 31st 1917

J. Vincent
Major
for Officer Comdg.
14th (S) Battalion
Royal Welsh Fusiliers

14th Batt. ROYAL WELSH FUSILIERS Vol 26

WAR DIARY.

FOR

JANUARY 1918.

J.H. 26.C.

Army Form C. 2118.

WAR DIARY
or
INTELLIGENCE SUMMARY.
(Erase heading not required.)

Instructions regarding War Diaries and Intelligence Summaries are contained in F. S. Regs., Part II. and the Staff Manual respectively. Title pages will be prepared in manuscript.

Place	Date	Hour	Summary of Events and Information	Remarks and references to Appendices
	Jan 1st/18		The Battalion relieved the 15th Bn R.W.F. in the Front Line Left Sub-Sector. Relief commenced at 4.30pm and was completed at 7.85 pm (Dispositions B & C Coys Right & Left Front Coys respectively. A & D Coys Right and Left Subsidiary Line Coys respectively.) Work done - Cable burying, carrying parties and wiring around LONDON BRIDGE. B Coy sent out a patrol of 1 N.C.O. & 3 men.	
	2/1/18		Battalion in Front Line. Own Artillery active (between 3.0pm & 4.0 pm.) Work done - Wire stopping Subsidiary line, carrying wiring material and wiring, erecting Baby elephant dug-outs in Right Coy Headquarters. C Coy sent out a fighting patrol from PATRICKS POST at 10.0 pm. No enemy patrols encountered.	
	3/1/18		Battalion in Front Line. Inter-Company relief A & D Coys relieving B & C Coys respectively. Hostile Artillery and Trench Mortars active on BURNT FARM and TRAMWAY AVENUE. No patrols sent out. Wiring carried out also revetting HAYMARKET.	

T2134. Wt. W708—776. 500000. 4/16. Sir J. C. & S.

WAR DIARY
or
INTELLIGENCE SUMMARY.
(Erase heading not required.)

Army Form C. 2118.

Place	Date	Hour	Summary of Events and Information	Remarks and references to Appendices
	4/1/18		Battalion in Front Line. A patrol of 1 Officer & 9 O.Rs leaving PATRICK POST at 10.0 p.m. and returning at 12.0 midnight - encountered no enemy patrols - works done - footstepping SUBSIDIARY LINE and erecting dug outs at Right Coy Headquarters	
	5/1/18		Battalion in Front Line. Inter Company relief B. C Coys. relieving A & D Coys. Hostile artillery fired about 12.7 p.m. Shells on PENSAM POST at 12.30 p.m. Patrol of 1 D.Co + 8 O.Rs. left PENSAM POST at 10.5 p.m. and returned at 11.55 p.m. having met no enemy patrols. Camouflage erected at the top of SHAFTESBURY AV. and bombing post on HAYMARKET at I 25 d. 20.55	
	6/1/18		Battalion in Front Line. Hostile Artillery fairly active on PENSAM POST. Camouflage erected in SHAFTESBURY AV. and wiring carried out during the night. B. Coy sent out a patrol. Battalion in Front Line Inter Company relief A + D Coys C	
	7/1/18		relieving B & C Coys. Patrol of 1 Officer & 8 O.Rs sent out by D. Coy from PAM POST at 10.0 p.m. to lie in wait at bridge in NO MANS	

Army Form C. 2118.

WAR DIARY
or
INTELLIGENCE SUMMARY.
(Erase heading not required.)

Instructions regarding War Diaries and Intelligence Summaries are contained in F.S. Regs., Part II. and the Staff Manual respectively. Title pages will be prepared in manuscript.

Place	Date	Hour	Summary of Events and Information	Remarks and references to Appendices
	7/1/18		LAND at I 26. b. 65. 65. No enemy seen. Patrols returned at 12. 0 midnight. Hostile Artillery active on PENSAM POST and LONDON BRIDGE between 3.0 pm & 4.0 pm.	
	8/1/18		Battalion in Front Line. About 8.30 pm a enemy hostile party attempted to raid PAN POST throwing two bombs into the Post. Raiding party withdrew on the Lewis Gun opening fire. A fighting patrol went out immediately but discovered no trace of the enemy.	
	9/1/18		Battalion in Front Line. Inter-Company relief "B" & "C" Coys relieving "A" & "D" Coys. Hostile Mortars active on Support Line and Joe's Joy. Patrol sent out from PERCY POST at 8.0 pm to lie in wait for hostile raiding party at I 26 a. 90. 70. No enemy seen. — Works:- repairing trenches damaged by hostile trench Mortars, and preparing trenches for all round defence of B.H.Q.	
	10/1/18		Battalion in Front Line. Hostile trench Mortars very active during the day and up to midnight. Considerable material damage done to COLLEGE GREEN, TRAMWAY AVENUE, SUPPORT LINE & PATRICK day	

T2134. Wt. W708—776. 500000. 4/15. Stv J. C. & S.

WAR DIARY
or
INTELLIGENCE SUMMARY.
(Erase heading not required.)

Army Form C. 2118.

Place	Date	Hour	Summary of Events and Information	Remarks and references to Appendices
	10/8		At 4.30 am a patrol was sent out from P.W. POST to select a spot invisible from our front line but visible from the enemy front line, and a defensive position for a Lewis Gun to cover this spot. Position selected I.26.b.30.15. - Work:- repairing trenches. Battalion in front line.	
	11/8		Relieving "B" & "C" Coys. At 3.30 am the enemy opened a heavy trench mortar bombardment on our right boy front and on the front of the 15th Bn R.W.Fus. on our right. Hostile party attempting to raid left post of 15th Bn R.W.Fus. was dispersed. Between 9.30 am & 11.0 am and 6.0 pm & 7.0 pm the enemy bombarded with trench mortars the left Company front especially the Support Line, doing considerable material damage. Patrol sent out from P.W. POST encountered no enemy. All available labour devoted to repairing trenches. Battalion in front line. Considerable hostile trench mortar	
	12/8		activity on left Company front, especially between 9.0am & 9.45am. when about 70 heavy trench mortars were fired, and from 7.20 pm	

T2134. Wt. W708—776. 500000. 4/15. Sir J.C. & S.

WAR DIARY
or
INTELLIGENCE SUMMARY.
(Erase heading not required.)

Army Form C. 2118.

Place	Date	Hour	Summary of Events and Information	Remarks and references to Appendices
	12/1/18	10.0.15 pm	shew the bombardment became very intense, doing considerable material damage. A patrol was sent out from PAN POST but encountered no hostile parties. All available labour put on repairing trenches. A dummy figure was placed at I.26.b.40.25. which position had been selected on 10th instant.	
	13/1/18		Battalion in front line. Hostile bench Mortars fired a few rounds on left Coy. front but were very quiet compared with the previous four days. Work - repairing trenches. At 5.0 pm a fighting patrol was sent out to lie in wait for the enemy near the dummy figure which had been put out at I.26.b.40.25. on the 12th. No enemy appeared and the dummy was brought in at 6.20 pm.	
	14/1/18		Battalion in front line, relieved by 6th Batt (Queens) R. West Surrey Regiment. Relief complete at 8.0 pm Battalion marched to BRUAY at BAC ST MAUR.	
	15/1/18	9.30 am	Battalion marches from BAC St MAUR to ROBERMETZ starting at 9.30 am	

WAR DIARY
or
INTELLIGENCE SUMMARY.
(Erase heading not required.)

Army Form C. 2118.

Instructions regarding War Diaries and Intelligence Summaries are contained in F. S. Regs., Part II. and the Staff Manual respectively. Title pages will be prepared in manuscript.

Place	Date	Hour	Summary of Events and Information	Remarks and references to Appendices
	16/8		Day devoted to cleaning up and baths.	
	17/8		Progressive programme of training comprising Musketry, close order drill and Physical Training & Bayonet fighting commenced.	
	18/8		Company training.	
	19/8		Company training.	
	20/8		Church parade.	
	21/8		Company training. The Battalion paraded at 11.0am for the Comdg. Officers inspection.	
	22/8		Company training. Inter Company tug of War competition - won by B Coy.	
	23/8		Company training. The Brigade Commander Lt. Col. J.B. Cockburn inspected the billets and the Companies during training.	
	24/8		Company training. "C" "D" Coys on the range.	
	25/8		Company training - mainly Musketry. A Coy on range.	
	26/8		Company training - Musketry, Bayonet fighting & Close Order drill, C & D Coys on range.	
	27/8		Divine Services for C & E.. Non-conformists & R.Cs. "C" Coy. plays	

Army Form C. 2118.

WAR DIARY
or
INTELLIGENCE SUMMARY.
(Erase heading not required.)

Instructions regarding War Diaries and Intelligence Summaries are contained in F. S. Regs., Part II. and the Staff Manual respectively. Title pages will be prepared in manuscript.

Place	Date	Hour	Summary of Events and Information	Remarks and references to Appendices
	27/8		"A" Coy 13th Rustro. at Association Football in the Divisional Recreation Programme and 1st were beaten 1 goal - nothing.	
	28/8		Company training - Musketry Bayonet & Close Order drill A & B Coys on range	
	29/8		Company training - Subject to Baths for all Coys. 'B' Coy on Billet + Bayonet Course in the Forest of Nieppe.	
	30/8		Company training - Musketry Bayonet Close Order - C & D Coys on range. "A" Coy Team entered for Brigade Cross Country run & came in second. "B" Coy won tug of war event.	
	31/8		Company training "D" Coy on range. euphedies by Major General Blackader, G.O.C. Division	

W.C.Webs
Major for off Comdg
13th Rutmulars

T2134. Wt. W708—776. 500000. 4/15. Sir J. C. & S.

Vol 27

27.C.
7 sheets

War Diary.

14th Battalion Royal Welch Fusrs.

February 1918.

Army Form C. 2118.

WAR DIARY
or
INTELLIGENCE SUMMARY.
(Erase heading not required.)

Instructions regarding War Diaries and Intelligence Summaries are contained in F. S. Regs., Part II. and the Staff Manual respectively. Title pages will be prepared in manuscript.

Place	Date	Hour	Summary of Events and Information	Remarks and references to Appendices
	Feb. 1st/18	10 a.m	The Battalion paraded at 10 a.m. in the following order Battalion HQ, C, A & B Coys and marched to GUARBECQUE arriving there at 2.30pm where the Unit was billets for the night.	
	2/18	8 a.m	The Battalion paraded at 8 HQ and at GUARBECQUE in the following order. Adjut, D, A, B, C, Coys and marched to billets at ST HILAIRE COTTES arriving there at 12.30 p.m	
	3/18		Divine Service held in the morning for C of E. Nonconformists & RCs and the afternoon devoted to Recreational Training	
	4/18		Coys training. A & B Coys on the range and all Coy Lewis Gunners, all Coys carry on Close Order Drill and Bayonet fighting, paying special instruction to musketry.	
	5/18		Coys training for all Coys except A Coy which was detailed for work on the Bullet & Bayonet Course "B" & "A" Coys on the range	
	6/18		The whole Battalion paraded at 10.30 am at the range at T 15 a to observe a demonstration in Platoon drill and tactical exercise by a platoon of the HAC (Royal Fusiliers)	

T2134. Wt. W708-776. 500000. 4/15. Sir J. C. & S.

WAR DIARY
or
INTELLIGENCE SUMMARY.
(Erase heading not required.)

Army Form C. 2118.

Place	Date	Hour	Summary of Events and Information	Remarks and references to Appendices
	6/18		In the afternoon at 2.30 the Battalion also paraded to watch a demonstration in Musketry instruction and practice by the Lewis platoon. During the day 6 Officers and about 100 men from the 15th Rifle Brigade (now Pioneers) reported to this Unit and were posted to Companies.	
	7/18		Coys. training owing to bad weather, much of the training was carried on indoors. In the afternoon the Battalion Rugby football team played the 16th Rif. and was beaten & had to nothing.	
	8/18		Lt Col Cust P Uniacke DSO surrendered to Hospital - Major W.P. Kelson DSO assumed command of the Battalion vice Lt Col Cust P Uniacke DSO. Coy. working on B & B Guards - Coy. lisening to in morning "C" Coy. during afternoon.	
	9/18		Coy. training. Inter Company Competitions held:- Cooking - won by A Coy. Runners won by A Coy.	
	10/18		Divine Services held during the morning. Capt E Nonconformists + R.C.	

WAR DIARY
or
INTELLIGENCE SUMMARY.
(Erase heading not required.)

Army Form C. 2118.

Place	Date	Hour	Summary of Events and Information	Remarks and references to Appendices
	11/7/18		Coy having A + B Coys on Bw [?] Range. Inter-Company Competitions held:-	
			Bombing . . . . D Coy.	
			B. Coy . . . . Best Shots	
			Lewis Gunners . . . . C Coy. — Rifle Bombing . . . B Coy.	
			. . . . — Riflemen . . . . A Coy.	
	12/7/18		Coy having C + D Coys on 300 yds range	
			Finish of Brigade Competitions. Battalion won following Competitions. Shelter Beavers, Lewis Gunners & Best Coshing Band	
	13/7/18		Battalion paraded at 9.15 am and in the following order, Band, H.Q. A. B. C. & D Coys and marched to GUARBECQUE arriving there at 12.30 pm where the Unit was billeted for the night.	
	14/7/18		The Battalion paraded at GUARBECQUE at 9.30 am in the following order, Band, H.Q. B.C. & D Coys and marched to NEUF BERQUIN arriving at 1.30 pm where the Unit was billeted for the night.	
	15/7/18		The Battalion paraded at NEUF BERQUIN at 9.30 am in the following order, H.Q. B. A Coys. & C Coys and marches to	

WAR DIARY
or
~~INTELLIGENCE~~ SUMMARY.
(Erase heading not required.)

Army Form C. 2118.

Instructions regarding War Diaries and Intelligence Summaries are contained in F. S. Regs., Part II. and the Staff Manual respectively. Title pages will be prepared in manuscript.

Place	Date	Hour	Summary of Events and Information	Remarks and references to Appendices
	15/7/18		WATERLANDS CAMP (Brigade Reserve) arriving at 1.15 pm	
	16/7/18		Coy training "A" Coy on range - A Coy "Slans to" Company	
	17/7/18		Divine Services during morning - Cpl E Nonconformists. Major J Williams DSO assumed Command of Battalion vice Major WP Whalen DSO. Evacuated to hospital.	
	18/7/18		Battalion in Reserve at Waterlands Camp. Coy training + musketry carries out during the day	
	19/7/18		The Battalion relieves the Honorable Artillery Coy in Support at the Querries ERQUINGHEM.	
	20/7/18		Battalion in Support at the Querries. Training from 9.30 am to 12.30 pm	
	21/7/18		As on previous day.	
	22/7/18		The Battalion moves from the Querries to a new Support position near H 5 b 9 8. Dispositions B.Q. Asylum. "C" Coy Subsidiary Line A + B Coys billets near A 5 a 9 6.	
	23/7/18		The Battalion relieves the 16th Royal West Surrey Bn in the front line	

T2134. Wt. W708—776. 500000. 4/15. Sir J. C. & S.

WAR DIARY
or
INTELLIGENCE SUMMARY.
(Erase heading not required.)

Army Form C. 2118.

Place	Date	Hour	Summary of Events and Information	Remarks and references to Appendices
	23/7/18		Of the ARMENTIERES Sector from LEITH WALK to AUSTRALIA TRENCH. Dispositions: A Coy Right Front Coy. D. Coy Left Front Coy. B+C Coys right & left Subsidiary line Coys respectively. Relief Complete 8.15 a.m. A Coy sent out a patrol.	
	24/7/18		Battalion in front line. C. Coy sent out a patrol at 10.0 P.M. to reconnoitre the approaches to 1 N ANE Row. 1.5.B.20.50.	
	25/7/18		At 3.30 am the enemy opened out a heavy trench mortar & artillery barrage along the Batt. front which was very intense on the Right Coy. front especially about 1.16.B.90.15. The enemy ⟨deleted⟩ raided the 23 Post on the Left Coy Sector at 3.30 a.m. with a party of 2 Officers 60 other ranks and two machine guns. Hand to hand fighting ensued in the Post and our Casualties were 4 missing and 3 wounded. One dead and one wounded prisoner were left in our lines. According to the prisoners statements the intention of the raiders was to capture four of our posts to be Evel Annecta Co. delivered	

Army Form C. 2118.

WAR DIARY
or
INTELLIGENCE SUMMARY.
(Erase heading not required.)

Instructions regarding War Diaries and Intelligence Summaries are contained in F. S. Regs, Part II. and the Staff Manual respectively. Title pages will be prepared in manuscript.

Place	Date	Hour	Summary of Events and Information	Remarks and references to Appendices
	25/7/18		from Hospital. All available labour was put on wiring front posts and repairing damage done to trenches.	
	26/7/18		Battalion in front line. Work as on previous day. D Coy sent out a patrol from No 6 Post at 1.5 a.m. 2nd Lt Major W.P. Whelan DSO. returned from Hospital.	
	27/7/18		The Battalion was relieved in the front line by 13th Bn R.W. Fus. Relief Complete 6.30 pm. Battalion marched to Reserve in ERQUINGHEM.	
	28/7/18		The day was devoted to cleaning up and kit inspections. A Coy found working party of 100 men.	

25/7/18

WB Edwards Capt & Adjt

for Major & OC Coy
14th (S) Battalion
Royal Welsh Fusiliers

Vol 28

28.C
8 sheets

14TH. BATTN ROYAL WELSH FUSILIERS.

WAR DIARY

FOR

MARCH - 1918

WAR DIARY
or
INTELLIGENCE SUMMARY.
(Erase heading not required.)

Army Form C. 2118.

Place	Date	Hour	Summary of Events and Information	Remarks and references to Appendices
	March 1st 1918		Battalion in Reserve in ERQUINGHEM. RE working parties found during the day. St David's Day dinner for all Companies.	
	March 2nd 1918		Battalion in Reserve RE Working parties found during the day	
	March 3rd 1918		The Battalion relieved 13th Bn RWF in Front line Dispositions after relief :- B Coy Right front. C Coy Left front. A Coy Right Subsidiary D Coy Left Subsidiary. B Coy sent out a Patrol from I.10.b.9.0.20 at 10.30 p.m.	
	March 4th 1918		Battalion in front line. All the men of the Subsidiary Companies were on Brigade RE Working parties during the tour in the line. C Coy sent out a patrol from I.5.a.50.80. at 11.50 p.m. No enemy seen or heard.	
	March 5th 1918		Battalion in front line. Patrol of 1 Officer and 7 O.Rs sent out from I.S.a.55.40 at 1.0 am, found no traces of the enemy in No Man's Land.	
	March 6th 1918		Battalion in front line. A & D Coys relieved B & C Coys respectively. Heavy hostile shelling on the Battalion sector and several	

WAR DIARY
or
INTELLIGENCE SUMMARY.

(Erase heading not required.)

Army Form C. 2118.

Place	Date	Hour	Summary of Events and Information	Remarks and references to Appendices
	March 6th (contd)		Gas shells near Battalion headquarters. "C" Coy sent out a patrol from I.5.a.50.30 at 1.25am to endeavour to locate hostile listening post at about I.5.08.45. Patrol was under the command of 2Lt N.P.VANDERBIJT, and when it got to I.5.a.80.10 a low whistle was heard and a working party in the enemy lines opposite suddenly ceased work. Patrol lay in wait for a time, and then withdrew.	
	March 7th		Battalion in front line. Heavy hostile shelling on Battalion front. Two Officers of the 38th Sniping Coy. seriously wounded in a dug-out near Battn. Hdqrs. "A" Coy sent out a patrol of 8 O.Rs under the command of 2Lt L.D.Williams O.C.M. from I.10.b.95.30 at 3.0 am. Whilst our patrol was still in our own wire it was fired at from our own left flank range and bombed by a hostile patrol or raiding party of about 25. Hand to hand fighting ensued, and the enemy withdrew. Our casualties were one killed and three wounded, who were	

WAR DIARY
or
INTELLIGENCE SUMMARY.
(Erase heading not required.)

Army Form C. 2118.

Place	Date	Hour	Summary of Events and Information	Remarks and references to Appendices
	March 8th (contd) March 8/1/1918		brought in after the hostile patrol was chased with fire. Battalion in front line. Heavy shelling on the Battalion Sector by hostile Guns and Trench Mortars. Patrol of 9 O.Rs left our lines at 15.a.60.70 at 3:30 a.m. under the command of 2/Lt F.E. LEYSHON, but returned after finding no enemy in NO MAN'S LAND.	
	March 9th 1918.		Battalion in front line. A hostile raid on our Right Coy. having been suspected, fire front line Coys on the Right Coy. Sector were withdrawn to the Support line, and listening posts were sent forward. The Battalion was relieved by the 13th Bn R.W.F. and moved into Support with Battn Hdqrs and 'A' Coy in huts near H.6.A.10.90. "B" Coy in the BRICKFIELD at I.8.b.20.65. 'C' Coy in Cellars near SACRE COEUR CHURCH. c.26.d.25. and 'D' Coy in the Asylum I.2.a.40.20.	
	March 10th 1918.		Battalion in Support. News received of a hostile raid on the	

T2134. Wt. W708—776. 500000. 4/15. Sir J.C. & S.

WAR DIARY
or
INTELLIGENCE SUMMARY.
(Erase heading not required.)

Army Form C. 2118.

Place	Date	Hour	Summary of Events and Information	Remarks and references to Appendices
	March 10th 1918 (Cont'd)		Left Coy Sector of the 13th Bn R.W.F. with total casualties of 34. In view of a probable hostile attack, Major W.P. Whelden D.S.O. two Coy. Commanders and a proportionate detail of Specialist from each platoon were sent back to Brigade School.	
	March 11th 1918.		Battalion in support. In view of the impending attack B.H.Q. moved up to ASYLUM, and 'A' Coy to cellars near SACRÉ COEUR CHURCH.	
	March 12th 1918.		Battalion in Support. Lt. Col. E.W.P. Murcacke D.S.O. left for Brigade School owing to ill-health and Major W.P. Whelden D.S.O. assumed of command of the Battalion	
	13/3/18 to 19/3/18.		Battalion in Support. All men working on R.E. parties. Officers reconnoitring positions for the defence of the CROSS out and the ASYLUM, + FME. DES. JARDINS Sectors. The enemy displayed a great deal of activity with Gas Shells during this period	
	20/3/18		Battalion relieved the 16th Bn R.W.Fus. in the front line. Dispositions after relief 'B' + 'C' Coys. Right + Left front Coys. respectively	

WAR DIARY
or
INTELLIGENCE SUMMARY.
(Erase heading not required.)

Army Form C. 2118.

Place	Date	Hour	Summary of Events and Information	Remarks and references to Appendices
	March 20th (cont'd)		'A' & 'B' Coys. Right & Left Subsector line Coys. 'C' Coy sent out a fighting patrol. No enemy encountered.	
	March 21st 1918.		Battalion in front line. 'B' & 'C' Coys sent out fighting patrols but both returned having encountered no enemy.	
	March 22nd 1918.		Battalion in front line. The enemy carried out a silent raid on No 14 Post at 1.40 am on the 22nd/23rd. Wounding 1 NCO and the enemy captured this man and a Lewis Gun. One of our men was killed. At 4.45 am the enemy attempted to raid No 9 Post with a party 40/50 strong but the raiders were completely repulsed by Lewis Gun fire from Posts 8 & 11.	
	March 23rd 1918.		Battalion in front line. 'B' Coy sent out a patrol, 1 Officer and 9 men to search the ground between Posts 1 & 3 Posts and to give warning of any attempted hostile raid. Patrol went out at 12.0 midnight and returned at 5.0 am. No enemy encountered.	
	March 24th 1918.		Battalion was relieved by the 13th Bn R.W. Fus., and after relief came into reserve, with Battn H.Q. = 'B' Coy in huts near M.6.a.10.90.	

Army Form C. 2118.

WAR DIARY
or
INTELLIGENCE SUMMARY.
(Erase heading not required.)

Instructions regarding War Diaries and Intelligence Summaries are contained in F. S. Regs., Part II. and the Staff Manual respectively. Title pages will be prepared in manuscript.

Place	Date	Hour	Summary of Events and Information	Remarks and references to Appendices
	March 24th (cont'd)		A, B & C Coys in the Laundries ERQUINGHEM.	
	March 25th 1918		Battalion in Reserve. All the men being employed on Divisional working parties.	
	March 26th 1918		Re-distribution of the Divisional front took place, so as to have two Brigades holding the line and one in reserve. The Battalion moved into the Laundries H.5.a.50.70. and furnish part of the troops Reserve. All men on night working parties.	
	March 27th 1918		Battalion in Corps Reserve. All men on night working parties, and two hours Company training by day.	
	March 28th 1918		Battalion in Corps Reserve. All men on night working parties and two hours Company training by day.	
	March 29th 1918		The Battalion was relieved by 15th Battn Royal Scots of the 34th Division. Battalion marched into Billets at VIEUX BERQUIN arriving at 8.5 p.m.	
	March 30th 1918		The Battalion moved to the STEENBECQUE Area by lorry, leaving VIEUX BERQUIN at 8.0 p.m.	

WAR DIARY
or
INTELLIGENCE SUMMARY.

(Erase heading not required.)

Place	Date	Hour	Summary of Events and Information	Remarks and references to Appendices
March 31st	1918		Battalion in huts in STEENBEEQUE. Divine Service during morning. Major B. Wellin's 8 hrs. assumed command of the Battalion vice Lt Col P.M. Unwood who handed over sick.	

W Wold
Major 2. So.
1st(s) Battalion
Royal Welsh Fusiliers

113th Inf.Bde.
38th Div.

WAR DIARY

14th BATTN. THE ROYAL WELCH FUSILIERS.

A P R I L

1 9 1 8

1st Battalion R.W. Fus.

Vol 29

War Diary
April 1918

E.M. 29.C.

Army Form C. 2118.

WAR DIARY
or
INTELLIGENCE SUMMARY.
(Erase heading not required.)

Place	Date	Hour	Summary of Events and Information	Remarks and references to Appendices
	April 1st 1918.		The Battalion with all transport entrained at STEENBECQUE Station at 8.0 a.m. and proceeded by train to DOULLENS and from there marched to TOUTENCOURT arriving there at 9.30 p.m. 'A' Coy. was detailed to loading party at STEENBECQUE for the Brigade, and did not arrive at TOUTENCOURT until the following day at 9.0 a.m.	
2. H. 18.			A reconnoitring party of 2 Officers + 2 runners per Coy (less 'A' Coy) under Major Wheldon D.S.O. left TOUTENCOURT at 9.0 a.m and proceeded to ENGLEBERMER to take over dispositions of the 2nd Division in that Sector, this Unit to be Battalion in Reserve upon relief. On arrival it was found that this Unit would relieve the 6th Brigade at ENGLEBERMER. Ultimately all orders for relief were cancelled, and the Battalion which had left TOUTENCOURT at 1.0 p.m. and arrived at FORCEVILLE at 3.30 p.m. were ordered to march back the following day to TOUTENCOURT whilst at FORCEVILLE the billets were shelled and the Adjutant + 2 other ranks were wounded.	
3. 4. 18.			The Battalion paraded at 7.15 a.m. and marched to TOUTENCOURT.	

WAR DIARY
or
INTELLIGENCE SUMMARY.
(Erase heading not required.)

Army Form C. 2118.

Place	Date	Hour	Summary of Events and Information	Remarks and references to Appendices
3.4.18 (contd)			and reached Billets Here at 10.15 am	
H.H.18			A very wet morning, and a Brigade tactical Scheme ordered for the morning had to be postponed. The Companies carried on with Musketry in Billets in the morning, and Company training was continued in the afternoon	
5.4.18			Company training carried on in Musketry carried on in the morning, but on return to billets at noon, orders were received to march forthwith to CONTAY. This was done and four Battle Surplus detail were withdrawn to TOUTENCOURT. First line transport remained with the Battalion, which bivouaced that night in a field adjacent to CONTAY, being in support to an Australian Division	
6.4.18			The Battalion remained at CONTAY until 4.0 pm when orders were received to move to RUBEMPRE area. The Battle detail proceeded to the Battalion. Billets were found at MIRVAUX and the whole Battalion was in billets by 9.0 pm	

WAR DIARY
INTELLIGENCE SUMMARY

Army Form C. 2118.

Place	Date	Hour	Summary of Events and Information	Remarks and references to Appendices
	7.4.18.		Church of England, R.C. & Nonconformist Services were held, and reconnaissances of the area N. & S. by Officers.	
	8.4.18		The day spent on a Brigade field exercise involving the selection and laying out of a bivouac camp and an Outpost scheme.	
	9.4.18.		The day spent on a Brigade field exercise involving an advance forward in Artillery formation, the taking up of an outpost line after attack and an enemy Counter attack.	
	10.4.18		The Battalion received orders to move forward and leaving MIRVAUX at 1.30 p.m. The Unit marched to bivouac at HARPONVILLE and blazed the night there. Reconnoitring parties went forward to SENLIS and BOUZINCOURT areas to view the forward positions.	
	11.4.18		Battle details (Surplus) under Major Whildon marches to CONTAY and VADENCOURT. The Battalion relieved the 6th Royal West Kents in support to the front line. Relief complete 2.45. a.m. (12/4/18)	

WAR DIARY or INTELLIGENCE SUMMARY.

Army Form C. 2118.

Place	Date	Hour	Summary of Events and Information	Remarks and references to Appendices
	12/7/15		SUPPORT DISPOSITIONS:- A Coy and H.Q. - W. 13. a. S. 8.; B Coy. - V. 24. t. C & D Coy. W. 13. d. Battalion in Support - working and wiring parties	
	13/7/15		Ditto	
	14/7/15		Ditto	
	15/7/15		Relieves 16th R.W.Fus in left Battn. front line. Dispositions B on left (W. 15 a + c) A Coy Centre (W. 15. c) C. Coy Right (W. 21. a) D Coy. Batt. Reserve (W. 14. t) Relief complete 11.30pm Battalion in front lines. All Companies in front sent out small reconnoitring patrols Ditto	
	16/7/15		Ditto	
	17/7/15			
	18/7/15		Relieved by 17th R.W.Fus. - Relief complete about 1.0 AM (19 & 18) Battalion moved back into position of Brigade in Reserve (W. 16. d.)	
	19/7/15		General cleaning up. Two Companies A + B on night working parties C + D Coys practises the attack, moving in Artillery formation over a replica	
	20/7/15		in view of the impending operations. A + B Coys on night working parties.	
	21/7/15		"C" + "D" Coys again practised the attack in morning. Compulsory rest for all during afternoon.	

Place	Date	Hour	Summary of Events and Information	Remarks and references to Appendices
	21/8		The Battalion relieved part of 17th Rus Fus, and part of 17th Battalion Royal Scots in front line. Dispositions "C" on Right "D" on left. A + B Coys in reserve. Relief complete 2.30 am (22 it 18) (Maps attached)	
	22/8		The 113th Inf Bde attacked. Zero hour 7.20 pm. Dispositions as per attached maps. Two Companies "C" + "D" moved forward in their waves at Zero hour at which time "B" Coy moved up and occupied the line vacated - Battn H.Q. + "A" Coy remained stationary. Our own barrage was somewhat ragged, the enemy put down a barrage very quickly near our front line. Their machine gun barrage was very accurate on our advancing lines and casualties were heavy. Neither Company reached their first objective but were held up, in a line about 150 yards in front of our original line. The 17th Rus Fus left flank only reached the auxiliary line. Consequently "C" Coy was withdrawn to the original line, "D" Coy was relieved by a platoon of "B" Coy. in their line of shell holes about 150 x ahead of our original line, and liaison was made with the 19th D.L.I. on the left	

WAR DIARY
or
INTELLIGENCE SUMMARY.
(Erase heading not required.)

Army Form C. 2118.

Place	Date	Hour	Summary of Events and Information	Remarks and references to Appendices
	22/4/18		During the action one officer 2nd Lt HUXLEY was killed. 2nd Lieut L. RICHARDS died of wounds and 2nd Lieut J.G. Holt and 2nd Lt. M. Evans were wounded. 2/Lt Elias JONES (R.O.M., M.M.(Bar)) died of wounds. The casualties among other ranks were 5 killed 95 wounded and 14 missing.	
	23/4/18		Battalion relieved in their sector of the front line by 18th Lanc. Regt. On completion of relief the dispositions were as follows. Battn H.Q. + A Coy W 14 b. B Coy Support line in W 14 d. C + D Coys in bank at W 13 d.	
	24/4/18		Battalion in Support. About 4.30 am the enemy counter-attacked the 13th K.L.Pho S.O.S signals were put up and repeated back to Brigade. The counter attack was repulsed and the Battalion was not called upon to move.	
	25/4/18		Battalion in Support. Relieved by 2nd Res. Pro Relief complete about 3.0 am (26.4.18) when Battalion moved to positions in W. 16. d.	
	26/4/18		Battalion in reserve, cleaning up and resting.	
	27/4/18		Battalion fell in at 6.25 am in following order Rho. L.G.B.R. and marches to HERRISART arriving there at 10-a.m. Remainder	

Army Form C. 2118.

WAR DIARY
or
INTELLIGENCE SUMMARY.
(Erase heading not required.)

Place	Date	Hour	Summary of Events and Information	Remarks and references to Appendices
	27/1/18		day devoted to cleaning up.	
	28/1/18		Divine services in morning. C/SE. Uninformed & R.C.	
	29/1/18		morning devoted to reorganisation of Companies. Lewis Gun training in the afternoon. the Battalion did an exercise in attack formations	
	30/1/18		Company training. A & B Coys. on the range in the morning. Lewis Gun class continued. Lecture in Major reading by the C.O. to Officers and N.C.O. in the afternoon.	

L Welden
Major for t/c
4th (S) Battalion
Royal Welsh Fusiliers

Map A

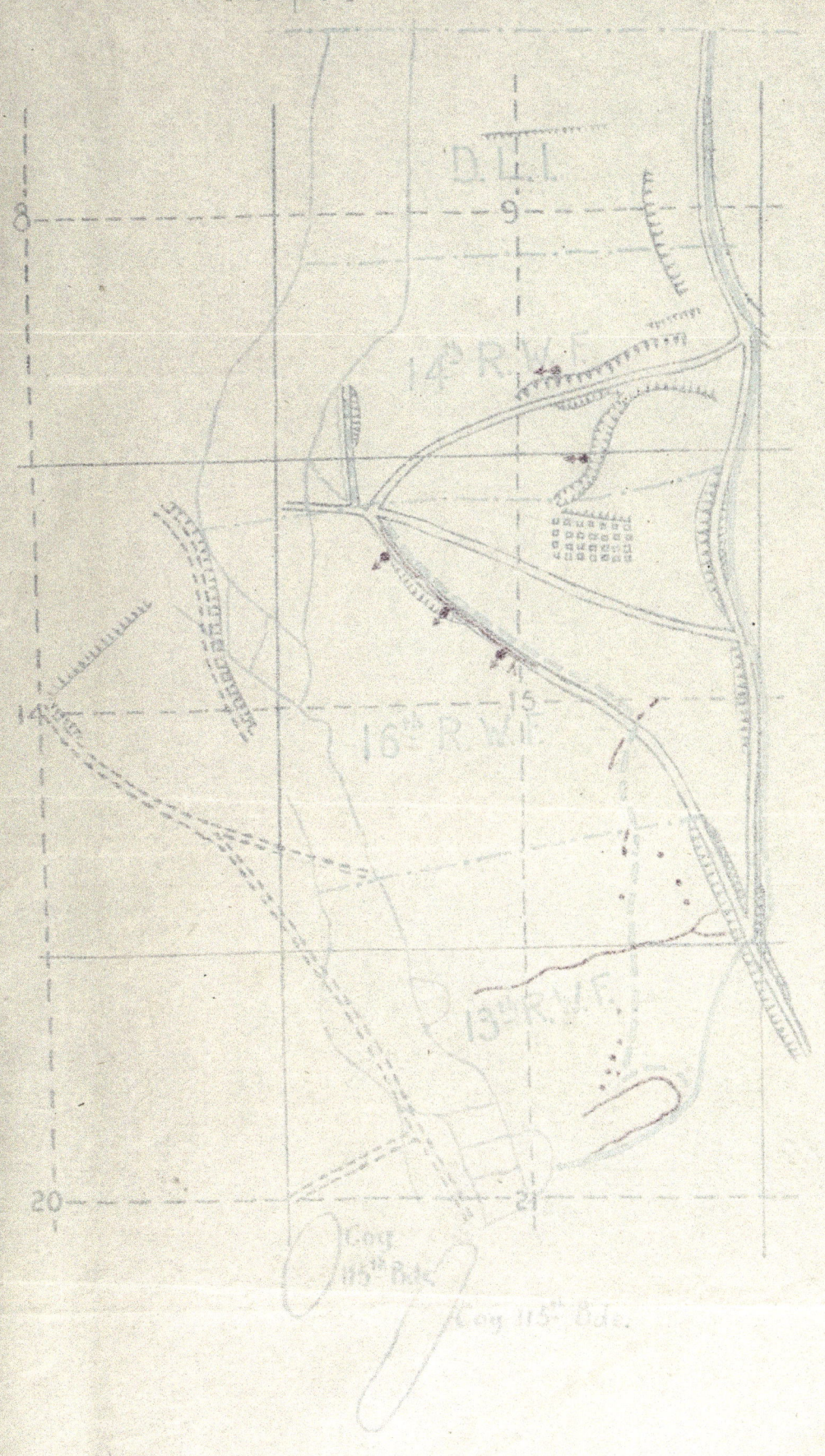

W 8 — 9 D.L.I.

14th R.W.F.

16th R.W.F.

13th R.W.F.

20 — 21

Coy 115th Bde
Coy 115th Bde.

Objective of 1st Wave.
    "   "   2nd   "
British Trenches.
German   "   & shell holes.

Map B

Distribution of units when assembled.

19th D.L.I.

14th R.W.F.

Coy 14th R.W.F.

Coy 14th R.W.F. — 14 R.W.F.

16 R.W.F.

13th R.W.F.

16th R.W.F. H.Qrs.

13th R.W.F.

▭ = Coy. Areas

Map C
Artillery Barrage

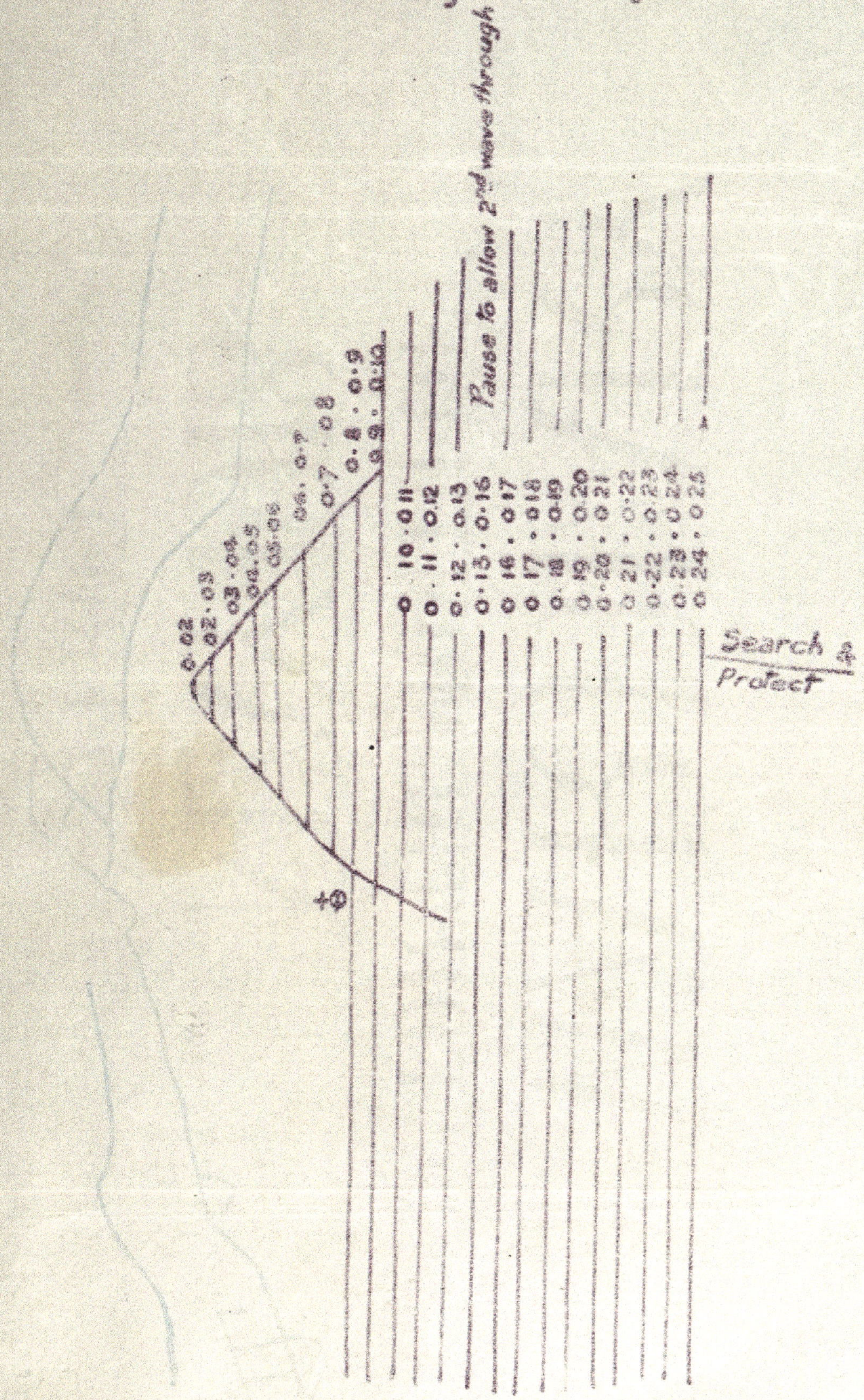

British Trenches.
Barrage Lines.

14 R.W.F. Vol 30

30.C
6 sheets

WAR DIARY
FOR THE MONTH OF
MAY 1918

14 R.W.F.

WAR DIARY
or
INTELLIGENCE SUMMARY.

(Erase heading not required.)

Army Form C. 2118.

Instructions regarding War Diaries and Intelligence Summaries are contained in F.S. Regs., Part II. and the Staff Manual respectively. Title pages will be prepared in manuscript.

Place	Date	Hour	Summary of Events and Information	Remarks and references to Appendices
	1/5/18		The Battalion paraded at 8.30 a.m. and marched to the Reserve positions in bivouacs near Neduinez then relieving the 13th H.L.I. at 1.0 p.m. The same evening the Battalion left Herrissart for Corps Reinforcement Camp.	
	2/5/18		Battalion rested in Reserve position until 8.30 p.m. and then moved up to Front Line. Left Battalion, Centre Brigade. Relief sector Dispositions "A" Front line, "B" in Support, "C" in Left Support in Martinsart Wood, "D" in Reserve. Relieving 19th A.S.L. Relief complete 11.30 p.m. – Bn HQ W1.a.90.10	
	3/5/18		Do. A Coy. sent out small reconnoitring patrol.	
	4/5/18		"C" Coy. moved into close support, being relieved in Martinsart Wood by a company of 114 Brigade. "A" Coy. sent out small reconnoitring patrol. "B" Coy. relieved "A" Coy. in front line. "A" Coy. moved into Rear Support. All available men digging new C.T. on left flank and wiring same.	
	5/5/18		All men digging or wiring in expectation of enemy attack. Reconnoitring patrol from "B" Coy. of OR	
	6/5/18		"D" Coy. moved from Reserve alongside of "A" in rear support. B/HQ. moved into position vacated by "D" Coy. W7.b.30.10. Attack expected at dawn.	
	7/5/18		Expected attack does not materialise. Situation normal, work continues – HQ. men employed such RE. at new B.HQ. W7.b.30.10	

A5834 Wt. W4973/M687 750,000 8/16 D. D. & L. Ltd. Forms/C.2118/13.

Army Form C. 2118.

WAR DIARY
or
INTELLIGENCE SUMMARY
(Erase heading not required.)

Instructions regarding War Diaries and Intelligence Summaries are contained in F. S. Regs., Part II. and the Staff Manual respectively. Title pages will be prepared in manuscript.

Place	Date	Hour	Summary of Events and Information	Remarks and references to Appendices
	9/5/18		Battalion relieved by 16th R.S. Rho. Relief complete 11.30 pm. Battalion moved into Bivouacs in reserve at V.5.a. D. Coy forward in Surples system.	
	10/5/18		69 men in 3 reliefs employed at new Brigade HQ. V & C. Curles. A Coy. moved forward to Surples system. Same party for Brigade HQ. All remaining men working on Surples system digging.	
	11/5/18		do	
	12/5/18		Battalion relieved 13th R.W.Fus. in Front Line. Right Battalion, Centre Brigade Artillery Sector. Dispositions D Coy Right Front. A Coy Left Front. C Coy Left Support. B Coy Right Support. Relief Complete 12.30 am.	
	13/5/18			
	14/5/18		All new wiring between Reserve and Support Lines. Reconnoitring Patrol with a view to raid later.	
	15/5/18		do	
	16/5/18		B Coy relieved A Coy in Front Line. 2 Officers (2/Lt Phillips, 2/Lt Bartley, D Coy) and 40 OR of A Coy withdrawn to practise raid. Patrol under 2/Lt Beveridge C Coy dispersed enemy working party.	
	17/5/18		Work as on previous days.	

A.5834. Wt. W.4973/M687. 750,000. 8/16. D. D. & L. Ltd. Forms/C.2118/13.

WAR DIARY or INTELLIGENCE SUMMARY

Army Form C. 2118.

(Erase heading not required.)

Place	Date	Hour	Summary of Events and Information	Remarks and references to Appendices
	17/5/18		Reconnoitring patrol by "C" Coy. "B" Coy relieve "D" Coy in front line.	
	18/5/18		Raiding Party returns to Lieut- Land carried out with a view to securing identifications and capturing enemy machine gun at W.9.b.20.15 - Zero hour 10.30 p.m. Result - One prisoner and one Machine Gun taken - two enemy killed - Our Casualties - 7 slightly wounded one missing	
	19/ 20/5/18		Battalion relieved by 17th Royal Scots and marched to Maryville where breakfasts were served at 7.15 am and the Battalion then marched to hut in Camp at Rubempré.	
	21/5/18		Day spent by all Companies in cleaning, refitting and reorganising platoons. At 5 pm the C.O. inspected the Battalion	
	22/5/18		Company training carried on by all Coys. Great attention being paid to Musketry & Lewis Gun work	
	23/5/18		Company training continued - Musketry, Lewis Gun and the abodes handling of a platoon. A successful Concert was held in the evening	
	24/5/18		Company training continued as before but was considerably interrupted by continuous rain.	

Army Form C. 2118.

WAR DIARY
or
INTELLIGENCE SUMMARY.
(Erase heading not required.)

Instructions regarding War Diaries and Intelligence Summaries are contained in F. S. Regs., Part II. and the Staff Manual respectively. Title pages will be prepared in manuscript.

Place	Date	Hour	Summary of Events and Information	Remarks and references to Appendices
	25/5/18		Company training continued, special attention being given to Musketry, Lewis Gun and Tactical Schemes for Platoons.	
	26/5/18		Church of England. Reconformist R.C. parades in the morning. Each Coy. did One hour Musketry in the afternoon.	
	27/5/18		Company training mentioned as before, and the Battalion was inspected by G.O.C. Third Army (Sir Julian Byng, K.C.B.) in its Musketry training.	
	28/5/18		On the morning Company training continued and in the afternoon the Battalion took part in a Brigade exercise with tanks. The Corps Commander and the Divisional Commander were present.	
	29/5/18		Company training continued. All Coys. on ranges and in the afternoon officers and Senior NCOs were engaged upon a tactical exercise without troops.	
	30/5/18		In the morning the Battalion paraded with the rest of the Brigade in Review Order by way of practice for the Corps Commanders inspection the following day. The rest of the morning spent in Company training	

WAR DIARY
or
INTELLIGENCE SUMMARY.
(Erase heading not required.)

Army Form C. 2118.

Place	Date	Hour	Summary of Events and Information	Remarks and references to Appendices
	3/5/18		and the afternoon in recreational training	
			the Brigade and the Transport of all Units inspected by the Corps Commander. Major General D. Shute. C.B., C.M.G. who also presented medal ribbons to several Officers, N.C.Os & men who were recently awarded medals. The Corps Commander expressed himself as pleased with the appearance of the men and transport. In the afternoon all Companies went through a Gas test for the respirator.	
	31/5/18			

C. P. Weedon
Major for Officer Commanding
1st/4th Battalion Royal Welsh Fus[ilier]s

14th BATT. ROYAL WELSH FUSILIERS.

WAR DIARY

FOR

JUNE 1918.

Army Form C. 2118.

WAR DIARY
or
INTELLIGENCE SUMMARY
(Erase heading not required.)

Instructions regarding War Diaries and Intelligence Summaries are contained in F. S. Regs., Part II. and the Staff Manual respectively. Title pages will be prepared in manuscript.

Place	Date	Hour	Summary of Events and Information	Remarks and references to Appendices
	1/1/18		Usual bayonet training in the morning and specialist training in afternoon. It has fallen badly with "influenza" which has touched every officer, N.C.O.	
	2/1/18		Church of England and non-conformist services held. Bayonet competition held in the afternoon – No entries from the Battalions for the Divisional Inter-Platoon Competition on the 110 yards range. No 3 Platoon are the entries which entered other events.	
	3/1/18		Company continued usual training in the morning. In the afternoon & evening, actively prepared by the packs, kit etc. for entry into the trenches.	
	4/1/18		Battalion prepared to move to the line. 38th Division relieving 63rd Division relieving R.N.D. as supporting battalion at HAMEL-MESNIL. Left 4th C.A. 2 relieving R.N.V.R. 113 Brigade in the line on left Brigade of Right Division. 17th Division in the left, in MAILLY-MAILLET – BUCHONVILLERS area. Battalion moved off 6.10 pm under command of Major Waldron and marched to its position for the night in PUCHEVILLERS ROAD. Beaufort molested on the way.	
	5/1/18		Battalion moved up to its position at dusk. B+D Coys in front Right, Supported in Coad bank of Valley E. of ENGLEBELMER, C+D coys in Railway bank on left, between QUARRIES ALLEY and CHARLES STREET relieving 2 R.M.L.I. Relief complete at 2.30 am.	
	6/1/18		Dispositions relieved Battalion organised in depth, to be used front line at MESNIL outposts, D in support along BARN TRENCH and RAILWAY front face at MESNIL. Marched in area E. of HILL 142 and B Coy W of HILL 142. – On a	

WAR DIARY
or
INTELLIGENCE SUMMARY

Army Form C. 2118.

Place	Date	Hour	Summary of Events and Information	Remarks and references to Appendices
	6/18		matter of fact A. L/O Coys bivouacked in ENGLEBELMER VALLEY Bank with BHQ. B's Coys to in trucks on HILL 142 where BHQ Lewis Guns also held tactical positions - 13th Rus. Rgt. held front & support line on left W. of HAMEL - & 16th Rus. Rgt. in dispositions to their rear with Reyns on front line 17th Division behind Brigade on our right, with Rus Rgts in reserve. Relief proceeded with little doubt New and 10th S.W.B. in reserve. The front held by the Battalion as consequently part of HAMEL outposts and MESNIL outposts from (Map 57D SE) Q.29.d.9.3 to Q.29.d.1.8. The front on our right up to BOUZELUY WOOD and the 13th Rus Rgt who are apt to recoil West of HAMEL VILLAGE. The feature of the front is the valley of the ANCRE with road and railway 50-60 metres with the crest of our ridge and facing it the old Battlefield of THIEPVAL WOOD Beaucourt to the west apparently more or less in MESNIL outposts, and appears to have a few M.G. posts on the crest about the ridge and one at the junction of MESNIL - HAMEL Road and Main Road running South.	
	7/18		No moments fighting patrols enough in new front after dusk & located to HQ and relieved the General working parties on GUIT'S AVENUE - No Main C.T. back to BHQ and in deep dugouts in the front 32 Q 26 a. Q 26 c.	
	8/18		Nothing unusual. The 19th Div carried out a two battalion raid on our BEAUMONT-HAMEL Company M.G.s / prisoners. Blank working parties in the evening into Company relief. C's in the front line relieved by A Coy and D's in dug out reserve by B Coy.	
	9/18		HQ relieved by Brig moved round to the Report Centre in complete tth Sav. 9/10.14 By CHARLES Manor Rgts by CHARLES Manor	

WAR DIARY
or
INTELLIGENCE SUMMARY

(Erase heading not required.)

Army Form C. 2118.

Place	Date	Hour	Summary of Events and Information	Remarks and references to Appendices
	10/9		Orders having been received to retire for a futile raid, dispositions of Brigade are altered to enable withdraws, to move back for having "B" get held to VITERMONT MILL and 19" to QUARRY RLY; "C" get back west of ENGELBEZMER and "D" Major remain in the bank.	
	11/9		Headquarters & "D" get back and trenches W. of ENGELBEZMER too far. Major etc in dugouts taken over from R.E. consequently Battalion placed in the evening by 10th R.I.B. but rally not complete during the night who take on the trenches	
	12/9		12/13/9 R.O. and type of these trenches were unsatisfactory and no steady activity not amongst men during daylight. The principal fatigue was to carry rations from ENGELBEZMER & NESLE RD Valley where our transport to be in Daylight. A position of 500 frequently snipers at H.E. treated in ENGELBEZMER. On the Battalion moved out from ENGELBEZMER to FORCEVILLE new 700 yielding along valley in P. 23 and 24. Trenches in old trenches E. of FORCEVILLE the nearest. Trenches in new area by Rouen of ground for said. Companies abandoned their area by Rouen from Batt HQtrs. Trenches at Coy HQts in the men running from Coy HQts separately at different times during operations.	
	13/9		Total work to field to practice and I am remaining in new Battalion orders out details for the 18 + Filled up from CO. etc Coy. D, B, & C Coy details for Brigade General type had about some training in withdrawal of dugouts and ammunition. Otherwise work good. Checks by General Inspection of men and kit by Brigadier General type, had about some training in withdrawal of dugouts and ammunition. Otherwise work good. Checks by General General Britt. Cecile Brunswick white, and these technical staffs total	
	14/9			

WAR DIARY
or
INTELLIGENCE SUMMARY.
(Erase heading not required.)

Army Form C. 2118.

Place	Date	Hour	Summary of Events and Information	Remarks and references to Appendices
	15/8		[illegible] the to reconnoitre. Practised with Company training and Rest Parade on Africa Area. Lunch and Tea were on the ground. Brigadier Vipping inspected each section in detail on this Parade and men were in very good form. Divisional General Ronald [?] and returning to BOISCEVILLE [?] visited General Fanshawe after Parade and they thanked everyone [illegible] front and returned with excellent luncheon state.	
	16/8		Day of fine weather bearing. Had during morning. Rehearsed over rehearsal ground at 10.0pm. Brigadier present. Battalion back in billets 10.45am out to 6.0pm.	
	17/8 18/8		Battalion Rhodes [?] Raid a coud [?] 5am - 5.30pm. Inspected by Brigadier-General Burry who attended by Colonel in charge of the new scheme. Proceeded to Practise ground, Brigadier inspected scheme for 19/8 Operations as to laying out Tapis Cutting etc, under Command of Self Major Pt. Denny now 2nd Capt. O.C. Coys in 2nd. Battalion returned to bivouacs.	
	19/8		[illegible] Coys in action in Preparation for Operations at 2.5am on the morning of 19/8, carrying out Tapis Ground [?] to Front line to tapes out a Raid from B Coy to the [illegible] line to practise [illegible] with assembly and [illegible] running of the enemy [illegible] 1/203 Taping out the assembly Trenches to the Trench for the new front. Plans is attached Showing the assembly points off Platoons pinned in and how time Objectives divided cover at with A Copy of Operation Orders is also attached.	Nº D 29.

Instructions regarding War Diaries and Intelligence Summaries are contained in F. S. Regs., Part II. and the Staff Manual respectively. Title pages will be prepared in manuscript.

WAR DIARY

or

~~INTELLIGENCE SUMMARY.~~

(Erase heading not required.)

Army Form C. 2118.

Place	Date	Hour	Summary of Events and Information	Remarks and references to Appendices
	20/8/18.		During the evening and night light rain fell. After a good meal in bivouacs at FORCEVILLE, the raiding party composed of A B & C Coys made up to strength by picked men from D Coy started up the line by platoons at 100 yards interval - the whole party being clear of near B Hill near the support front line by BARN TRENCH by midnight. All arrangements worked out according to plan, and the raiders returned upon the given signal. The results owing to very few enemy posts being encountered were not great but one Bosche Machine Gun was captured owing to great enterprise shown by [illegible] Parsons who although officially assigned to be holding the front line with his party while the Raiders went over, joined in the hunt and went over with No 2 Platoon A Coy., saw a Bosch M.G. retiring near the Fork Roads chased them, and succeeded in capturing the gun which the enemy abandoned. They were fired at while attempting to escape into cover along the Ancre, it is believed some were killed or wounded but this could not be followed up. All other dugouts and a T.M. dugout were blown up by the rest of the Raiding Party all of whom reached their objectives, assisted by parties of R.Es attached to the Raiders. The barrage put down by our guns at Zero included smoke bombs which are alleged to have lit up the ground while they burst so that some of the enemy near the posts were able to see the raiders coming down on them, and consequently escaped into thick wired bushes beyond our objectives. Casualties were light. [illegible] J. Rawlings of A Coy was severely wounded while in the support trench and subsequently died also Corporal J.H. Thomas of A Coy also died of wounds. There were twelve other slightly wounded including two officers. The principal fact established by the raid was that this sector is only lightly held by patrols with a Machine Gun post South of the village of HAMEL.	

D. D. & L., London, E.C.
(A10266) Wt W5300/P713 750,000 2/18 Sch. 52 Forms/C2118/16

WAR DIARY
or
INTELLIGENCE SUMMARY.
(Erase heading not required.)

Army Form C. 2118.

Place	Date	Hour	Summary of Events and Information	Remarks and references to Appendices
	21/6/18		All ranks made their way back by dawn to FORCEVILLE where the day was spent in rest.	
	22/6/18		Working parties of 60 from each Company sent out to work on Brown Line also bathing near Toronto. Remainder of Battalion Company training.	
	23/6/18		Working parties to be supplied as on previous day. Bands concert held by 6th West Yorks in evening.	
	24/6/18		Testing patrols on Brown line east of FORCEVILLE and cable burying near Toronto. Remainder of Battalion Company training.	
	25/6/18		Battalion marched to ACHEUX WOOD where Company was assembled and in the morning and after dinner a lecture stood where was carried out. The Commanding Officer went round to an attend through the Wood in two places ad Companies in the fire a defends sector, owned in four different columns; trying exclusions to attack. Company then marched and without falling out similarly platoon and Section Commanders were required to go to the head.	
	26/6/18		Company training and bathing during the day. In the evening the Battalion proceeded to purple line East of MARTINSART to work at digging and wiring. Work continued till midnight when men found way back to day remainder by Officer & men. Company and sections.	

Army Form C. 2118.

WAR DIARY
or
INTELLIGENCE SUMMARY.
(Erase heading not required.)

Instructions regarding War Diaries and Intelligence Summaries are contained in F. S. Regs., Part II. and the Staff Manual respectively. Title pages will be prepared in manuscript.

Place	Date	Hour	Summary of Events and Information	Remarks and references to Appendices
	24/6/18		Battalion returned from town at 1 am. Rested until 10 am. 100 Runs firing on the range, and in the evening at 8.30 pm proceeded to PURPLE system again to continue work started on the previous night.	
	25/6		Battalion rested till 10 am. Company training and firing on the range.	
	29/6		Battalion rested till 10 am. One Company on the reserve position of BERTHUY put in out post. One platoon on VARENNES and FORCEVILLE, and one company at GROVE Alley trenches, one East of FORCEVILLE.	
	30/6/18		Battalion paraded twice at 10 am in the Orchard at FORCEVILLE and at the Cmd. Brigade service in the same place at 11 am. Capt. Humphreys Brown and 6th Bays reconnoitred the left platform front line (MAESNIL SECTOR) with a view to relieving the 10th S. & D. the following night.	

N P Wheeler
Major Commanding
14th (S) Batn. RW Fusiliers

D. D. & L., London, E.C.
(A10260 Wt W4500/P7713 750,000 2/18 Sch. 52 Forms/C2118/16

SECRET.

14th BATTALION. ROYAL WELSH FUSILIERS.

OPERATION ORDER NO. 30.

Ref. Map Sheet 57 D., 1/40,000.

OBJECTIVE. 1. At a date and time to be notified later the 14th Battn. Royal Welsh Fusiliers will carry out a Raid on the Railway between Q.29.d.40.50. and Q.23.d.67.00. and the road between Q.29.b.90.70 and 60.60., with a view to killing or capturing Germans, blowing up dugouts, capturing Machine Guns, and obtaining identifications.
The 115th Infantry Brigade will carry out a Raid at the same time on the Railway from Q.29.d.40.45. to AVELUY WOOD exclusive.

INFORMATION REGARDING THE ENEMY. 2. All known information regarding the enemy, his Machine Guns, dugouts, and Trench Mortars in or near the objective is given in Map "A" attached.

GENERAL PLAN. 3. The general plan of action willbe for the Infantry to push the position from tthe MESNIL HAMEL outpost Line under cover of a smoke barrage from 4" Trench Mortars, combined with an Artillery, Machine Gun, and Trench Mortar Barrage on all positions from which the enemy might interfere with the raid by fire or counter-attack.
On the previous night at 3;0. a,m. the 4" Mortars will discharge Gas mixed with smoke on the objective and neighbouring points so as to make the enemy think on the night of the raid when they see smoke that Gas is being discharged, and that they must put on their respirators.

DETAILED PLAN. 4. The Raid will be carried out by three Companies; namely 'C', "B" and "A" Companiesm "D" Company will hold the front line during the raid., and furnish the parties for laying out the 'forming up' tape and for covering the assembly of the raiders.
OBJECTIVES.
'C' Company will attack from Q.29.d.40.45., to Q.29.b.50.30.
'B' Company from Q.29.b.50.30. to Q.29.b.60.60.
'A' Company from Q.29.b.60.60. to Q.23.d.67.00.
At ZERO minus 15 minutes the Raiding Party will be drawn up as in Map 'A' attached on a taped line whibh will be set out by an Officer's Patrol detailed by O.C. "D" Coy. This taped line will be ready by ZERO minus 60 minus 60 minutes, and O.C. "D" Company will report to O.C. Raid at that time that this has been done.
At ZERO the Reserve Platoons will fire one Rifle Bomb each at the objective, and to do this will be extended by ZERO minus 15 minutes as follows:-
'C' Coy. 1 platoon from Q.29.d.05.75 to Q.29.b.05.10.
'B' Coy. 2 platoons from Q.29.b.05.10 to Q.29.b.05.70.
'A' Coy. 1 platoon from Q.29.b.05.70 to Q.23.d.05.10.
This extension allows for 1 Rifle Bomber to 9 yards of front.

ACTION OF ARTILLERY, TRENCH MORTARS AND MACHINE GUNS. 5. At ZERO 4" Mortars will fire 12 rounds on the objective Artillery, Heavy Trench Mortars, and 6" Trench Mortars and L.T.M's will open a standing barrage on targets as shown in aptached Map 'B'.

ACTION OF ATTACKING PLATOONS.	6.	At ZERO the attacking platoons will rush forward to their objectives as shown on Map 'A' as follows:-
'C' Company. ... 3 platoons.
'B' Company. ... 2 Platoons.
'A' Company. ... 3 Platoons.
METHOD OF ATTACK.	7.	The method of attack for all Platoons, with one exception which will be notified later, will be as follows:-
The Riflemen and Bombing Sections will attack and capture any enemy and enemy Machine Guns found at the objectives shown on Map 'A'. The Rifle Bombers Section will be immediately in rear, as shown on Map "A", and will provide covering fire where necessary.
The Lewis Gun Sections will in each case rush forward of the railway, as shown on Map "A", and open covering fire for the sections in rear, leap-frogging past the Rifle and Bombing Sections. All Sections will rush to their objectives in sections ~~in files~~ in file.
(a) In the case of the Right Attacking Platoon of 'A' Coy. no Lewis Gun will be taken, but each section will act as Riflemen and Bombers and will attack the four dugouts on the road as indicated in Map 'A'.
(b) 'C' Company will arrange for the Right Platoon to furnish a Liaison Section which will maintain touch with the 115th Infantry Brigade on the objective.
	8.	After firing one Rifle Grenade each the Reserve Platoons will move forward to the areas shown on Map 'A', where they can be used as required.
At ZERO plus 1 minute the Machine Gun Barrage opens on targets as shown on Map "B".
At ZERO plus 30 minutes the raiders commence to withdraw. Standing Barrage ceases.
WITHDRAWAL.	9.	The signal for withdrawal will be :-
(a) The cessation of the standing barrage.
(b) Thermite bomb.
ORDER OF WITHDRAWAL.	10.	The Lewis Gun Sections will first withdraw to the two attacking sections, and upon the arrival of the Lewis Gun sections the attacking sections will withdraw to our front line, being covered by the Lewis Gun Sections.
The Lewis Gun Sections will then withdraw to our front line and will be covered by the reserve platoons in their withdrawal.
In each Platoon the Reserve ~~Platoon~~ Section will withdraw last.
In each Company the Reserve Platoon will withdraw last.
The Right Platoon of "A" Company will withdraw at ZERO plus 30 minutes to the advanced position of the Reserve Platoon of 'A' Company on the MESNIL - HAMEL Road, and their further withdrawal to our front line will be covered by the Reserve Platoon.
	11.	Each Company will arrange a Tally post in the Front Line, and each section will report to its respective Company Tally Post upon withdrawal to the front line.
Tally Posts will be stationed as follows:-
'C' Company at Junction with DRAKE AVENUE.
'B' Company at Junction with MESNIL - HAMEL Road.
'A' Company at Junction with GRASS STREET.
Company Quarter Master Sergeants will be present at their respective Company Tally Posts to check all men as they come in.
PRISONERS, CAPTURED MACHINE GUNS, DOCUMENTS, etc.	12.	All prisoners, Machine Guns, documents, and other identifications captured will be immediately passed back to the Reserve Platoons who will each have four men detailed to condct any captures to Battalion Hdqrs.

EQUIPMENT & ARMS.

13. <u>All Ranks.</u> = Box Respirator in 'Alert' Position, Steel Helmets.

   <u>Each Officer.</u> = Revolver, 24 rounds ammunition, Electric torch, whistle, 2 hand grenades.

   <u>Other ranks.</u> = No equipment except in case of Rifle Bombers who will wear a belt.

   <u>Rifle Sections</u> = Rifle, Bayonet, 50 rds. in pocket, 2 Hand Grenades per man.

   <u>Lewis Gun Sections</u> = Lewis Gun and 6 drums per section Each drum loaded with 8 tracer and 39 ordinary rounds in series of 2 tracer and 10 ordinary.
   1 Hand Grenade per man.

   <u>Rifle Bomber Sections.</u> = 7 Rifle Bombs, Rifle, Belt, and Bayonet, 50 rds. S.A.A per man.

   <u>Bombing Sections.</u> = Bayonet men, throwers and leaders 6 bombs each, carriers 10 ordinary bombs and 2 'P' Bombs each. Rifle, bayonet, and 50 rounds S.A.A. per man.

   <u>Section Commander</u> = Whistle each in addition to above.

   <u>Platoon Sergeants</u> = Rifle, bayonet, 50 rounds, whistle, Electric torch each.

   <u>Sections.</u> = In each section :-
   (1) 2 men will carry 2 sandbags each for bringing away papers, maps, shoulder badges etc., from dead or living men and from dugouts.

   (2). 1 man will carry a large wirecutter attached by string to his shoulder.

   (3) 2 men will have wirecutters fixed to rifles.

14. No maps, badges, or anything that may give a clue to the enemy as to who took part in the raid, will be carried. Patrol identity discs will be carried.

15. Apart from the "B.A.B". Code, page 23, the following special code words will be used:-
    "Have captured (number) prisoners" = BBB followed by No.
    "Identifications received obtained" = CCC followed by Battn. Regt. and Div. No.
    "Estimated enemy killed". = DDD followed by No.
    "Have captured (number) Machine Guns" = EEE followed by number.

16. Orders regarding Medical arrangements will be issued later.

17. Nothing concerning the raid is to be spoken on the telephone except during the actual riad if the tactical situation require it.

18. Orders regarding synchronization of watches will be issued later.

19. Battalion Headquarters will be at Q.28.a.,9-8.

ACKNOWLEDGE.

                          (Signed)   W. P. WHELDON.
                                                Major,

                                                    Commanding,

                                          14th (S) Battalion,
                                      ROYAL WELSH FUSILIERS.

12th HJUNE, 1918.

<u>Copies to</u>:-

Commanding Officer:-
2nd in Command.
O.'A' Coy.
O.C. 'B' Coy.
O.C. 'C' Coy.
P.C. 'D' Coy.
113th Infantry Brigade.
2nd Battn. R.W.Fus,
War Diary (2 copies)

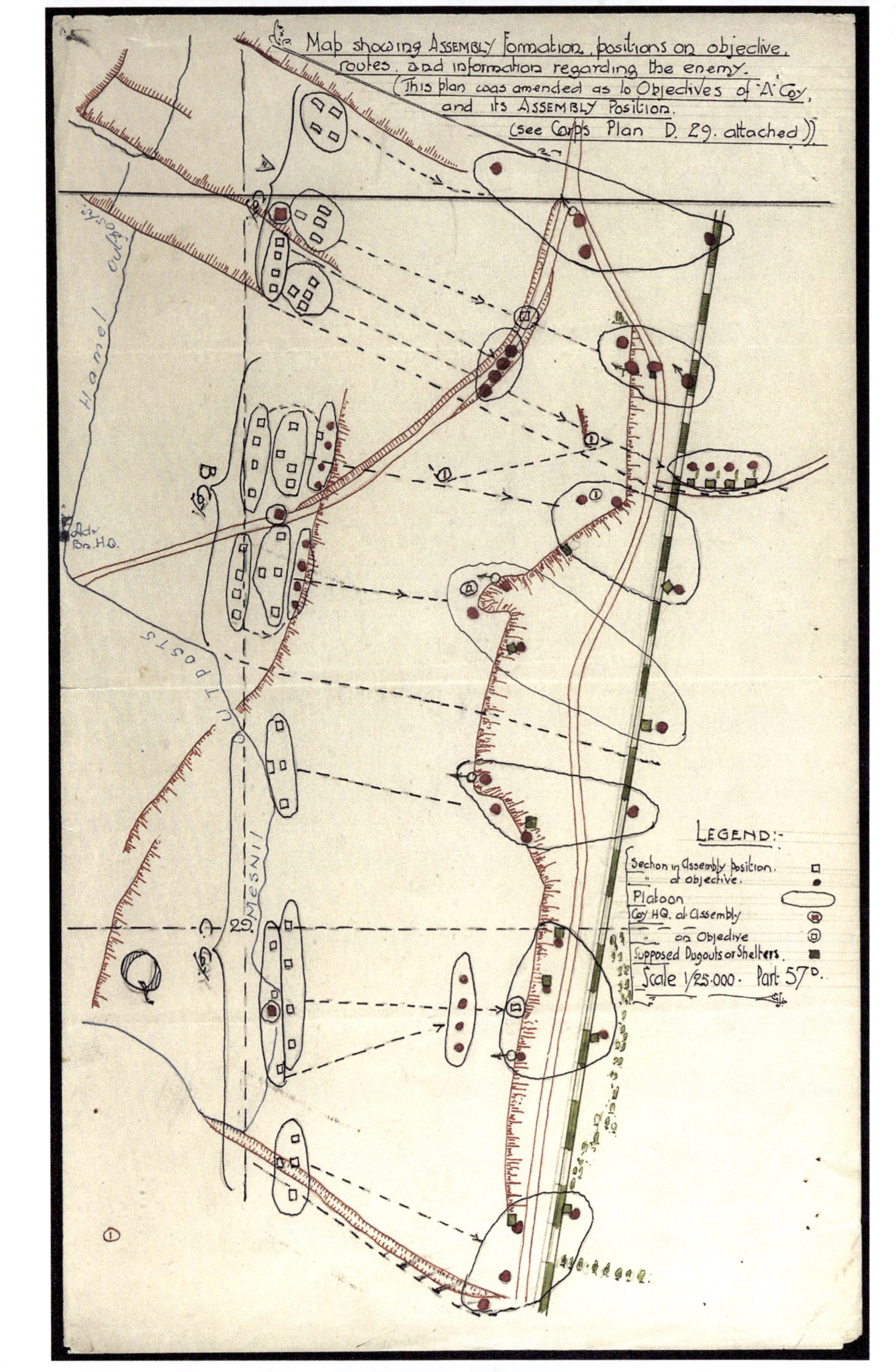

Map showing ASSEMBLY Formation, positions on objective, routes, and information regarding the enemy.
(This plan was amended as to Objectives of "A" Coy, and its ASSEMBLY Position.
(see Corps Plan D.29. attached))

LEGEND:-
Section in Assembly Position.
" at objective.
Platoon
Coy HQ. at Assembly
" on Objective
Supposed Dugouts or Shelters.
Scale 1/25.000. Part 57D.

Scale 1/5,000
Sheet 57c
A Coy
B Coy
C Coy
29
B2
Railway bank along eastern edge
REFERENCE
ENEMY TRENCHES =
WIRE = x x x x x
Machine Guns.
T.M. Positions
Tracks in Use.
Small British R.E Dump.
Dugouts.
Note: Enemy Positions along Railway in Q29 vary constantly.
3 Platoons Objective.
(Copied from Corps Topo. N° D29
14th Bn. RW Fus.)
F.B.
Damaged.

14TH BATT. ROYAL WELSH FUSILIERS WAR DIARY FOR JULY 1918

Vol 3²

WAR DIARY
INTELLIGENCE SUMMARY.
(Erase heading not required.)

Army Form C. 2118.

Place	Date	Hour	Summary of Events and Information	Remarks and references to Appendices
	1/7/18		14th R.W. Fus relieved 10th Bn. S.W.B. in MESNIL beds during night 1/2nd July 1918. The dispositions held were from QUAKER ALLEY and Q 23 a 30 80 (Sheet 57 D) on the left to DRAKE ALLEY exclusive on the Right. D Coy. under Lt. Roderick held the front as far back as Ridge Support and B Coy. under Lieut. John held the front (Right) from Q 29 a 80 Southwest to DRAKE and as far Southward as B2 R.N. Support. Battalion Headquarters at Q 28 a 53 80. C Coy. under Captain a Royal Jones in support along QUAKER ALLEY and A Coy under the dispositions of Left Supporting Battalion about Q 21 b 10 80. Major Wheeler left for Senior Officers School at Aldershot and Captain Humphreys-Owen took the Battalion over the line. The Naval Division (63rd) held depts on our left and the 13th R.W.Fus held the Sector on our Right. Two Battalions of the Brigade being in the Front Line and one Battalion (N.Z.) being in Support at ENGLEBELMER. Companies patrol their front.	N.U.
	2/8		Hostile activity below normal, our own artillery active. Two fighting patrols sent out by Right & Left front line Companies to enemy Line Lines of HAMEL and to the main road running South to AVELUY. No enemy encountered but concentration wire defences.	
	3/8		Quiet day on both sides. Two patrols sent out as on previous night.	
	4/8		Our Artillery shot a shoot on HAMEL and the ground between the Village and River ANCRE. Minor hostile retaliation on our front and support line about 4.0 p.m. Patrols went out in the evening.	

Army Form C. 2118.

WAR DIARY
or
INTELLIGENCE SUMMARY.
(Erase heading not required.)

Instructions regarding War Diaries and Intelligence Summaries are contained in F. S. Regs., Part II. and the Staff Manual respectively. Title pages will be prepared in manuscript.

Place	Date	Hour	Summary of Events and Information	Remarks and references to Appendices
	5/7		Our Artillery did a shoot with heavy shells on enemy M.G. emplacements & J.M.S. in HAMEL and drew a feeble retaliation. Lt. Hunter M.C. was wounded in the arm by a splinter and evacuated. In the evening with company reliefs was carried out. D Coy going into support, B going to the left supporting Battalion (16th R.W.Sh.) and A & C Coys going into the front line. 2/Lt. Parsons to receive the Military Cross for work done on the raid in June.	
	6/7		Our Artillery fairly active. North guns shelled BHQ for about an hour before lunch - slightly wounding the Officers' Mess cook. Enemy everything normal. Major T. Cartland M.C. 2 R.W. Fus came to act ng 2 i/c in command. retns	
	7/7		Position normal. No unusual activity on either side. Two patrols go out at night. Owing to his flying many planes over our lines about 5. O am during previous two mornings. Officers from RFC came up to report and arrangements made to deal with them, but without result. Patrols sent out on night & left flanks.	
	8/7		Nothing abnormal. Battn relieved in front line by 2nd R.Sc Fus in evening	
	9/7		14th R.W.F. relieved by 16th R.W.Sh. in the evening 9pm/10pm. Nugents South of FORCEVILLE during night 9pm/10pm	
	10/7		Day spent in resting & cleaning up.	

D. D. & L., London, E.C.
(A10260) W1 W5306/P73 750,000 1/16 Sch. 83 Forms/C2118/16

WAR DIARY
or
INTELLIGENCE SUMMARY

Army Form C. 2118.

(Erase heading not required.)

Instructions regarding War Diaries and Intelligence Summaries are contained in F. S. Regs., Part II and the Staff Manual respectively. Title pages will be prepared in manuscript.

Place	Date	Hour	Summary of Events and Information	Remarks and references to Appendices
	11/8		Working parties detailed for trench digging and cable laying in the BROWN System the material salvaged by the Battalion during their tour in the line amounted to four times that obtained by the other two Battalions of the Brigade	
	12/8		Major Brock Williams of 11th Welsh Regiment assumes Acting Command of the Battalion. Working parties and musketry carried out.	
	13th/6 14th/6		Battalion engaged in working parties on the Brown System receiving drafts of Officers and men from Reinforcement Camp at MAMETZ. Training is also carried out in Lewis Gun, Musketry, Rifle Bombs & Drill.	
	15/8		Battalion moves into Brown System at V.14.b. Division goes out of the line.	
	17/8 16/8		Daily working parties are furnished for work at SENLIS BOUZINCOURT and on the Brown System.	
	20/8		Remainder of the men continue training. Musketry on the ranges and preparation for Brigade & Divisional Sports. A good deal of the time is spelt by the wet weather.	
	30/8		The Battalion found working parties in morning and marches to ARQUEVES in the afternoon arriving in billets about 8 pm	

Army Form C. 2118.

WAR DIARY
or
INTELLIGENCE SUMMARY.
(Erase heading not required.)

Instructions regarding War Diaries and Intelligence Summaries are contained in F. S. Regs., Part II. and the Staff Manual respectively. Title pages will be prepared in manuscript.

Place	Date	Hour	Summary of Events and Information	Remarks and references to Appendices
	3/18		Training. Tactical scheme. The C.O. explained Lewis Gun tactics and method of tacking same.	
	3/18			

[signature]
Major for O.C.
Hinton Royal Welsh Fusiliers

14th BATT ROYAL WELSH FUSILIERS Vol 33

WAR DIARY
FOR
AUGUST 1918

33.C.
10 sheets

WAR DIARY
or
INTELLIGENCE SUMMARY.

Army Form C. 2118.

Place	Date	Hour	Summary of Events and Information	Remarks and references to Appendices
	1/8/18		Battalion paraded as strong as possible for the range at 9 a.m. During the morning the battalion was inspected at work by the Army Commander. Battalion marched past in column of fours on its way back to billets. Brigade Sports were held in the afternoon.	
	2/8/18		Training Battalion carried out a tactical exercise. Moving off from billets at 5-0 a.m. Two Coys were tasked & battalion "to hold" & defend the HEDAUVILLE SWITCH at 4-0 a.m. The scheme was to counter attack in accordance with Brigade Defence Scheme. M.G. Coy took part. Came on to rain very hard at 9-30 a.m. & battalion marched back to billets at 10-0 a.m. Lieut. Col. (b.d.) Collier arrived from Sick leave in England in the afternoon.	
	3/8/18		Training Battalion formed up on the range to watch a demonstration of fire effect by Tracer Ammunition. A wet morning. Funeral Sports in the afternoon.	
	4/8/18		Training - Musketry & Range. Received orders to move to HERISSART. Paraded in full marching order at 10 p.m and arrived at camp on Northern edge of HERISSART at 2 A.M. (5.8.18.)	
	5/8/18		C.O. & Coy Comdrs went up by bus to reconoitre the intermediate system Vim AVELUY LISFT Sector. Battalion spent day packing up & preparing for the line. A demonstration of Message Carrying Rocket was to have been held but did not take place owing to the transmitter who was arranging it having a nasty bicycle accident. Battle Surplus moved to VALHEUREUX by Road.	

Army Form C. 2118.

WAR DIARY
or
INTELLIGENCE SUMMARY.
(Erase heading not required.)

Instructions regarding War Diaries and Intelligence Summaries are contained in F. S. Regs., Part II. and the Staff Manual respectively. Title pages will be prepared in manuscript.

Place	Date	Hour	Summary of Events and Information	Remarks and references to Appendices
	6/8/18		Battalion moved off from HERISSART in fighting order at 9 AM with 100 yds between Coys to relieve the 9th Bn. South of Wellington Regt in reserve position in the AVELUY Sector. Batn marched past the B.G. Comdg on the line of march. Halted from 12 noon till 8 pm near FORCEVILLE. Relief was reported complete at 1.30 AM.	
	7/8/18		Battalion rested during the day. Training was carried out from 5 to 7 PM. Day passed quietly.	
	8/8/18		Training from 9 AM to 1 PM. Quiet day.	
	9/8/18		Training tactical scheme. Two companies marched to FORCEVILLE & attacked ENGLEBELMER which was held by another company. Fourth Coy trained in Camp. Musketry 107 & 13.F.	
	10/8/18		Training 9 AM to 1 PM. Baths at WARLOY in the afternoon. Battalion moved to billets in FORCEVILLE in the evening.	
	11/8/18		Training. Extended order drill and artillery formations. No Church services were held. The village was bombed during the night.	
	12/8/18		Rested by day & relieved to 1/5th R.W.Fus in support in AVELUY Sector at 11 pm. 1/3th Bn. R.W.Fus was relieved by American troops in the front line. Ordinary Trench routine. Day passed quietly.	
	13/8/18		Commanding Officer reconnoitred front line positions in AVELUY WOOD. Brigadier General Commanding inspected the battle positions of the battalion. Quiet day.	
	14/8/18		Orders were received at 8 pm that enemy was retiring through BEAUMONT-HAMEL and orders to send 1 Company across the River ANCRE and capture THIEPVAL Ridge. The Coy "C" got through	

WAR DIARY
or
INTELLIGENCE SUMMARY.
(Erase heading not required.)

Army Form C. 2118.

Place	Date	Hour	Summary of Events and Information	Remarks and references to Appendices
	15.8.18		the marshes but failed to cross the main stream. There were no bridges and no material was available. Battalion remained in support SE of ENGLEBELMER. On night 15/16 "A" Coy attempted to cross river ANCRE in 2 places. 2nd Lt Phillips platoon proceeded along causeway at Q29a83. They crossed one branch of the ANCRE but failed to cross main stream. 2nd Lt Mason's platoon proceeded along bridges at AUTHUILLE & had better success. Lt Mason & four men reached the far bank, but it was impossible to take a platoon across.	
Sheet 57d S.E.	16.8.18		The battalion was relieved by 10th Bn S.W.B. and marched to TOUTENCOURT. Day was spent in cleaning up & resting. Parades under Coy arrangements.	
	17.8.18		Battalion took part in a Brigade scheme being battalion in support. The scheme was a proposed wheel of crossing the ANCRE and attacking towards THIEPVAL and LA BOISELLE.	
	18.8.18		Training. All companies on the range. Orders received to move up to BROWN Line via cross country tracks to ENGINEER VALLEY at 8.30 pm	
	19.8.18		Battalion moved off arriving in BROWN Line at 11 pm.	
	20.8.18		Training under Coy arrangements. Reconnaissance parties were sent forward to look for best tracks to AVELUY WOOD Sector. Lt C.E. Jones was in charge of the party.	
	21.8.18		Training. Battalion standing by to move at a moments notice. The old scheme was cancelled and orders that Brigade might have to exploit success on our right were received.	

WAR DIARY
or
INTELLIGENCE SUMMARY.
(Erase heading not required.)

Army Form C. 2118.

Place	Date	Hour	Summary of Events and Information	Remarks and references to Appendices
	22.8.18		In the morning battalion moved forward to a position N of HENENCOURT in V.21.b. The Brigade assembled there & prepared for action. At 12.30pm Brigade moved off in the order 13th RWF. 16th RWF. 14th Bn. RWF. 14th Bn. RWF moved to a position in ADELAIDE St south of BOUZINCOURT in W.13 & W.19.F. Here it remained till night. At 9.30pm battalion moved through ALBERT to assemble for attack next morning. Order of Coys – B Coy. P.V.O. The battalion was in support to 13th Bn. R.W.Fus. The officers with the battalion going into action were Hq Coy Lt Col. R.H. Collier. Capt. A.E. Humphreys Owen, Lt Dunkin. 2nd Lt W.G. Evans. "A" Coy Capt Murray, Lt R.J. Phillips. 2nd Lt Haycock. "B" Coy Capt J. Jack. 2nd Lt H. Williams. 2nd Lt D.D. Roberts. 2nd Lt B. Law. "C" Coy Lt Pringle. 2nd Lt R. Seel. Lt C.E. Jones. "D" Coy Capt Roderick. Lt K.O. Parsons. Lt Farrell & 2nd Lt J. Bartley. Lt G.R. Wilson accompanied the battalion as Med: Officer.	
	23.8.18		Zero hour was 4.45 AM. 14th Bn. followed close behind the 13th Bn. In a number of cases our men joined the 13th Bn & went on in the front wave to the first objective. Objective of battalion was sunken road up W.23 c.2. 29.1. (Sheet 57d SE) Casualties were moderate. Three officers were wounded. Captain Humphreys Owen, acting 2nd in Command was wounded while objective was being consolidated. Lt K.O. Parsons was wounded during the attack & Lt W.O. Roberts at the assembly point. About 100 prisoners were taken at H.M. Guns. At 7pm "A" Coy moved up on the right to support the 13th & "B" Coy moved up on the left. Two platoons of "C" Coy were sent to the left flank to hold the chalk pit. 2nd Lt Seel led his platoon to the flank and attacked a strong point. Capturing	

WAR DIARY
or
INTELLIGENCE SUMMARY.
(Erase heading not required.)

Army Form C. 2118.

Place	Date	Hour	Summary of Events and Information	Remarks and references to Appendices
	24.8.18		2 M.Guns & 17 prisoners. The remainder of "C" Coy & whole of "D" Coy remained in objective as reserve. Early morning of 24th the Battalion formed up at far objective for an attack towards La BOISELLE – GRANDCOURT. C&D Coys were in front line with B & A in support. At 1AM the Battalion moved forward. 17th Bn. R.W. Fus. on the left & 16th Bn. on the right. Very little opposition was met with until the far slope was reached in the craters 2 strong points at X.13.a (Sheet 57d SE) in front of La BOISELLE. Here there was a general mix up of battalions & it was some time before they were sorted out. The 14th Bn. held the strong point on the left, capturing over 100 prisoners and 12 M.Guns. The enemy counter attacked B Coy unsuccessfully, leaving 30 prisoners in our hands. 2nd Lt R.J.Phillips M.C. was wounded during the attack, also the R.S.M. Sgn Tucker. At 5 am 24th orders were received to move forward through the valley in X.13, 8.3 towards OVILLERS-LA-BOISELLE mopping up as they went. C&D Coys moved forward supported by B&A. They reached the crest of valley, our left at X.9.C.3.5 and right at X.15.a.28. Here the enemy Lewis fire on the Bn. & Bn. had to work round the left flank. Capt Jack M.C. moved B Coy round to the left flank & here it secured "A"Coy remained in support. The Bn. had to held a line of shell holes as the enemy fire was too strong to advance against. 16th Bn. on our left 2nd Lt Farrell was wounded whilst attempting to gain touch with 16th Bn. on our right.	
	25.8.18		At 1AM the Bn. formed up for attack towards COURTALMAISON. C & D front line, B & A in support. 1st objective was sunken road at X.11.c, X.17.a. (57d SE) and Lido reached without any opposition. "C" Coy took 2	

(A.10260) Wt W.3886/P713 750,000 7/18 Sch. 52 Forms/C2118/16

WAR DIARY or INTELLIGENCE SUMMARY

Army Form C. 2118.

Place	Date	Hour	Summary of Events and Information	Remarks and references to Appendices
	26.8.18		prisoners. Here touch was gained with 16th Bn on right & the 10th Bn S.W.13 on the left. From here the Bn moved forward taking up a position looking down to MAMETZ WOOD. This was held all morning and at 2pm Bn moved to valley in X 12 & 9.18 a, where they prepared for the attack through MAMETZ WOOD towards BAZENTIN-LE-GRAND. At 6 A.M. the attack commenced. 13th Bn were in front supported on left by 14 L. on right by 16th Bn. The attack went well until 13th R.W. Fus. lost direction. 14 R. Bn got to 13th Bn objective to find 13th to far to the right. Heavy M. Gun fire was brought to bear on the Bn & both flanks were exposed. "B" Coy moved forward & drove the enemy out of BAZENTIN-LE-GRAND & followed them up the road as far as the Cross Roads in S.16.a (Sheet 57C SW) from here they were forced back to cross roads at BAZENTIN-LE-GRAND. Two platoons of "C" Coy were sent to the left to capture a strong point which was holding up the advance. They surrounded the position and on the 10th/S.W.Bs coming up. "C" Coy took the strong point capturing 2 M. Guns & 30 prisoners including 2 officers. They then held the windmill at S.9.c.4.9 (57C SW) the remainder of the Bn formed up in shelter of bank at S.15.a and made an attack on high ground on the right. Two platoons of "C" Coy & "D" Coy were on the left and "A" Coy on the right. The M. Guns were cleared off the ridge & over 100 prisoners taken with 8 M. Guns. The hill was cleared as far as S.16 and & then the 13th Bn. moved up into support at road running through S.16.a.	

WAR DIARY or INTELLIGENCE SUMMARY

Army Form C. 2118.

Place	Date	Hour	Summary of Events and Information	Remarks and references to Appendices
			This was the heaviest fighting the Bn. had experienced since the beginning of operations & for tired men a wonderful dash & spirit were shewn. Lieut. G. Jones was wounded while leading an attack against a M. Gun. nest. 2nd Lt. Egerton was killed in attempting to rush a M. Gun. 2nd Lt. W. G. Evans, Intelligence officer, was wounded in the attack on BAZENTIN-LE-GRAND. Capt. John Jack M.C. was wounded while leading his company forward on the left flank. The Bn. took up a position in the afternoon nearly 1000 yds in front of the rest of our line with left on S.7a.22 and right on S.16.d.29 with A & D Coys in front line, "C" Coy in support & "B" Coy in reserve. The enemy counter attacked at 5 pm & as both flanks were in the air & ammunition running short the C.O. decided to withdraw to conform to the rest of our line. This was done in perfect order & the battalion took up a position in front of 13th R.W.F. about S.16.a Central. Captain Murray commanding "A" Coy was wounded during the counter attack and Lt. Meyrick was killed. Major J. Cuthbert M.C. joined the battalion.	
	27/8/18		At 3.30 am. orders were received to advance to a position just in front of Longueval, 13th Batt. leading, 14th Batt. in support & 16th Batt. in reserve. 13th Batt. was held up by heavy M.G. fire on the edge of LONGUEVAL. The attack commenced at 11-30 am & the withdrawal to sunken road at 4-30 pm. Half hours barrage in LONGUEVAL from 6-30 pm to 7-0 pm. At 7-15 pm. orders were received not to push from 13th Batt. and withdraw to reserve & 14th Batt. field on outpost line from S.14.a.7.9. to S.14.a.45.25 with 10th S.W.B. on left & 16th R.W.F. on the right. "B" Coy & half of "A" Coy outpost line with "A" "D" Coys in support & "C" Coy in reserve.	

WAR DIARY
or
INTELLIGENCE SUMMARY.
(Erase heading not required.)

Place	Date	Hour	Summary of Events and Information	Remarks and references to Appendices
	28/8/18		Their positions were held till the afternoon of 28th. Lt Seel & 3 O.Ranks patrolled through LONGUEVAL & found the village empty, whereupon Lt Pringle took "C" Coy forward and occupied a line 200 yards in advance of main LONGUEVAL - FLERS Road with his right at S.17 & 65 and his left at S.11 a 60.	
	29/8/18		At midnight 28/29th orders arrived to occupy the high ground beyond GUINCHY. We were to follow a creeping barrage. The 115 Bde were to move by the north side of the Wood & join us in our objective at 7.8 a 50. The 114 Bde were to mop up DEVILLE WOOD. Bde formed up by 4.45 am. 14th Bn on right & 13th Bn on left. 16th Bn on right & 13th Bn in reserve. 14th Bn left to move 200 yards south of southern edge of wood. The barrage came down promptly at 5.15 am & Bde moved forward at 5.31 in accordance with barrage table. Both Bns were leading with A & D in support. No opposition was met with & Bde reached objective at 7.9 am, linking up with 17 R.W.Fus at T.8 a 50 & 16 R.W.Fus at T.14 b 80. Battle patrols were at once sent out & came into touch with enemy on the forward slopes of MORVAL Ridge. At 6 p.m. 14th Bn pushed forward and occupied a position from about T.0 c 85 to T.6 a 88. 16th Bn on the right occupied a position further down the valley but we did not get in touch with them during the night. Our left flank was in the air. Bn was heavily shelled with Blue Cross Gas & H. Explosive.	
	30/8/18		Early on morning of 30th the 114 Bde passed through the 113 Bde in an attack on MORVAL but in the evening the battalion was withdrawn to GINCHY in reserve. Lt A.S. John was wounded by shell fire on the way to reserve position.	

Army Form C. 2118.

WAR DIARY
or
INTELLIGENCE SUMMARY.

(Erase heading not required.)

Instructions regarding War Diaries and Intelligence Summaries are contained in F. S. Regs., Part II. and the Staff Manual respectively. Title pages will be prepared in manuscript.

Place	Date	Hour	Summary of Events and Information	Remarks and references to Appendices
	31.8.16		Bn resting & refitting as much as possible in GUINCHY.	

Wilfred Kelp
2nd i/c Co.
Cmdr 14th Bn. R.W.F.

WAR DIARY.
for September 1918

14TH. BATT. ROYAL WELSH FUSILIERS.

Army Form C. 2118.

WAR DIARY
or
INTELLIGENCE SUMMARY.
(Erase heading not required.)

Instructions regarding War Diaries and Intelligence Summaries are contained in F. S. Regs., Part II. and the Staff Manual respectively. Title pages will be prepared in manuscript.

Place	Date	Hour	Summary of Events and Information	Remarks and references to Appendices
	1/9/18.		"C" Company was sent to assist 114th Brigade and captured 20 prisoners on the right of MORVAL. At 6.0 p.m. the 113th Brigade attacked SAILLY-SAILLISEL with 16th R.W.F. on the right. 13th R.W.F. on the left and 14th R.W.F. in reserve. Enemy put up a stubborn resistance. We held a position just west of the village.	
	2/9/18.		At 5.0 p.m. we attacked with MESNIL-EN-ARROUAISE as our objective, 115th Brigade on our right and 17th Division on our left. 13th and 16th R.W.F. were in support and reserve. The attack was held up on the SAILLY-SAILLISEL - LE TRANSLOY ROAD by very heavy M.G. fire. Captain A. Floyd Jones M.C. and Lieut. Smalley were wounded. The Battalion consolidated near the road and a number of big fires were to be seen behind the enemy lines.	
	3/9/18.		We were ordered to advance to MESNIL-EN-ARROUAISE at 2.30 p.m. which was carried out in conjunction with the Battalion consolidated S.E. of the village with the 13th R.W.F. on the left and 16th R.W.F. in support. No signs of the enemy and strong opposition was met. 114th Brigade advanced to the CANAL-DU-NORD where remains near MESNIL-EN-ARROUAISE. Colonel Collier takes over command of 113th Brigade. Major Cuthbert M.C. assumes command of the Battalion. Orders are received about 5 p.m. to be ready for 13th R.W.F. and 14th R.W.F. to hold the Spurs in V.2. and V.7. respectively and bring up to bear on enemy on the opposite side of the CANAL DU NORD while the 16th R.W.F. crossed the Canal. This order was cancelled and we were ordered to hold ourselves in readiness to move forward when the 114 Brigade & 115th Brigade - CANAL DU NORD had been crossed by the 114 Brigade. Capt. A.F. Jones M.C. was buried at CONTALMAISON. Battalion remained near MESNIL-EN-ARROUAISE.	
	4/9/18 5/9/18		Relieved by 21st Division intensive marched to billets on N. side of DELVILLE WOOD via COMBLES.	

Army Form C. 2118.

WAR DIARY
or
INTELLIGENCE-SUMMARY.
(Erase heading not required.)

Instructions regarding War Diaries and Intelligence Summaries are contained in F.S. Regs., Part II. and the Staff Manual respectively. Title pages will be prepared in manuscript.

Place	Date	Hour	Summary of Events and Information	Remarks and references to Appendices
	6/9/16		A day of rest.	
	7/9/16		Battalion rested and refitted. A Battalion open air concert was given which was a great success.	
	8/9/16		Brigade parade services near Brigade Hdqrs. In the afternoon a memorial cross was erected on the SOUTHERN edge of MAMETZ WOOD in memory of the Officers NCOs and men of the Battalion who fell on the 8th July 1916.	
	9/9/16		Rest and refitting continued.	
	10/9/16		Battalion marched to Billets at ROCQUIGNY.	
	11/9/16		Reconnoitring parties are sent forward. to reconnoitre the position W of DESSART WOOD of the 7th Borden Regt. who we relieved at 5.30 p.m. Bn. in Support Bn. to the Support Bde. Batts Inflrs were sent to BEAULEN COURT-	
	12/9/16		All Officers reconnoitred the front Battalions of 113th & 115th Brigades - 114th Brigade were in Support.	
	13/9/16		Training was carried out in the valley behind our position (N.6.c.) 2nd Lieut Harding was wounded. In the early morning enemy gas shelled A & C companies. About 4/5 m. 30 men reported "gassed" and were evacuated. Battalion practised attack scheme in the afternoon.	
	14/9/16		Total gas casualties amounted to 5 Officers 2Lt. LtQ. Williams. Brown. Lt. Williams Edwards and Jenkins aged 76 men. Training carried out as yesterday. Carrying parties were provided for Div. Trench Mortars and special carrying parties in making new dugouts.	
	15/9/16		Battle Surplus again. Battle Surplus again. Orders were received for the attack.	
	16/9/16		Battalion rested and was equipped for action.	
	17/9/16		Battalion marched to its assembly position in front of GOUZEAUCOURT. on the GREEN LINE. All coys were ready in position by 4.15am	
	18/9/16		14th R.W.F. was on the right. 16th R.W.F. on the left. 13th R.W.F. in Support.	

(A10260) Wt.W5300/P713 750,000 2/15 Sch. 52 Forms/C2118/16 D.D. & L., London, E.C.

WAR DIARY
or
INTELLIGENCE SUMMARY.
(Erase heading not required.)

Army Form C. 2118.

Place	Date	Hour	Summary of Events and Information	Remarks and references to Appendices
	19/9/18		Battalion dispositions were:- "D"Coy on the right, "A"Coy Centre, "B"Coy left and "C"Coy Support. Zero hour was 5.20 p.m. Officers going into action were:- Headquarters: Lt. Col. B.W. Collery, Lt. W.J.C. Humphrey, 2.Lt. O. Llewelyn, 2.Lt. F. Keyshaw, 2.Lt. S.S. Jackson, "A"Coy:- 2.Lt. Evans, 2.Lt. Hancock, 2.Lt. Parker; "B"Coy: 2.Lt. Bewley, 2.Lt. J.D. Roberts. 2.Lt. Darnill. "C"Coy: 2.Lt. Beveridge, 2.Lt. Gates. "D"Coy: 2.Lt. Roberts, 2.Lt. Mathews. The attack was held up on the left by a M.G. nest at Q. 35.a. Central. "A" and "D" Coys got through to the final objective on the GREEN LINE. The 16th R.W.F. were held up on our left by M.G. fire. The 114th Brigade on our right got through to their final objective on the GREEN LINE. "A" and "D" Coys held Q. 36.c. 10. 30 to Q. 35.6. 90.15. "B" and "C" Coys fell back to AFRICAN SUPPORT after numerous attempts to push on. 16th R.W.? held AFRICAN SUPPORT on our left. 2.Lt. J.D. Roberts was missing, 2.Lt. Darnill was killed, 2.Lt. Beveridge and 2.Lt. Roberts were wounded. At 2.30 p.m. "B" & "C"Coys made a bombing attack assisted by artillery up C.T. from Q. 35.c. 10.80 to AFRICAN TRENCH and then North along the trench to the M.G. nest at Q. 35.a. Central. We established our line in AFRICAN TRENCH and captured eight M.G.s and nine prisoners. 13th R.W.? relieved the 16th R.W.? and held the line Q. 35.6.90.30. to Q. 35.a. 55.30 along AFRICAN TRENCH to Q. 35.a. Central then down C.T. to AFRICAN SUPPORT. and Northwards along this hange to Q. 25.d. 90.45. "B" and "C"Coys Enemy attacked at 6.30 a.m. and captured AFRICAN TRENCH. Helped by artillery and trench mortars. made a bombing attack at 12 p.m. up C.T. to Q. 35.c. 60 95 and then Northwards along AFRICAN TRENCH. Simultaneously the 13th R.W.? made a bombing attack up C.T. from Q. 35. a. 20. 55. both attacks converging in Q. 35.a. Central. The attack was successful and we captured three M.Gs. 2.Lt. Jarks was wounded. During the day the enemy attacked "A" and "D" Coys. Six times, capturing their line in the last attempt. Our Companies had run short of S.A.A. and bombs and no supplies could be sent them. Only about 25 men got back to AFRICAN TRENCH. 2.Lt. Ywans. 2.Lt. Hancock and 2.Lt. Parker D.O. & L. missing: the last named officer was wounded in killed.	

WAR DIARY or INTELLIGENCE SUMMARY.

Army Form C. 2118.

(Erase heading not required.)

Place	Date	Hour	Summary of Events and Information	Remarks and references to Appendices
	20/9/18		Relieved by 115th Brigade - Relief complete by 4.30 a.m. after which we marched to PRICKLE POSS TRENCH, west of DESSART WOOD. 9/RSM. Newman was killed at BHQ Q.34.a.20.50. We marched to billets near ROCQUIGNY arriving about 5pm. 9/RSM Newman was buried in cemetery at ROCQUIGNY.	
	21/9/18		Battalion resting. Brigade parade service in YMCA hut.	
	22/9/18		Periods under company arrangements - reorganising etc. 3.0 p.m. the Commanding Officer took all Officers and Platoon commanders in Map Reading and tactical exercises.	
	23/9/18		All companies on the ranges from 9.0 a.m. to 1.0 p.m. P. v B.T. also carried out. 3.0 p.m. the C.O. took all Officers and Platoon commanders in Map Reading etc.	
	24/9/18		Coy training from 9.0 a.m. to 1.0 p.m. P. v B.T. Musketry, Bombing, Platoon drill carried out near camp.	
	25/9/18		Company training as before. During the morning all men pass through a gas chamber at Bde. Hdqrs. to test Box Respirators.	
	26/9/18		All Companies firing on the ranges from 9.0 a.m. to 10.0 p.m. Battalion resting and re-equipping for the line. Battle Cartridge was issued at 6.0 p.m. and advanced at 8.0 p.m.	
	27/9/18		Battalion embussed at ROCQUIGNY at 6.0 p.m. and marched to positions half a mile S.E. of HEUDECOURT. Battalion is under orders to move at an hour's notice. Major Cuthbert M.C. is in command.	
	28/9/18		Battalion remains in positions S.E. of HEUDECOURT. Lieut. Col. Collin D.S.O. rejoins Battalion. Battalion moved to positions S.E. of HEUDECOURT.	
	29/9/18		Battalion remains in positions S.E. of HEUDECOURT.	
	30/9/18			

Cuthbert Major.
14(S) Bn. Royal Welch Fusiliers

Vol 36 / 118/38

35.C.
8 sheets

14 RWT
WARDISKY
FOR OCTOBER
1918

WAR DIARY
or
INTELLIGENCE SUMMARY.
(Erase heading not required.)

Army Form C. 2118.

Place	Date	Hour	Summary of Events and Information	Remarks and references to Appendices
	1/10/18 2/10/18		Battalion at HENDECOURT and did Company training.	
	3/10/18		Battalion at HENDECOURT and when on Battalion training, orders were received to advance and the Battalion moved at 16:15 hrs to trenches in X.25 and 26 (57 S.E.)	
	4/10/18		The Bn. moved again to trenches next to and West of BONY and remained that night.	
	5/10/18		'A' Coy was detailed to deal with a pocket of the enemy in the HINDEBURG line at S.21, S.26, S.27 (Sheet 57.B) and moved off under Lieut PRINGLE at 04.00 hrs but found only eight enemy who were captured. The remainder of the Battalion moved forward as Advance Guard to the Bde at 11:15 hrs, marching through BONY to W- of MORTHO WOOD T.1. and T.7. but were held up by M.n machine gun fire and broke up a position in the LE CATELET - MAURCOY line. Patrols sent out and located machine guns in the wood. Patrols again sent out to recce a way through the wood, but found it strongly held & no progress made. Patrols succeeded in establishing posts forward of MORTHO WOOD and in the sunken road East of the wood.	
	6/10/18			
	7/10/18			

WAR DIARY
INTELLIGENCE SUMMARY

Army Form C. 2118.

Place	Date	Hour	Summary of Events and Information	Remarks and references to Appendices
	8/10/16		At 01.00 hours the Bn. took part in a Prepared attack on the PEAR RESERVOIR Line. The Bn. reinforcements to the 16th and 13th Battns. which attacked on the Right and Left respectively. All Coys were in position by 00.30 hours. (B 18th Inst.) and the right hand Coy of the Right & Left flank Companies of the 13th & 76th Bns Rgt made progress and the Coys at the attack were held up in front & North of MORTHO WOOD by strong wire and enemy machine guns at our break in the junction with Rink of the 14 Brigade, whereupon moved forward to reinforce positions in T.B.d. The whole line moved forward and the Coys at this Battalion co-operating with a section of the 54ths cleared the wood and the trenches forward and reached ANGLE'S ORCHARD at T.8.d and the trenches to the NORTH of it. The 114 Bde. failed through at 11.30 hours and Jones the enemy in free flight. The Bn. late in the day moved to trenches in m.T.3.C and d (57B Sw) and remained there the night. The Cas: received in this operation were not heavy. 10 Killed, 45 wounded & 25 missing; 8 Men drowned; 1 officer wounded, Lieut. B.LAW. Killed, 2nd Lt. D. EVANS & 1 Officer Missing.	

WAR DIARY
or
INTELLIGENCE SUMMARY.

Army Form C. 2118.

Place	Date	Hour	Summary of Events and Information	Remarks and references to Appendices
	9/10/18		The Bn moved at 16:00 hours to billets at MALINCOURT.	
	10/10/18		Recon[naissance] & return to MALINCOURT.	
	11/10/18		Bn training MALINCOURT.	
	12/10/18		Bn marched to BERTRY across country, traversing totally [un]known ground. Arrived at BERTRY about 14.30 hrs. Officer reconnoitred front area. Major Wheler D.S.O. in command.	
	13/10/18		About 05:00 hours shell hit factory in which Bn war billeted, killing 6 and wounding 15. Bn moved to billets in village.	
	14/10/18		Bn training at BERTRY	
	15/10/18		Bn training at BERTRY; 3 Officers reconnoitred crossing R over River SELLE.	
	16/10/18 17/10/18		Bn command BERTRY; training found for construction of dugouts. (Headquarters) in forward area. Reconnaissance of forward area by all Coys.	
	18/10/18		General Curzlon D[ivisional] Commander of dugouts from Battle Surplus and examined a Coy of the 2/R.N.F. in front line. Lt Col Bn GILLERD.S.O. who is in Command D.C. relieves 12 Commanders West Coy.	

WAR DIARY or INTELLIGENCE SUMMARY

Army Form C. 2118.

Place	Date	Hour	Summary of Events and Information	Remarks and references to Appendices
	19/10/16		Morning devoted to taking out & equipping for the next battle. At 20.30 hrs the Bn. less C Coy paraded and marched across country to the assembly position East of MARTIN STREET, preparatory to an attack. Advance party of all Coys had formed ahead to lay out the tapes from which we were to the assembly position. The 10th Batln. D.L.I. was in command. The assembly worked without a hitch all Companies being in position and unaware by 0.00 hours.	
	20/10/16		Zero hour at 02.00 hrs – A & C Coys were detailed to take the first objective and then moved with the barrage at 02.00 hours. Capturing their 1st objective 100 yards N.E. of the railway after some stubborn resistance and the right of A Coy had some for casualties. Then B & D Coys moved through A & C Coys and attacked the enemy infantry and reached their final objective about 1000 yards E. of the railway. Thence some sporadic fighting took B + D Coys with enemy machine gun posts, but the Camerons were remarkably few. The night was very wet and misty and the attack manner scored a success, and, although our further advance of 1000 yards up the hill was opposed and our known nunnts were but a	

N[?] [signature] M.C. Lt. Col.

WAR DIARY
or
INTELLIGENCE SUMMARY.
(Erase heading not required.)

Army Form C. 2118.

Place	Date	Hour	Summary of Events and Information	Remarks and references to Appendices
	20/10/16		Lt Q.N. ROBERTS was killed, Lieut V. ETNELSON missing (since traced wounded) & others wounded & 9 other ranks killed & 27 wounded. 9 ans Cross the rise at dawn, but owing to the mist on the Steep hill Bomb C'ies made no further progress in the front. The Enemy shelled heavily all morning until about 12.00 hours but no attempt at a Counter attack on his part. The night was spent in vigorous patrolling forward where we had further advanced into the forest. Patrols ascertained that the enemy still held FOREST in some force.	
	21/10		By the morning the enemy shelling had greatly decreased and the day was spent in our relieving or being relieved. At dusk the whole Battalion was relieved by 1/5th Con. of the 10th Bn S.W.B. & left being Omplets at 20.30 hrs and the Battalion marches to billets at MERTEN.	
	22/10		Batln in billets. Baths, cleaning up & rest.	
	23/10		Batln paraded at 07.15 hrs under Lt Col Bro Osler D.S.O. and marches to TROISVILLE and after an hours halt there proceeded to MONTAY, from where it moved alone to assembly position West of FOREST and RICHEMONT with the intention of moving forward of RECOURT in Support of the 33rd Ann. Which had attacked that day.	

WAR DIARY or INTELLIGENCE SUMMARY

Army Form C. 2118.

Place	Date	Hour	Summary of Events and Information	Remarks and references to Appendices
	24/10/18		Battalion remained in vicinity of RICHEMONT - Battle Surplus and "B" Echelon moved to MONTAY.	
	25/10/18		Battalion still in RICHEMONT, Company training carried on.	
	26/10/18		The Battalion moved to positions East of VENDEGIES au BOIS with Batt HQrs in F.8.c. and d. and F.9.a. and c. (57b). Battle Surplus moved to FOREST.	
	27/10/18		Battalion remained in the same positions and carried on Coy. training. The 113 Bde were in support to the 115 Bde which held the line - the 114 Bde being in reserve.	
	28/10/18		Bn in same positions, training continues.	
	29/10/18			
	30/10/18		The Bn moved forward relieving the 13 R.W.F. in the left of the support Brigade front at POIX du NORD. Battle dispositions were taken up in F.4.d. and c. F.5.c and d. F.11.a and b (57b) + POIX du NORD. The Battalion was mainly billeted in houses in POIX du NORD during the night in shells which the front men of C & D Coys. Killing Lt O.M. JONES, 2Lt H.D. ROBERTS, 2Lt J. BARTLEY MC. and 2Lt G.H. CHARLES, also wounding Lt. T.A. PRINGLE MC & 2Lt E. SWAMPSON.	

Army Form C. 2118.

WAR DIARY
or
INTELLIGENCE SUMMARY.
(Erase heading not required.)

Instructions regarding War Diaries and Intelligence Summaries are contained in F. S. Regs., Part II. and the Staff Manual respectively. Title pages will be prepared in manuscript.

Place	Date	Hour	Summary of Events and Information	Remarks and references to Appendices
	31/10/16		The Battalion at POIX du NORD. Brunory owned a salvage work. Some trench shelling of the area but ordered in the afternoon.	

M. P. Wilson
Major
14th R. W. Fus.

36.C.
7 sheets

1st R.W.F. = 98.36

War Diary for

November 1918

WAR DIARY
or
INTELLIGENCE SUMMARY.

(Erase heading not required.)

Army Form C. 2118.

Place	Date	Hour	Summary of Events and Information	Remarks and references to Appendices
	1/11/18		Training continued at POIX-DU-NORD.	
	2/11/18		Battalion left POIX-DU-NORD for VENDEGIES-AU-BOIS to practice an attack through the Wood. They left by Companies after the attack for Gables at CROIX returning the same evening to POIX-DU-NORD.	
	3/11/18		Battalion in some positions and preparations being made for the attack on FORÊT-DE-MORMAL the following day. Lt. Col. B.W. Collins left the Battalion and proceeded to Base depots en route for England. Major W.R. Whalen DSO assumed command.	
	4/11/18		Battalion moved forward to assembly positions in A.2.a. and C.Ref. Sht. 51 S.W. and Sht. 57 N.W. (20,000) to arrive in these areas by 05.00 hours conforming to a line drawn N. and S. 200 yards in rear of the 10" I.N.B. Route to assembly positions across country through F.S.a. F.b.c. A.n.d. Companies moved to assembly positions in the following order:- "C" Coy. right front, "D" Coy. left front, moved at 02.00 hrs. "B" Coy. left rear, moved at 02.15 hrs. "A" Coy. right rear, moved at 03.00 hrs. "B" Coy. left rear in for protection from Artillery fire. On arrival at assembly positions Capt. Shey in for protection from Artillery fire. The objectives of the Infantry Bdes. of the Division were given:- 115th Brigade 1st Objective BLUE LINE. 113th Brigade 2nd Objective RED LINE. 114th Brigade 3rd Objective BROWN and GREEN LINES.	

WAR DIARY
or
INTELLIGENCE SUMMARY
(Erase heading not required.)

Army Form C. 2118.

Place	Date	Hour	Summary of Events and Information	Remarks and references to Appendices
			The 113 Infantry Brigade attacked with three Battalions abreast. 13th R.W.F on the right, 14th R.W.F. in the centre. 16th R.W.F on the left. Companies moved forward from the assembly positions in artillery formation to BLUE LINE and formed up for the attack by 08.30 hours. At 06.45 hours Coys. moved forward from the BLUE LINE. Method of attack. Coys and D Coys. attacked and captured the line of high ground between A.4.a.a.O. to S.28.a.0.2 thence along road to S.27.6.6.7. A and B. Coys. hopped through to the final objective. Headquarters. Major W.P. Whelden D.S.O., C. & B. Officers going into action:- "A" Company. A/Captain W.D. Roderick M.C. C. Hunkin M.C., 2nd Lieut. D. Llewellyn. "B" Coy; 2 Lieut. Jenkins. B/ Horton. "C" Coy; Captain B.J.S. Nicholls. R.C. Teil M.C., 2/Lt. While leaving their Hdqs. at POIX-DU-NORD at about 05.00 hours Major W.P. Whelden D.S.O. Lt. W.B. Chunkin M.C. was killed and 2/Lt. D. Llewellyn was wounded. Major Whelden carried on for a few hours afterwards. was killed. Major Bulbolia D.S.O. wanted to take command at about 1300 hours. Lt. Col. Bulbolia D.S.O. wanted to take command at the same time. 2/Lt. J.E. Leyshon returned from Battle Surplus at the same time. A/Captain W.D. Roderick was slightly wounded during the attack but carried on until the afternoon. After the BROWN LINE was captured the Battalion moved to positions of readiness in S.28.a.0.0. Major J. Lewis D.S.O. joined on this date.	

Army Form C. 2118.

WAR DIARY
or
INTELLIGENCE SUMMARY.
(Erase heading not required.)

Instructions regarding War Diaries and Intelligence Summaries are contained in F. S. Regs., Part II. and the Staff Manual respectively. Title pages will be prepared in manuscript.

Place	Date	Hour	Summary of Events and Information	Remarks and references to Appendices
	5/11/18.		Battalion moved forward from C.26.d. O.O. at 12.30 hours, arriving on the ROUTE-DE-SASSIGNIES about 15.30 hours. Remained in the wood during the night, which was very wet.	
	6/11/18.		Battalion moved forward at 13.15 hours and arrived in BERLAIMONT about 17.00 hrs., and good billets were found. The factories at D.26.d. and 27.c. which were on fire were shelled intermittently during the night. Orders received to be prepared to move at one hour notice from 0800 hrs. on the 7th inst.	
	7/11/18.		Battalion moved forward and crossed the RIVER SAMBRE about 0900 hrs. and proceeded to AULNOYE near the station when they remained until 16.30 hours. AULNOYE was heavily shelled during the afternoon. At 16.40 hrs. Brigade moved forward to relieve the 100 Brigade of the 33rd Division. The Battalion halted for some time at POT-DE-VIN before moving forward to assembly positions at DOURLERS. (Ref.Sh. 57A) D/24.75 to D.6.d.6.6.	
	8/11/18.		The attack was launched at 3.15 a.m. a/w a slight bombardment and the first objectives were gained with slight casualties. Owing to heavy machine gun fire from the second objective was not gained until the afternoon. 1st objective was the main MAUBEUGE ROAD. E.13.c. and at to E.1.c. and at 2nd objective, final, ROAD. E.3.c. and a. The attack was continued during the afternoon and the enemy retired during the night. Officers going into action. B/Col. B.W. Coffin D.S.O. Major J. Lined D.S.O. Lieut C.F. Dones D.S.O., Lt. F.L. Keyshan. "A" Coy. 2/Lt. Jenkins. "B" Coy. 2/Lt. O'Neil M.C. and	

WAR DIARY
or
INTELLIGENCE SUMMARY.
(Erase heading not required.)

Army Form C. 2118.

Place	Date	Hour	Summary of Events and Information	Remarks and references to Appendices
	9/11/18.		2.Lt. B.E. Horton, "C" Coy. Captain C.J.S. Nicholls "D" Coy. 2.Lt. W.J. Edwards. 2.Lt. Jenkins were wounded during the attack but carried on until the afternoon. During the afternoon 2.O. Linister returned and 4 new officers joined the Battalion.	
	10/11/18.		The Battalion moved forward at dawn and marched to Lillers at WATTIGNIES-LA-VICTOIRE. The cavalry were then in front. The Battalion moved on Lillers at DIMONT at 13.30 hours arriving here about 1500 hours.	
	11/11/18.		The Battalion at DIMONT cleaning up. "B" Echelon at POT-DE-VIN. Hostilities cease at 11.00 hours. Lt.Col. Collie D.S.O. left the Battalion during the afternoon to proceed to England. Major J. Sweet D.S.O. assumed command.	
	12/11/18.		Training continued in DIMONT (Ref. Sheet 57A) at F.7.6.	
	13/11/18.		Training continued in DIMONT	
	14/11/18.		Training continued in DIMONT. Battalion concert held during the evening in the mill.	
	15/11/18.		Training continued in DIMONT. Cpl. N. Weale awarded the V.C.	
	16/11/18.		Battalion left for DAMOUSIES (N.12) at 11.00 hrs. arriving at DAMOUSIES at 12.30 hrs	

Army Form C. 2118.

WAR DIARY
or
INTELLIGENCE SUMMARY.
(Erase heading not required.)

Instructions regarding War Diaries and Intelligence Summaries are contained in F. S. Regs., Part II. and the Staff Manual respectively. Title pages will be prepared in manuscript.

Place	Date	Hour	Summary of Events and Information	Remarks and references to Appendices
	17/11/18		Church parade: Thanksgiving service for victory. Nonconformists held their service in the village church. Col E. held their service in a field at W.12.d.5.3. Captain W.D. Roderick rejoined the Battalion.	
	18/11/18		Ceremonial parade in field (W.12.d.5.3) to Lieut General to Brigadier General Of. Rhys Price C.M.G., D.S.O. on his appointment as Director of Mobilization in India. Training continued.	
	19/11/18		Battalion marched to WATTIGNIES by Companies for baths. Training continued.	
	20/11/18		Training continued during the morning and recreational training during the afternoon.	
	21/11/18		Battalion paraded en mass at DAMOUSIES and marched to WATTIGNIES for the presentation of medal Ribbons to Officers and men of the 113 Brigade by Major General Bethill C.M.G, D.S.O. commanding 38th Division.	
	22/11/18		Training continued during the day. Advance parties left for new area in SARBARAS.	
	23/11/18		Battalion left DAMOUSIES at 0845 hours and arrived at SARBARAS at about 15.00 hours.	
	24/11/18		Church parades of different denominations.	
	25/11/18		Training continued and Salvage parties at work under 2.L. Edwards of "D" Coy.	

Army Form C. 2118.

WAR DIARY
or
INTELLIGENCE SUMMARY.
(Erase heading not required.)

Instructions regarding War Diaries and Intelligence Summaries are contained in F.S. Regs., Part II. and the Staff Manual respectively. Title pages will be prepared in manuscript.

Place	Date	Hour	Summary of Events and Information	Remarks and references to Appendices
	26/4/18		Battalion halted at SARBARAS, training and musing continued.	
	27/4/18		Battalion route march and training continued.	
	28/4/18		Battalion route march and training continued. Football match between 14th and 13th Battns. 14th won by 2 goals to nil.	
	29/4/18		Battalion training continued and also route march. Inter Coy. matches	
	30/4/18		Battalion route march and training continued during the afternoon.	

Fred Doel Major
Commanding 14th (S) Bn.
Royal Welsh Fusiliers

14th R.W.F.

WAR DIARY

FOR

DECEMBER 1918

WAR DIARY
or
INTELLIGENCE SUMMARY
(Erase heading not required.)

Army Form C. 2118.

Place	Date	Hour	Summary of Events and Information	Remarks and references to Appendices
	Dec 1st & 2nd/1918		Battalion in Billets in SARBRAES. Training continued, consisting of Route March, Close Order Drill & Saluting & Recreational training in afternoon. The following awards have been notified. No.27316 Sgt Jones A.T. "M.M" No.40055 Pte Llewelyn W "MM" B322 Pte Davies "MM" 2 Lieut. Jenkins A.J. — "M.C." No.28199, Sergt Prince G "D.C.M" 235433 L/Cpl Robinson J. "D.C.M" 255627 L/Cpl Horgan A.E. "D.C.M".	
	3/12/18		Battalion marched to B.G. L.22. (Sheet 57A) to be inspected by H.M. the King. The following award have been notified. No.20549 Sergt Jones H.G. D.C.M — M.M. 75339 " Watkins A.W. — M.M. 94348 " Sears J.R. — M.M. 235821 Pte Williams E. — M.M. Lt + QM. B.O. R.C.Loffrey joined for duty.	
	4/12/18		Training continued. do.	
	5/12/18		do.	

Army Form C. 2118.

WAR DIARY
or
INTELLIGENCE SUMMARY.
(Erase heading not required.)

Instructions regarding War Diaries and Intelligence Summaries are contained in F.S. Regs., Part II. and the Staff Manual respectively. Title pages will be prepared in manuscript.

Place	Date	Hour	Summary of Events and Information	Remarks and references to Appendices
	5/12/18		The following awards have been notified.	
			No.60007 Pte Williams R.A. — M.M.	
			235290 " Brinson J. — M.M.	
			37383 " Roberts J.E. — M.M.	
			56407 L/Cpl Bran G.W. — M.M.	
	6/12/18		Training continued.	
	7/12/18		Training continued.	
	8/12/18		Church Parade. The following Officers joined for duty:-	
			2Lt. G.E. Thomas, 2Lt. D.G. Williams, 2Lt. G.R. Davies.	
	9/12/18		Training continued.	
	10/12/18		Battalion left SARBARA and moved to billets in BERLAIMONT.	
	11/12/18		Training continued.	
	12/12/18		Training continued.	
	13/12/18		Training continued.	
	14/12/18		Training continued.	
	15/12/18		Church Parade.	
	16/12/18		Training continued	

WAR DIARY
or
INTELLIGENCE SUMMARY

Army Form C. 2118.

Place	Date	Hour	Summary of Events and Information	Remarks and references to Appendices
	16/12/18 (contd)		(a). The following awards of the M.M. have been notified:- Lo. 27027 Cpl Baker A.R, 235.72 Pte Hogan J.J, 10515 Cpl. J. Rogers. 16758 L/Cpl. L. Edwards, 37563 Pte. J.R. Lloyd, 20161 Pte L. V. Lewis. 23582. Pte J. Williams, 27428 Cpl. W. McGregor, 20700 L/Cpl. A. Jones. 29227. Pte L. Howard, 60690 Pte. J. Dyson, 87433 Pte. S.L. Baker. 60772 Pte. W.A. Jones, 61398 Pte. B. Thomas, 40295. L/Cpl W. Jones, 56905 L/Sgt Saunders, N.C. 26849 L/Cpl. W. Bates 26799. Pte W. Blackmur, 20994 Sgt. J. Thomas, 21135 L/Cpl K. Brown 24873 Cpl W.H. Williams.	
	17/12/18		Training continued. Lt. Colonel L.C. Norman D.S.O, returned from leave and assumed temporary command of 113th Inf. Brigade vice Lt. Col. J. Lomax 13th R.W. Fus. The following Officers joined the Battalion for duty:- Lt. J. Fisher 2/Lt A.L. Brown.	
	18/12/18		Training continued	
	19/12/18		Training continued	

WAR DIARY
or
INTELLIGENCE SUMMARY

(Erase heading not required.)

Army Form C. 2118.

Instructions regarding War Diaries and Intelligence Summaries are contained in F.S. Regs., Part II. and the Staff Manual respectively. Title pages will be prepared in manuscript.

Place	Date	Hour	Summary of Events and Information	Remarks and references to Appendices
	20/12/18		Training continued	
	21/12/18		Training continued. Lt Col C.C. Norman D.S.O. assumed Command of the Battalion.	
	22/12/18		Church Parade.	
	23/12/18		Training continued.	
	24/12/18		Training continued.	
	25/12/18		Christmas Day. Church Parade in morning. Men dined by Companies today and spent a very enjoyable afternoon and evening. All Officers of the Battalion dined together in the evening.	
	26/12/18		Preparations for move to WARLOY area. Billets in Berlaimont thoroughly cleaned, and transport packed as far as possible for the move.	
	27/12/18		Battalion left Berlaimont at 8.45 hrs and marched to Englefontaine. Rained heavily during march, and men arrived in billets very wet, about 1 p.m.	

Army Form C. 2118.

WAR DIARY
or
INTELLIGENCE SUMMARY.
(Erase heading not required.)

Instructions regarding War Diaries and Intelligence Summaries are contained in F. S. Regs., Part II. and the Staff Manual respectively. Title pages will be prepared in manuscript.

Place	Date	Hour	Summary of Events and Information	Remarks and references to Appendices
	28/12/18		Continued march. Left Englefontaine at 9.0 a.m. and marched to INCHY, arriving there about 1 pm. Rained heavily the whole time, and men got very wet again	
	29/12/18		Continued journey to WARLOY by bus. Left Inchy about 8.30 a.m. and arrived at WARLOY about 3.30 p.m. Took over a new hutment camp at WARLOY which was not quite finished	
	30/12/18		Day spent in settling down in new camp, and generally cleaning up	
	31/12/18		Commanding Officers' inspection of camp. Owing to rain no parades were possible, and remainder of day was spent in cleaning up generally. During the month 272 Gunners have been demobilized. Also 80 Drivers, and 2 Other Ranks have also been demobilized.	

The Week.
Major Command
4th Bgd R.W. Fus hire

P17

14TH BATTN. ROYAL WELSH FUS Vol 38

WAR DIARY

FOR

JANUARY – 1919.

38 C.
5 sheets

Army Form C. 2118.

WAR DIARY
or
INTELLIGENCE SUMMARY.
(Erase heading not required.)

Instructions regarding War Diaries and Intelligence Summaries are contained in F. S. Regs. Part II. and the Staff Manual respectively. Title pages will be prepared in manuscript.

Place	Date	Hour	Summary of Events and Information	Remarks and references to Appendices
	1-1-19		Battalion in Nissan Hut Camp at WARLOY, 7 miles N.W of ALBERT. Companies went for route march in morning. Remainder of day spent in getting Camp in order.	
	2-1-19		Training consisting of route march & P.T., B.F.	
	3-1-19		Training continued, also improvement of Camp.	
	4-1-19		-do-	
	5-1-19		Battalion attended Church Parades in morning.	
	6-1-19		Battalion paraded & marched to Baths at VADENCOURT. When not at Baths Coys. carried on with usual training & improvements to Camp. Lt.Col. C.C.Norman assumed command of 113 Infantry Brigade during absence of Brig. General. Major F. Ewer 2i/C took over command of the Battalion.	
	7-1-19		Continuation of training and work in Camp. Div. Commander inspected Transport in morning.	
	8-1-19		Continuation of training and work on Camp.	
	9-1-19		-do-	
	10-1-19		-do-	
			The following award was notified:- 2Lt.(A/Captain) W.B.Roderick M.C. awarded D.S.O. Lt.Col. C.C.Norman DSO returned from Brigade and took over command of the Battalion.	
	11-1-19		Training and work on Camp continued.	

Army Form C. 2118.

WAR DIARY
or
INTELLIGENCE SUMMARY.
(Erase heading not required.)

Instructions regarding War Diaries and Intelligence Summaries are contained in F.S. Regs., Part II. and the Staff Manual respectively. Title pages will be prepared in manuscript.

Place	Date	Hour	Summary of Events and Information	Remarks and references to Appendices
	12-1-19		Battalion attended Church Parades in morning.	
	13-1-19		Training and work in camp continued.	
	14-1-19		Battalion went to Baths in morning and afterwards carried on with the work in camp.	
	15-1-19		Training and work as usual.	
	16-1-19		A presentation of colours was made today by Major Gen. T.A. Cubitt. CB. CMG. DSO. comdg the 38th (Welsh) Division. On behalf of His Majesty the King George V the Maj. Gen. presented each Infant. Batt. in the Division (except the 2nd RWFus) with a silk union jack. The presentation was made at ALLONVILLE. Lieut J.E. Williams as Senior Subaltern received the colours for the Battalion.	
	17-1-19		Training and work in camp as usual.	
	18-1-19		-do-	
	19-1-19		Battalion attended Church Parades in morning.	
	20-1-19		Battalion went to Baths in morning and afterwards carried on work in camp. 2/Lieut. H.J. DYE joined the Battalion for duty	
	21-1-19		Parades and work in camp as usual.	
	22-1-19		-do-	
	23-1-19		-do-	
	24-1-19		-do-	
	25-1-19		-do-	

Army Form C. 2118.

WAR DIARY
or
INTELLIGENCE SUMMARY.
(Erase heading not required.)

Instructions regarding War Diaries and Intelligence Summaries are contained in F. S. Regs., Part II. and the Staff Manual respectively. Title pages will be prepared in manuscript.

Place	Date	Hour	Summary of Events and Information	Remarks and references to Appendices
	26-1-19.		The following award was notified:— "MSM" No. 19651. RQMS. Smith H.	
	27-1-19.		Battalion attended Church Parades in morning. Battalion at Baths during the morning. When not at the Baths, carried on with work in camp. Lt Col. Norman DSO. assumed temporary command of 113" Infantry Brigade during absence on leave of G.O.C. Major J Sinel DSO took over temporary command of the Battalion.	
	28-1-19.		Work continued in camp.	
	29-1-19.		—do—	
	30-1-19.		—do— No parades.	
			The following awards were notified:— D.C.M. 20010 L/Sgt Byrne R. 55849 Pte Byrne Ja. (all Bn. RWF) Mentioned in Despatches. Lieut Col. L.b. Norman DSO. Lieut E.W. Mason. 20586 C.S.M. Anton E.S.	

Army Form C. 2118.

WAR DIARY
or
INTELLIGENCE SUMMARY.
(Erase heading not required.)

Instructions regarding War Diaries and Intelligence Summaries are contained in F. S. Regs., Part II. and the Staff Manual respectively. Title pages will be prepared in manuscript.

Place	Date	Hour	Summary of Events and Information	Remarks and references to Appendices
	31-1-19.		No parades — Work continued on Camp.	

Fred Sweet
Major
Commanding 14" Bn. Royal Welsh Fusiliers

WAR DIARY
or
INTELLIGENCE SUMMARY.
(Erase heading not required.)

Army Form C. 2118.

14 R.W.F. 39.C. 2 sheet

Place	Date	Hour	Summary of Events and Information	Remarks and references to Appendices
	1/2/19		Battalion at Baths at Hadicourt on "Prospect" in the after noon "Army"	Lt Col Robinson leaves
	2/2/19		Church Parade. Major R.A. Rigby assumed command of the Battalion vice Major J. Shea to leave.	
	3/2/19 4/2/19		Parades and work on camp.	
	5/2/19		A.R.A. Prince of Wales visits the Battalion and inspects the camp.	
	6/2/19		Battalion at Baths. Battalion reorganised into two companies	
	7/2/19		Battalion reorganised as under:-	
	8/2/19		Men for Army of Occupation. do do Demobilisation do do Cadre	
	9/2/19		Church Parade.	
	10/2/19		Wood Collecting & Working parties	
	11/2/19		Award of Belgian Decoration Militaire to 27703 Pte J. O'Board notified All Demobilisation Stores handed in to O.M.	

WAR DIARY
or
INTELLIGENCE SUMMARY
(Erase heading not required.)

Army Form C. 2118.

Place	Date	Hour	Summary of Events and Information	Remarks and references to Appendices
	12/2/19		Draft of 50 O.R. for Army of Occupation inspected by Major General Forestier Walker.	
			7. A. CURITT - Baths at Vadencourt used by Battalion	
	13/14		Working parties in Camp	
	15/2/19			
	16/2/19		Battalion proceeded to baths at Vadencourt.	
	17/2/19		Working parties in Camp	
	18/2/19		Working parties in Camp	
	19/2/19		Baths and working parties	
	20/2/19		Draft of Lieut. J. Billam 2Lt H. Aspe and 50 other ranks proceeded to join 26th Bn R. W. Fusiliers	
	21/22/ 2/19		Working parties in Camp	
	23/2/19		Church service	
	24-25/ 2/19		Working parties	
	28/2/19		Ration Strength of Battalion Feb 28th 12 officers 170 other ranks	

Ted Snel
Major
Comdg
14th R. W. Fus.

14 R.W.F.
WD 70

40C
2chels

WAR DIARY
or
INTELLIGENCE SUMMARY.

Army Form C. 2118.

(Erase heading not required.)

Instructions regarding War Diaries and Intelligence Summaries are contained in F. S. Regs., Part II. and the Staff Manual respectively. Title pages will be prepared in manuscript.

Place	Date	Hour	Summary of Events and Information	Remarks and references to Appendices
	1/3/19		St Davids Day. Owing to depleted state of Battalion no special parades took place. Working parties as usual.	
	2/3/19		Church Service.	
	3/3/19 8/3/19		Working Parties in Camp.	
	9/3/19		Church Service.	
	10/3/19 13/3/19		Working Parties in Camp. as usual.	
	14/3/19		Working Parties in Camp as usual. Major General S. Ashby C.M.G. O.B., C.M.G. 9.30. visited the Battalion to say "Goodbye" on giving up the command of the 38th (Welsh) Division.	
	15/3/19		Working Parties in Camp.	
	16/3/19		Church Service	

Army Form C. 2118.

WAR DIARY
or
INTELLIGENCE SUMMARY.
(Erase heading not required.)

Instructions regarding War Diaries and Intelligence Summaries are contained in F. S. Regs., Part II. and the Staff Manual respectively. Title pages will be prepared in manuscript.

Place	Date	Hour	Summary of Events and Information	Remarks and references to Appendices
	17/3/19		The Battalion left camp at WORLOY-BAILLON and marched to new camp at BLANGY-TRONVILLE. The bodies of the 13th, 14th & 16th Bns "O. Bns." are concentrated in this camp.	
	18/3/19		Day spent in settling down in new camp.	
	19/3/19		Baths in morning. Fatigues for the remainder of the day.	
	20/3/19		Fatigues in camp.	
	22/3/19			
	23/3/19		Church service	
	24/3/19		Fatigues in camp	
	26/3/19			
	28/3/19		Camp inspected by Brig Genl. A.J. de Pree, CB., CMG. Comdg 3rd Div Inf. Bde.	
	28/3/19		Fatigues in camp	
	29/3/19			
	30/3/19		Church Service	
	31/3/19		Fatigues in camp	

Fred Tweed
Major
14th R.W. Faithies

Army Form C. 2118.

WAR DIARY
or
INTELLIGENCE SUMMARY.

(Erase heading not required.)

Vol 41

Instructions regarding War Diaries and Intelligence Summaries are contained in F. S. Regs., Part II. and the Staff Manual respectively. Title pages will be prepared in manuscript.

Place	Date	Hour	Summary of Events and Information	Remarks and references to Appendices
Blargy Troisville	April 1917 1st		Parades & Fatigues in Camp.	
	2			
	3			
	4			
	5		Church Service Route March	
	6			
	7			
	8		Parades & Fatigues in Camp	
	9			
	10			
	11			
	12		Church Service Route March	
	13			
	14		Parades & Fatigues in Camp. Church Services & Fatigues	
	15			
	16			
	17		Good Friday - Church Service & Fatigues	
	18		Parades & Fatigues in Camp.	
	19		Church Services	
	20			
	21			
	22		Parades & Fatigues in Camp.	
	23			
	24			
	25			
	26			
	27		Church Services	
	28			
	29		Parades & Fatigues in Camp.	
	30			

Ivel Sweet
Major
14th (S) Bn. R.W. Fus

HIC
1 sheet

Lightning Source UK Ltd.
Milton Keynes UK
UKOW07f2230060716

277808UK00005B/44/P